Metrolingualism

This book is about language and the city. Pennycook and Otsuji introduce the notion of 'metrolingualism', showing how language and the city are deeply involved in a broader cultural exchange between people, history, migration, architecture, urban landscapes and linguistic resources. Cities and languages are in constant change, as speakers with new repertoires come into contact as a result of globalization and the increased mobility of people and languages.

Metrolingualism sheds light on the ordinariness of linguistic diversity as people go about their daily lives, getting things done, eating and drinking, buying and selling, talking and joking, drawing on whatever linguistic resources are available. Engaging with current debates about multilingualism, and developing a new way of thinking about language, the authors explore language within a number of contemporary urban situations, including cafés, restaurants, shops, streets, construction sites and other places of work, in two diverse cities, Sydney and Tokyo. This is a valuable look at how people of different backgrounds get by linguistically.

Metrolingualism: Language in the city will be of special interest to advanced undergraduate and postgraduate students and researchers of sociolinguistics and applied linguistics.

Alastair Pennycook is Professor of Language in Education at the University of Technology Sydney. He is the author of many titles, including *Language as a Local Practice* (2010) and *Global Englishes and Transcultural Flows* (2007).

Emi Otsuji is a Senior Lecturer at the University of Technology Sydney. She is the co-editor of the book *Languages and Identities in a Transitional Japan: From Internationalization to Globalization* (2015) and the Japanese editor for *The Japan Journal of Multilingualism and Multiculturalism*.

Metrolingualism

Language in the city

Alastair Pennycook and Emi Otsuji

Routledge
Taylor & Francis Group

LONDON AND NEW YORK

First published 2015
by Routledge
2 Park Square, Milton Park, Abingdon, Oxon OX14 4RN

and by Routledge
711 Third Avenue, New York, NY 10017

Routledge is an imprint of the Taylor & Francis Group, an informa business

British Library Cataloguing-in-Publication Data
A catalogue record for this book is available from the British Library

Library of Congress Cataloging-in-Publication Data
Pennycook, Alastair, 1957- author.
Metrolingualism : language in the city / By Alastair Pennycook and Emi Otsuji.
pages cm
Includes bibliographical references and index.
1. Urban dialects. 2. Multilingualism--Social aspects. 3. Language and languages--Variation. 4. Urban dialects--Australia--Sydney. 5. Urban dialects--Japan--Tokyo. 6. Sociolinguistics. I. Otsuji, Emi, author. II. Title.
P40.5.U73P46 2015
306.44'6091732--dc23
2014038517

ISBN: 978-0-415-83163-5 (hbk)
ISBN: 978-0-415-83165-9 (pbk)
ISBN: 978-1-315-72422-5 (ebk)

Typeset in Times New Roman
by Saxon Graphics Ltd, Derby
Printed in Great Britain by Ashford Colour Press Ltd.

Contents

Images

Preface and acknowledgements

This book is the product of a multifaceted and exhilarating journey in and around cafés, restaurants, shops, streets, construction sites and other places of work in Sydney and Tokyo. We owe a great debt to all those who helped us with this research, talking about their work and lives, agreeing to be recorded at work, sitting down with us again when we came back with questions. We also owe many thanks to those who helped along the way, introducing us to different people and research sites, and making it possible for us to make a range of connections across city networks. The idea of conviviality discussed in Chapter 5 emerged in part from the extraordinary generosity and friendliness of our many research participants (even while they often couldn't see what was supposedly so interesting about the everyday language practices of their lives).

We are also deeply indebted to all those who worked on the research, and especially to our principal research assistant Astrid Lorange. Astrid worked with us on all aspects of this project, from interviewing to recording, from ethnographic note-taking to finding references, from transcribing to suggesting new research possibilities. The choice of Astrid as a research assistant was also part of our attempt to think differently about language and the city: Astrid is more of a poet than a sociolinguist, an expert on Gertrude Stein (Lorange, 2014) rather than William Labov, but we felt (rightly as it turned out) that a poet who can do sociolinguistics and is interested in cities might be more valuable than a sociolinguist who can't do poetry or cities. As we try to make clear in our research notes at the end of various chapters, the interactions and discussions of our research team were crucial to this endeavour, and the many times Emi, Astrid and Alastair sat, walked, hung out, drank coffee, swapped notes and talked were the dynamic heart of this project.

In addition to this core team, many others have assisted in this project. When Astrid left for a full-time academic position (a 'real job'), Julie Choi stepped in and worked with us on the data and the book manuscript, and also contributed in multiple ways to the final development of this book. Others who worked on transcribing and translating include: Jo Bu (who also accompanied us on visits to markets and market gardens, and gave us a range of insights into some of these parts of the project), Smiljana Glisovic, Mehal Krayem, Amina Singh, Krzysztof Komsta, Akiko Hiratsuka, Saori Kawazoe, Narelle Fletcher and Kelly Chan. One of the characteristics and challenges was to capture the soundscape of the space but also to make the recording more transcribable, and for this we are indebted to Edward Hopely and Alan Lem for 'cleaning' the sound files. Thanks to our meticulous and thoughtful indexer Tom Melick. Finally, we should thank the Australian Research Council (ARC) for making all this possible by funding the Discovery Project (DP110101014) *Metrolingual language practices in four urban sites: Talking in the city.*

In the broader context of researching and writing, we have, over a number of years, engaged in some highly productive and interesting discussions on cities, metrolingualism, multilingualism, translanguaging and so on and we owe a great debt to all those who have taken the time to talk, argue, critique, help and encourage. These include John Maher, Jan Blommaert, Sari Pietikäinen, Nik Coupland, Theo van Leeuwen, Brigitta Busch, Monica Heller, Alexandre Duchêne, Claire Kramsch, Ophelia García, Stephen May, Li Wei, Adrian Blackledge, Angela Creese, Ryuko Kubota, Lynn Mario Menezes de Souza, Dipesh Chakrabarty, Mary Louise Pratt, Sirpa Leppännen, Kimie Takahashi, Elana Shohamy, Bonny Norton, Tim McNamara, Steve Thorne, Brian Morgan, Sinfree Makoni, Ikuko Nakane, Chihiro Thomson, Hideo Hosokawa, Suresh Canagarajah, Chris Stroud, Norman Jørgensen, Martha Sif Karrebæk, Janus Møller, Tommaso Milani, Tope Omoniyi, Samy Alim, Awad Ibrahim, Ruanni Tupas, Beatriz Lorente, Angel Lin, Andy Kirkpatrick, Luisa Martin Rojo, Melissa Moyer, David Block, Ben Rampton, Christina Higgins, Ahmar Mahboob, Ingrid Piller, Cynthia Nelson, Ros Appleby, Brian Paltridge, Bong Jeong Lee, Shaila Sultana, Sender Dovchin, Véronique Conte, Misako Tajima and many others.

Earlier versions of some sections of this book have been published as journal articles and book chapters (Otsuji & Pennycook, 2010, 2014; Pennycook & Otsuji, 2014a, b) and we would like to thank the publishers – John Wiley and Sons, Taylor and Francis and Multilingual Matters – for permission to publish these revised versions, as well as the editors and reviewers of these publications for their critical input into our work. Louisa Semleyen at Routledge should also be thanked for her patience and trust and advice. Writing a book such as this incurs debts to many, and as we think back over its ever-changing forms and the many different contexts in which it was written – including the hugely productive Kangaroo Valley writing retreat in December 2013 with Emi, Alastair, Astrid and Dominique Estival (who also supported this project in numerous ways) – we hope we have acknowledged all those who have been part of this.

1 Morning markets and metrolingual multitasking

The Produce Market: *Salamu alaykum* mate

It's a little after five o'clock in the morning. While much of the rest of the city is still asleep in the predawn gloom, Sydney Produce Market is alight and buzzing. As we travel across the dark city in time for the busiest period of the morning, we traverse the rhythmic urban patterns as the city breathes in and out. Unlike the quiet of the tree-lined suburbs, Oxford Street is alive and noisy, brawny dark-clothed bouncers watching nightclub patrons spilling out onto the pavement. Taxis hover: The night shift changed over at 3 a.m., and fresh drivers are patrolling the streets looking for a late night (for the clubbers) or early morning (for the drivers) ride before public transport gets moving. Early morning garbage trucks are starting up; road workers are closing up after a night job.

Meanwhile, the produce market is humming with activity: Giant trailer trucks are pulled up alongside loading bays, stacked high with bananas and other tropical fruit (transported down south from Queensland overnight), or packed with vegetables and stone fruit from Canberra and Shepparton to the southwest, or apples from Tasmania even further south. Their cargoes of fruit and vegetables are whisked away on forklifts. Everywhere forklifts – hundreds of them, lights on, hurtling backwards (the loads piled up on the forks make driving forwards impossible), turning in tight circles, moving pallets of oranges, onions, pineapples, bananas, beetroot, potatoes from one place to another.[1] This is the largest fresh food market in Australia, and one of the largest in the world. It is estimated that 2,500,000 tonnes of fresh fruit and vegetables are sold through this market annually, through the hundreds of wholesalers, produce growers and flower grower-sellers.

Among the movements of products and people, Muhibb and Talib are busy.

Excerpt 1.1 (M: Muhibb, T: Talib, P: Passerby)
(Transcription conventions are provided in appendix 1) Arabic: *italics*; English: plain (translation in brackets)
1. M: Hey! Johnny fix up the stand! Here move these cherry tomatoes put them with them. Let them do it. Let them do Hog's Breath … If you wanna do anything … if my dad's not doing it start here.

2.   T: *Ed da calaphak? Etnan?* (How much did it cost you? Two?)
3.   M: Sorry. *Eh tnanan* dollar! (Yeah two dollars)
[Ten seconds pause]
[phone conversation]
4.   T: Joe … good morning, Can you send me one ras one blues please. Thank you very much. See ya buddy! Coles is on special. Dollar seventy and dollar sixty on u::mm on on what do you call it … two dollars.
5.   P: *Salamu alaykum* mate (*Peace be upon you,* mate)
6.   M: *Wa alaykum assalam* (*Peace upon you too*)

At their stall on the floor of the giant warehouse – the size of three football pitches – Talib and Muhibb are hard at work. The different areas are being set up, pallets of goods piling up for sale. Each area has a portable desk, dropped off and removed by a forklift. This is where the deals are done, the paperwork is shifted, the cash changes hands. They are surrounded by food on the move, workers loading and unloading fruit and vegetables, forklifts picking up loaded pallets and bringing new loads of tomatoes or beans or strawberries or onions.

This is the north end, generally understood as the 'Lebanese section' (a walk from the south of the warehouse takes one through sections recognized as Chinese, Vietnamese, Maltese, Italian, Lebanese). On the side of the brothers' desk is a Ramadan calendar. The brothers – second generation Lebanese Australian – are strongly built, hair cut short, beards bulky. In T-shirts, they are dressed to work. Others in the warehouse wear the traditional leather market aprons. The two brothers run this movable business with their father and one other brother (and seven other employees of Turkish, Pakistani, Moroccan, Sudanese-Egyptian, Somalian and Filipino backgrounds), a business that comes and goes with the forklifts. As we discuss further in the next chapter, the 'Lebaneseness' of this section of the market is also constructed from a sense of Lebanese being the default Arabic community in Sydney, whereas, as we see from the backgrounds of these co-workers, there are in fact far more complex sets of linguistic, regional, religious and migrationary affiliations at play across the workforce.

Such interactions capture much of what we wish to get at in this book: They are, first of all, an example of what we have elsewhere (Pennycook & Otsuji, 2014a) called *metrolingual multitasking,* a term we use to capture the ways in which linguistic resources, everyday tasks and social space are intertwined. The seamless management of linguistic resources and interlinked practices are very evident in the previous extract as the two brothers organize their working area (line 1) with instructions to their other workers, work out prices (lines 2 and 3), call suppliers (line 4) and greet other workers (lines 5 and 6). The linguistic resources of this workspace are generally drawn from English and Lebanese Arabic, though the two brothers use a considerable variety of styles and registers (modifying both their English and their Arabic according to different customers and contexts). They employ a particular local variety of 'market talk': 'one ras one blues' for raspberries and blueberries, and elsewhere 'caulies' for cauliflower, 'rocky' for rockmelon, alongside alternations between mixed terms such as *allettuce* and *khass* (using the Arabic article 'al' with 'lettuce' in the first case, and the Arabic word for lettuce in the second). They frequently mix English and Arabic (Sorry. *Eh tnanan* dollar!), as do other people in the market (*Salamu alaykum* mate).

For Wood and Landry (2008) 'the market – both as a concept and a physical location – is central to any understanding of intercultural exchange' (p. 148). The market place, they go on, 'for many throughout history – and still today – is the place where, for the first time, people physically encounter someone who is visibly distinct from them, who speaks and dresses differently and who offers unusual cultural goods and experiences' (p. 148). Markets, more than any other city space, perhaps define human engagement with difference. While language is crucial for Talib and Muhibb in getting their business done, they are not 'language workers' in the sense that language is a central tool of their trade (unlike, say, call centre workers, translators, teachers, lawyers). Language is important to them in their constant transactions but so too is the price of parsley. This is a place where stuff gets done, where the quality and price of the onions convinces a buyer; and as we shall discuss later (Chapter 8), the languages of these markets – spoken in interwoven mixes by working people – may indeed have little 'market value' in the broader sense. It is also a place where the longstanding relation with the customer matters, where the ability to convince the buyer about the cucumbers, mangoes or zucchini is a skill, and where the interaction between workers and customers, buying, selling, loading a pallet for pickup or delivery, getting more produce brought in on a forklift, happens multimodally.

Our aim in this book is to develop an understanding of the relationship among the use of such diverse linguistic resources (drawn from different languages, varieties and registers), the repertoires of such workers, the activities in which they are engaged, and the larger space in which this occurs. This focus brings together metrolingual practices and the city; it is about getting things done, everyday language use and local language practices in relation to urban space (see Chapter 2). The focus on metrolingualism is part of our attempt to understand linguistic resources in relation to the city, to show how *everyday multilingualism* operates in markets, cafés, streets, shops and other social city spaces. The term *metrolingualism*, which will be explored throughout this book, was originally developed by extending the notion of *metroethnicity* (Maher, 2005) to refer to 'creative linguistic conditions across space and borders of culture, history and politics, as a way to move beyond current terms such as multilingualism and multiculturalism' (Otsuji & Pennycook, 2010, p. 244). As we defined the term then, metrolingualism 'describes the ways in which people of different and mixed backgrounds use, play with and negotiate identities through language'. Rather than assuming connections between language and culture, ethnicity, nationality or geography, metrolingualism 'seeks to explore how such relations are produced, resisted, defied or rearranged; its focus is not on language systems but on languages as emergent from contexts of interaction' (p. 246).

Since then, as explained in further detail in Chapter 3, our use of the term has shifted away from a focus on playful or wilful creativity towards an understanding of everyday language use in the city. Like other recent thinking that has sought to challenge the language of bilingualism, code-mixing and code-switching, and instead has focused on the mobility of linguistic resources (Blommaert, 2010), translanguaging (Blackledge & Creese, 2010; Garcia, 2009; Li Wei, 2011), transglossia (Garcia, 2013, 2014; Sultana, Dovchin & Pennycook, 2015) or polylingual languaging (Jørgensen, 2008a; Møller, 2008), we have aimed to open up a way of thinking about multilingualism centred around the everyday use of mobile linguistic resources in relation to *urban space* (McQuire, 2008). Unlike these approaches, however, with their focus on resources and individual repertoires, metrolingualism makes central the relations between language practices and the city.

This chapter raises a number of the central themes of this book by sketching some of the language practices of the Produce Market complex and looking at the interrelationship between language practices, spatial relations and getting things done. We are not so much interested therefore in a mundane mapping of the languages used, nor the impossible task of grasping the entirety of language practices in the market, but rather are focusing on 'mobile resources rather than immobile languages' (Blommaert, 2010, p. 197). We are interested in the dynamic ways in which the layered languages, tasks, practices and spaces combine together to produce *spatial repertoires* (Chapter 4) and the *metrolingua francas* (Chapter 8) of such urban markets. That these interactions will involve a diverse array of linguistic and other resources we take as a given, and while we note with a certain delight the possibility of an Australian-Lebanese-Arabic phrase such as '*Salamu alaykum* mate' as one worker passes a stall in the predawn business of the Market, we do not intend to emphasize the 'mixing' or 'hybridity' of such language use but rather to take it as the norm (Otsuji & Pennycook, 2014).

Languages of the market: lingo-ing in their own language

How, then, might we go about understanding the languages of this market? As already suggested, we are not so much interested in a demolinguistic approach to this – mapping percentages of language backgrounds – but in the daily practices. Joseph, who runs the two cafés at either end of this vast expanse of fruit and vegetables, is useful on this. The cafés, which open at midnight, provide the expected breakfast foods – burgers, bacon and eggs – but also a mix of other foods. While the café his son runs at the other 'Lebanese' end of the warehouse has food such as Lebanese bread with *za'atar*, Joseph's café, at the more 'Chinese' end has a range of other dishes, such as *wonton* soup, *satay* chicken and Mongolian beef hotpot, among Portuguese chicken and bacon and egg rolls. The staff are of various backgrounds: the cooks Chinese, the woman making the coffee Korean, the owner, Joseph, Lebanese. English is a common language of the café, but others, especially Arabic and Cantonese, are also in use.

This market is where Joseph has always worked – selling vegetables, driving a forklift – since he arrived in Sydney 36 years before: 'Well, put it that way, they picked me up from the airport ... drove me to the bottom gate down there, and I'm still stuck over here in this maze, I haven't got out of that maze yet!' (Joseph, interview, August, 8, 2012). His 24-year-old son runs the other café. As he explains, his son speaks English to his second generation Lebanese Australian mother but 'speaks Lebanese, fluent Lebanese with me. Fluent. On the same dinner table, we'll be together, he turns around, I'm on the left he goes he speaks to me in Lebanese, and he speaks to his mother in English'. We shall return particularly in Chapter 6 to the significance of the combination between food, language and eating together (commensality), the intertwining of culinary and linguistic resources. For Joseph it is the dinner table that is a site of sociolinguistic interaction, which he discusses in everyday local language terminology ('fluent Lebanese'), both a picture of the very ordinariness of mixed language use and also a source of pride.

The overarching common language of this market is, not surprisingly, English (whatever exactly is meant by that label), but what gets used when and with whom also depends on the day of the week, who is buying from whom and where the interaction takes place. 'But if between a buyer and a seller that is a common language of their background is spoken they do use it, OK, they feel more comfortable they feel more comfortable lingo-ing in their own language' (Joseph, interview, August, 8, 2012). The two dominant languages of the market are Lebanese Arabic and Cantonese, though this varies by area:

> Door 1, 2, down to door 5 ... very very populated area with Lebanese background people. And they use, very often they use broken English and lingo in Lebanese. Past that area there's no traders of Lebanese people, so we go back to different nationalities. Maltese, Italian, Greeks, we go back and use our common language, our first language is English.
>
> (Joseph, interview, August 8, 2012)

At weekends it changes too: 'on a Saturday, it goes back to different languages, more Italians and Greeks and so on.' Joseph's account of the language patterns of the market is centred on the traders, a view that differs from the public signage aimed at customers (see Image 1.1) here in English, Vietnamese, Arabic and Chinese. More importantly they show again the everydayness of language flows and terminologies as workers 'use broken English and lingo in Lebanese' while different languages come and go with the changing faces of the market.

Those like Joseph who've been there a long time also get to know a bit of each others' languages: 'There's always jokes about languages, where we pick all the bad words and naughty words. We throw at each other ... but not in a nasty way, just ah, a friendly thing, to say, "yeah I know a little bit about your language and you know a bit about mine".' In the two examples below, we see two aspects of this: On the one hand, Talib adjusts his English to accommodate a customer of Maltese background; on the other we see the same customer intervening in Talib and Muhibb's use of Arabic.

Image 1.1 Public sign: produce market.

Excerpt 1.2 (M: Muhibb, T: Talib, CM: Maltese Customer)

1. CM: I am back.
2. T: You are back huh?
3. CM: Lionel talk to you?
4. T: Yeah.
5. CM: He say he want more zu, [Maltese accent]
6. T: Zu::cchi::ni:: [enunciates and prolongs each syllable]
7. CM: Extra extra large … like mine.
8. T: No. Extra large like yours no good. [Customer laughs] That's small one. [syllable-timed and spoken slowly, mimicking the pronunciation of the customer]
9. CM: How do you know it's a small one!
10. T: Your extra large and my extra large are two different things,

In dealing with a customer of Maltese background in this excerpt, Talib appears to playfully mimic Maltese pronunciation (line 6). He speaks slowly as he enunciates and prolongs the syllables when pronouncing 'Zucchini'. The customer's response takes up this humorous exchange in line 7: 'Extra extra large … like mine'. Talib subsequently appears to imitate, or at least synchronize, the accents as he speaks in English more slowly, with syllable rather than stress timing, and with additional syntactic simplifications: 'No. Extra large like yours no good' in line 8. Metrolingualism, it should be said, is not only about the use of linguistic resources from different languages, but may equally describe those harmonizing (or sometimes parodying) practices of adjustment within codes, as well as certain forms of styling. Indeed, once we start to question the very categories of language that underlie notions such as bi- and multilingualism (Otsuji & Pennycook, 2010; 2014), we need to see how metrolingualism is less dependent on the identification of specifically different codes at use at the same time, and more dependent on the integration of diverse linguistic resources in the city.

In excerpt 1.3, Muhibb and Talib are working out prices and quantities of zucchini for the same customer of Maltese background.

Excerpt 1.3 (M: Muhibb, T: Talib, CM: Maltese Customer)

Arabic: *italics;* English: plain (translation in brackets)

1. M: How many boxes does he want?
2. T: *Tamana?* (eight?) *Siteh?* (six?) *Arba?* (four?) Oh four.
3. M: Yeah no worries!
4. T: Tell him *arba wa ashreen* (24) I told him. He wants to try and get it for cheaper. *Arba wa ashreen.* (24)

[opening a box of zucchini]

5. T: *Hadol misfareen. Misfareen hadol.* (These are yellowing. They've gone yellow.)

6. CM: *Isfar* (Yellow) … we understand *isfar* in Lebanese … *isfaree isfaree* (Yellow, yellow) yellow.
7. T: Get that one and we'll get you another one. [to the customer]

Between lines 1 and 4, Muhibb and Talib continue to deal with the zucchini order, confirming the number of boxes and price and using English and Arabic resources in a mixture common to second generation immigrants working in such an environment. Here, however, Talib's use of Arabic to acknowledge that the zucchini they are trying to sell have turned yellow (line 5) is picked up by the customer: He knows the meaning of *isfar* (lines 6). This seems to concur with Joseph's view that they know a bit of each other's languages, though in the case of Maltese and Arabic, this is not wholly surprising (*isfar* is also the Maltese for yellow). More generally, however, this shows how people draw on their own resources in achieving tasks at hand and how items such as yellow zucchini (the food rather than the linguistic form) play a mediating role in the metrolingual action. Metrolingual practices concern the whole package of linguistic resources, personal trajectories and repertoires, objects and space.

Talib and Muhibb speak both English and Lebanese Arabic, and the interactions between them frequently contain both. Arabic is commonly used for numbers and quantities, but here it may also have the capacity to conceal their discussions from the customer, though this appears to backfire when the customer recognizes the Arabic/Maltese for yellow. With other workers on their part of the floor speaking a variety of languages, English and Arabic may be used separately or together, depending on the people with whom they are interacting. In the fast-paced buying and selling, moving and ordering of this space, however, patterns of language use are not easily predictable. With varied linguistic trajectories and repertoires, with varied possibilities for 'lingo-ing', the patterns are always emergent in the local interaction. This is more than 'feeling comfortable to lingo in [their] own background' but is rather the process of management and engagement of linguistic resources as part of wider metrolingual practices involving people, space and vegetables.

This example also shows again the layers of action, interaction and transaction in metrolingual multitasking practices, as the brothers move around, assess prices and quantities, check the quality of the vegetables and negotiate with customers. It is to capture this relationship between the linguistic resources (which include varieties of Arabic, varieties of English and a range of mixed practices), everyday tasks (the buying and selling of vegetables, the stacking of pallets as orders are filled, the lifting of boxes, and updates on supermarket special deals) and social space (the size of their operation within this warehouse, its location around 'Door 2' at the 'Lebanese end', the predominantly male sociality of the customers, workers and cafés) that we focus on metrolingual multitasking. This metrolingual multitasking then needs to be understood in relation to the spatial repertoires (discussed further in Chapter 4) of this workplace.

This understanding of repertoires of linguistic resources draws on the earlier work of Gumperz, who described linguistic repertoires as 'the totality of linguistic forms regularly employed in the course of socially significant interaction' (1964, p. 137).

Questioning the idea of the speech community on which Gumperz's work depended, more recent approaches to this idea have focused on the historical trajectories of individuals as they move through time and space, including the bodily, emotional and historical-political dimensions of life trajectories (Busch, 2012b; 2013). Repertoires, from Blommaert and Backus' (2013) point of view are therefore 'individual, biographically organized complexes of resources' that 'follow the rhythms of actual human lives' (p. 15) and 'reflect the polycentricity of the learning environments in which the speaker dwells' (p. 20).

Lest repertoires are seen as located only within and at the disposal of the individual, however, we have developed the idea of *spatial repertoires*, akin in some ways (see discussion in Chapter 4) to Li Wei's notion of *translanguaging space* (2011, p. 1223). Talib and Muhibb bring to their work their own linguistic repertoires based on their particular histories as second generation Lebanese-Australian market workers. These linguistic resources, however, can only be understood in relation to the practices they engage in (buying, selling, ordering, stacking) and the other linguistic resources that people bring to this space (varieties of Arabic, English and other languages) and which then form such spatial repertoires. From our point of view, then, we need to understand the relations between personal trajectories, current activities and spatial repertoires in order to account more fully for the language practices of market places and other contexts of metrolingual interaction.

Multilingualism from below

We have drawn attention here to the everydayness of metrolingual practices. This view we are connecting more broadly to Higgins and Coen's (2000) views on the *ordinariness of diversity* whereby 'diversity is the given reality of human social action – it does not have to be found; it is already there' (p. 15). We are also drawing here on ideas of multiculturalism and globalization from below. For Wise and Velayutham (2009), multiculturalism from below, or everyday multi-culturalism, is understood as 'a grounded approach to looking at the *everyday practice* and lived experience of diversity in specific situations and spaces of encounter' (p. 3). Rather than the policy-oriented, top-down approaches to multiculturalism that look at ethnic groups in terms of rights, entities and social groupings, the attempt here is to get at everyday practices, at the ways, for example, that young people work their way through cultural diversity in multicultural cities and suburbs (Harris, 2013), at the small-scale local encounters of 'intercultural "rubbing along" in the public spaces of the city' (Watson, 2009, p. 126). From this point of view, we can only understand everyday multiculturalism or metrolingualism 'in its local sociocultural specificity' (p. 127). This is the space of ordinary or working class cosmopolitanism, of the 'incremental and dialogic construction of lived identities' (Ang, 2001, p. 159) in mundane interactions over fruit, vegetables, prices, and other market practices.

Wise (2009) develops the notion of *quotidian tansversality* to describe the ways in which 'individuals in everyday spaces use particular modes of sociality to produce or smooth interrelations across cultural difference' (p. 23). Quotidian tansversality, she explains, is neither hybridity nor code-mixing; nor is it an assimilationist or integrationist notion of exchange requiring unbalanced forms of accommodation. Instead, the focus here is on 'how cultural difference can be the basis for commensality and exchange; where identities are not left behind, but can be shifted and opened up in moments of non-hierarchical reciprocity, and are sometimes mutually reconfigured in the process' (p. 23). Everyday forms of exchange – fruit, vegetables and garden produce between neighbours, for example – 'produce capacities for the recognition or acknowledgement of otherness in situational specificity' (p. 35). A central part of this, from our point of view, is the *quotidian translinguality* used in such encounters, the negotiation of language resources, the deployment of multiple semiotic codes in interactive moments. Everyday urban multilingualism – metrolingualism – is that form of quotidian translingual exchange that is part of how the city works, how language and identity are negotiated. And while Wise focuses on cultural difference as the basis for commensality, we shall focus in coming chapters (see Chapter 6) on the linguistic differences in relation to commensality.

As Noble (2009) notes, the *super-diversity* described by Vertovec (2006) and taken up by many others (e.g. Blommaert, 2010) to account for the increasing diversity in European cities, has long been part of the common reality in Australian cities. The idea of super-diversity is largely a European reaction to the recent necessary engagement with urban diversity. But the rest of the world has been doing diversity for a lot longer. What is now going on in Australian cities, Noble argues, discussing a study of Australian diversity (Ang *et al.*, 2006), is a form of *hyper-diversity*:

> it wasn't just that people lived hybrid lives, or lived them in polyethnic neighbourhoods, but that complexity and its subsequent forms of interaction were of such a nature that they went beyond typical understandings of multiculturalism and corresponded to the claim that diversity was becoming more diverse.
>
> (p. 47)

In trying to understand everyday cosmopolitanism, Noble (2009) argues for the need to study *unpanicked multiculturalism*: 'spaces of cultural complexity which don't become subject to conflict or anxieties regarding social fragmentation' (pp. 50–51). From this point of view, rather than viewing cosmopolitanism in terms of some moral ideal of openness and interaction, it can be viewed as 'forms of situated, strategic, transactional labour' (p. 52). Likewise, our focus is not on some idealized state of marvelous multilingualism but rather on the everyday work of unpanicked metrolingual practices. The mischievous challenges in the zucchini transactions shown previously are not so much panicked multilingualism as everyday metrolingual exchanges.

This also ties in with the idea of *globalization from below*, a term used to describe 'globalization as experienced by most of the world's people' or more explicitly as 'the transnational flow of people and goods involving relatively small amounts of capital and informal, often semi-legal or illegal transactions' (Mathews & Vega, 2012, p. 1). Globalization from below is similar to Appadurai's (2001) *grassroots globalization*, part of his understanding that 'we are functioning in a world fundamentally characterized by objects in motion', which include 'ideas and ideologies, people and goods, images and messages, technologies and techniques' (p. 5). An understanding of globalization from below typically involves a focus on market places and cities with large informal economies (Guangzhou, Mexico City, Kolkata, Cairo and São Paolo are typical examples; Mathews, 2012), but it also occurs in all those local markets and interactions across many smaller domains.

These local yet global markets are all around us. In a small shopping plaza in a northern Sydney suburb, alongside the Japanese grocery store, butcher, Indian spice shop, and the African and Nepalese restaurants, an Indian arts and crafts shop sells saris to Anglo-Bollywood party goers. The owner, who is from Punjab and tells us he speaks Hindi, Dogri, Punjabi, Kashmiri, Haryanyi and English, goes to India every six months to purchase Indian arts, crafts and jewellery to supply the niche Sydney market for Bollywood parties. Meanwhile, the very produce market complex where Muhibb and Talib sell cherry tomatoes and extra large zucchini becomes on Fridays a market where products such as leather jackets, cosmetics, batik clothes, wigs, music and CDs, herbs and spices converge from all over the world.

And on the weekend, it becomes a produce market where, as Joseph explains, recently arrived refugees from Iraq and Afghanistan take advantage of the bulk food prices: 'They've settled in Sydney district over here and they use the market to do their shopping in bulk for their family. So they've obviously done their homework and they do it that way' (Joseph, interview, August 8, 2012). In the multiethnic Sydney suburb of Marrickville, Song's Discount Store sells anything from plastic flowers and kitchenware to framed texts from the Koran alongside models of Genesha, the Hindu elephant-headed deity, Christian iconography, including a plastic model of the last supper, and gold 'Lucky Cats' gesturing with their left paw at passers-by. Song herself, the co-owner, speaks Thai, Lao and Teochow (her 'mother tongue'), as well as Mandarin and bits and pieces of Cantonese, Vietnamese and Greek that she has picked up from her interactions with her diverse clientele (see Chapter 5). The products in her store, cheaply produced, cheaply sold, make their way to such outlets through the diverse pathways of grassroots globalization. These places, therefore, are diverse not only in terms of the products stacked up alongside each other but also in terms of the cultural and linguistic diversity of the people who shop here.

These 'markets, flows, and trade networks that are part of globalization from below' relate to what Ribeiro (2012, p. 221) calls 'the non-hegemonic world system', an alternative to the dominant and homogenizing forces of globalization: 'Globalization from below is structured by flows of people, goods, information, and capital among different production centres and market places which, in turn, are the nodes of the non-hegemonic world-system' (p. 223). Many participants and activities in these informal economic relations are considered illegal or criminal, involving as they often do pirated and copied goods, informal and non-taxed cash economies and the transport of goods across borders without legal sanction. As Ribeiro argues, however, such judgments of legality and illegality, and claims to a moral monopoly over the rules of trade, are always in the hands of the powerful, of those intent on protecting their own modes of trade: 'It is the rich and powerful who, through the control of state apparatuses and wider political structures, create a transgressive image of the workers and entrepreneurs of the non-hegemonic system' (p. 230). While the multilingualism from below that interests us here is not legally (un)sanctioned in the same way, it nevertheless sits outside the strictures of much analysis of multilingualism from above, with its preference for languages as clearly defined and countable entities. It is informal multilingualism from below, the non-hegemonic world of daily language use, that interests us, processes of communication that often occur precisely in these same contexts of informal economies. We shall return to this discussion of languages and market value in Chapter 8.

The idea of *multilingualism from below*, then, is central to our project. This idea, however, may be understood in various ways. Webb (2010) for example, asks whether South Africa will become 'meaningfully multilingual from below' and answers in the negative: 'South Africa is not a multilingual country, nor is it likely to become one, despite all the top-down "prescriptions" (the constitution, national provincial, municipal and institutional policies) and bottom-up activities (of activists) which have taken place since 1994' (p. 143). While there are reasons to be sceptical about the kind of multilingualism represented by official South African language policy, the argument that South Africa is not multilingual, especially when looking 'from below', seems an unlikely conclusion. Webb's position is based on his definition of mutilingualism as 'the use and recognition of more than two languages in high-function public contexts in the major domains and at all the different levels, that is, that more than two languages are accepted as linguistically equal and have parity of esteem in the public domain' (p. 143).

This framing of multilingualism from below as the recognition of language equality and use at a local level differs in several ways from our approach, which does not assume that equality is in any way necessary for the recognition of multilingualism. Indeed, everyday metrolingual practices are inevitably bound up with social and economic disparities. Our interest is in understanding those metrolingual practices that are part of everyday life, and to do so not through predefined versions of languages in terms of equitable language policies but instead through local language ideologies. Multilingualism from below, then, is about the ways in which people get by linguistically and how they understand such linguistic practices from their perspectives. It is not therefore concerned with the extent to which local language policies and practices reflect top-down understandings of language (how language realities reflect language ideals) but rather is constantly challenging those very ideas of language that are employed in language policies (Pennycook, 2013).

Exploring multilingualism from below from a different perspective, van Camp and Juffermans (2010) respond to this challenge by taking up the question posed by Makoni and Mashiri (2007): Do we need a construct of language for language planning in Africa? In order to address this, the authors point out that we need to take up local understandings of language – language ideologies – as part of the investigation. This is why, in part, we take seriously Joseph's comments about Lebanese, lingo-ing and broken English. We need to understand the distinction Mohanty (2013) makes between 'grassroots multilingualism' – the use of 'multiple languages in daily life transcations' (p. 307) – and the language policies of Indian education. Blommaert's (2008) *grassroots literacy* is similarly concerned with 'writing performed by people who are not fully inserted into elite economies of information, language and literacy' (p. 7), and indeed Blommaert's discussion of 'grassroots literacy in globalisation' (pp. 194–197) links well with our understanding of globalization from below.

From a related perspective, Blommaert, Leppänen and Spotti (2012) talk of the need to understand the complexity of 'multilingualism-on-the-ground'. For people who speak a 'mixed, hybrid variety of language – a typical urban variety of language, in other words – they are not well served when their language is dissected and regarded as being composed of two or three other ones' (p. 18). Likewise Makoni, Makoni and Pennycook (2010) suggest that emergent urban varieties are 'multilanguages in themselves, diverse, shifting, and variable according to who is using them with whom, at what point, and to what effect' (p. 148). From this point of view, multilingualism from below describes not so much the capacity to use different linguistic codes, but rather 'a facility for handling a mobile multilanguage' (p. 148; and see Chapter 8).

Metrolingualism – as multilingualism from below – focuses therefore on local language practices rather than the local implementation and appropriation of top-down language policies. To understand multilingualism from below, we need sociolinguistic ethnographies of language in use that include local understandings of language and do not impose pregiven understandings of language and multilingualism. From this perspective, then, multilingualism from below is about how people get along with their multiple linguistic resources in their daily lives and also how they perceive and talk about this language use. This is about how Muhibb and Talib use (Lebanese-Australian) English with their multilingual workforce: 'Johnny fix up the stand! Here move these cherry tomatoes put them with them. Let them do it.' It is about how they mix English and Arabic with each other and respond to others' mixed utterances: 'Tell him *arba wa ashreen*'; '*Salamu alaykum* mate'. It also concerns the ways they sort out a problem when their use of Arabic *isfar* has been understood by a Maltese customer: 'Get that one and we'll get you another one.' It includes ways of modulating their English to match this same customer: 'Extra large like yours no good.' It also comprises the background of the intense predawn activity of the market. This is what we have termed metrolingual multitasking in order to capture the relations between language use, objects, accompanying activities and interactive space.

Metrolingual multitasking in a restaurant

In order to shed more light on the arguments we are making here, let us switch tracks, and places, and cities, and look at a short interaction in a restaurant in Tokyo. The excerpt below is another example of what we have termed *metrolingual multitasking*. We are using this phrase, as explained previously, in an attempt to grasp the ways in which linguistic resources, everyday tasks and social space are intertwined. Our central focus, therefore, is not only on the diversity of linguistic resources in 'unusual' combinations here but also on the dynamic relations between semiotic resources, activities, artefacts and space. Located next to a park that was famous in the nineteenth and early-twentieth centuries for its Geisha houses (*Karyūkai*), *Petit Paris'* establishment in Kagurazaka, whose small, sloping, cobbled streets dating from the Edo (seventeenth to nineteenth centuries) period are often said to recall Montmartre in Paris, is significant (Tauzin, 2009).

The management philosophy of *Petit Paris*, according to the owner Nabil who was born in the small city of Tipaza in Algeria, to a Moroccan mother and an Algerian father, is the 'reproduction' of a Paris bistro. With its old wooden wine boxes (with French text) as decoration around the counter, as well as the high bar stools, the atmosphere is more casual than formal. The customers are mainly Japanese, including students from the Institut Franco-Japonais de Tokyo (a nearby French language school). The staff comprise two chefs (Jean: from France, who worked in Cuba, Lebanon, Italy and Greece as a chef before moving to Tokyo 11 years ago; Pierre: from Réunion, who lived in Paris before coming to Tokyo), a Japanese manager (Hata san) from Tokyo and two floor staff (Nabil and Stéphane: born in Côte d'Ivoire and grew up in Morocco and New York as a child). The linguistic, cultural and gastronomic coming-together at *Petit Paris* thus entails a complex traffic and interaction of trajectories, historicities and mobilities.

The interaction below revolves around Nabil as he squeezes between tables, delivers meals, takes orders, and directs staff, interacting with the chef (line 1), a Japanese customer (lines 2 to 5) and another member of the floor staff of French background (line 6). The entire transaction takes place within 30 seconds.

Excerpt 1.4 (Na: Nabil, C: Customer)
French: **bold**; Japanese: *italics*[2]; Italian: ***bold italics;*** English: plain (translation in brackets)
1. Na: **Oui chef. Je suis là !** (Yes Chef. I'm coming!)
[a few exchanges in French between Nabil and chef about the food order]
2. Na: *Are*? (what?) Sorry sorry sorry sorry.
3. Na: Sorry **Chefterrine**. Sorry *gomen nasai ... to Hotate no* ***carpaccio.*** (Sorry excuse me ... and scallop carpaccio)
4. C: *a::: Sugoi* ! (wo :::w great !)
5. Na: **Voilà.** *Sumimasen.* **Voilà. Bon appétit!** (Here it is. Excuse me. Here. Have a nice dinner!)

6. Na: **pain** (bread) two people and two people *onegaishimasu*. (please)
    Encore une assiette. De pain. (One more plate. Bread.)

Within a short period of time, Nabil, the owner and floor staff of *Petit Paris*, whose own trajectory has brought him from his origins in Tipaza in the Maghreb, via Paris to Tokyo (with a few other stops on the way), moves around the restaurant floor, negotiating in French with the chef about the dish, passing between tables and managing customers in English and Japanese (Sorry *gomen nasai*). He serves food to customers (*hotate no **carpaccio:** scallop carpaccio*), the Japanese and Italian of the dish name combined like the ingredients and the cooking style, while also using the linguistic and culinary capital of French with customers (**voilà, bon appétit**). The orders for bread (**pain**) and another plate (**encore une assiette**), directed to other staff are in French, either side of a request to another member of the floor staff (who also speaks French) in English and Japanese to attend to two new customers who have just arrived (two people, and two people *onegaishimasu*).

As he moves between tables, takes orders, delivers meals, directs staff and manages the restaurant more generally, Nabil is thus engaged in a range of multimodal semiotic practices. Of importance here are the interrelationships between restaurant multitasking and linguistic resources, and the intricate patterning of movement, activity and semiotic supplies. Our interest is in the ways in which linguistic and non-linguistic resources are deployed in this busy (though not large) urban restaurant and how this, in turn, is related to an understanding of space. At any point in the flow of such activity, several different factors have to be understood together: There is Nabil with his own personal trajectory and linguistic repertoire (we return in Chapter 4 to a discussion of individual and spatial repertoires); particular customers and staff (though by no means an easily predictable pattern of language use according to their background); the material artefacts and activities involved (the bringing of scallops and bread, and request for another plate); the movement through the crowded restaurant (the layout of the restaurant and the small gaps between the tables are vital for an understanding of these interactions); and the social and cultural trajectory and identity of Kagurazaka, where all this occurs.

We shall come back to *Petit Paris* at various points in the book. Above all, what we wish to point to in this chapter is not so much the exotic hybridity of a French (Maghreb background) restaurant worker's use of English, French and Japanese, nor to the market value of the languages at play here. Of course it matters that Arabic seems to have no place in this restaurant while it frequently occurs in the discourse of Muhibb and Talib in the market, or that English plays a significant role in both, and that French retains a certain symbolic value, or perhaps, as Redder notes with respect to the use of Italian in a Hamburg restaurant, 'maintains the "dolce vita" counter world' (2013, p. 278). Rather, we wish to emphasize the everydayness of these deployments of multilingual resources and their interactions with the multiple tasks these people are engaged in.

Place, activity and language are intertwined and ordinary. By *metrolingualism*, then, we refer not so much to state-centric descriptions of diversity, but rather to local accounts of multiplicity, grounded accounts of language users, where multilingualism is not merely a plurality of languages but rather a creative space of language making, where rules and boundaries are crossed and changed. The *metro* as we understand it is the productive space provided by, though not limited to, the contemporary city to produce new language identities. Such an interpretation is intended to avoid the pluralization of languages and cultures, and to accommodate the complex ways in which fluid and fixed, as well as global and local, practices reconstitute language and identities.

Beyond monolingualism: Niemand ist einsprachig

Our non-count approach to diversity (metrolingualism rather than multilingualism) shifts the focus away from relations between languages (bilingualism, code-switching, multilingualism, translanguaging), or from how different languages are deployed in particular domains (demolinguistic mapping) or from how the individual is a container of various languages (competence, individual repertoires). Rather, the focus is on local language practices, which also has implications for the singularity of monolingualism. Unlike other work that has been critical of 'monolingualism', suggesting that we need to move beyond a 'monolingual mindset' in order to engage with multilingualism, we argue that all such arguments stem from the same problematic enumerative strategies. Multilingualism is all too often viewed in all-or-nothing terms. From this monological point of view, there are speakers and there are languages, and either a person speaks only one language, in which case they are 'monolingual', or they speak more than one, in which case they are bi- or multilingual. Either one speaks several languages or one does not.

We view this question differently. Not only do we note the obvious problems and prejudices in ideas such as *zerolingualism* – a pernicious Belgian coinage suggesting inadequate proficiency 'in either home or state languages, or more particularly of having an inadequate grounding in Dutch' (Jaspers, 2011, p. 1267) – and *semilingualism* or 'double semilingualism' (Skutnabb-Kangas, 1981, p. 250) – suggesting that a person's linguistic competence might be made up of two half competencies – but we also want to suggest that all these accounts, from zerolingualism and semilingualism, via monolingualism, to bilingualism, trilingualism and multilingualism, stem from similar problematic approaches to language enumeration.

A lot of work in the realm of multilingualism has sought both to show the richness and commonality of multilingualism and to critique what have been termed the *monolingual mindset* or *monolingual habitus*, those deep-seated tendencies to view monolingualism as the norm (Clyne, 2005; Gogolin, 1994). Some have gone as far as describing monolingualism as 'an illness, a disease which should be eradicated as soon as possible because it is dangerous for world peace' (Skutnabb-Kangas, 1988, p. 13; Skunabb-Kangas & Phillipson, 1989, p. 469). This critique has, quite rightly, focused on the problem that both popular and academic discussion of language in many contexts has for too long started from a baseline of monolingualism. Bilingualism and multilingualism have been seen as exceptional, as remarkable, as exotic even, and practices such as code-switching have been deemed in need of explanation: We have to explain why different languages are mixed together since they defy the norm of speaking one language at a time. The monolingual mindset has also been linked to the role that Global English plays since English speakers often appear to lack the will or motivation to learn other languages not only because they don't appear to need to, but also because they don't appear to understand the benefits of doing so. So despite the deep multilingualism of countries such as Australia, there remains a dominant Australian view that is Anglo-oriented, speaking only one language, poor at learning others and suspicious of the use of multiple languages (Clyne, 2005).

One of the aims of this book is to show how out of touch with everyday multilingualism such a view is. Yet while we are in accord with many of the critiques of blinkered monolingualism, we also want to insist that monolingualism (like zero-, semi-, bi- and mutilingualism) is an ideological construct rather than a linguistic reality. Just as Cummins (2000) concedes that his and others' use of the term *semilingualism* had 'no theoretical value and confuses rather than clarifies the issues' (pp. 104–105) (while also noting that 'liberating the field of applied linguistics from the construct of "semilingualism"' (p. 105) does not itself solve the problem of how we understand students' unequal access to and command of language resources), so we want to suggest here that the term monolingualism also has little theoretical value, and that while liberating the field of applied linguistics from this construct does not solve either the problem of unequal access to linguistic resources nor ignorance of everyday multilingualism, it allows us to address enumerative language ideologies that are equally part of the problem.

One difficulty with language enumeration can be seen in interviews with construction workers of Serbian backgrounds (for further discussion, see Chapter 2). As one of them explains, countering the divisions that have been created after the break up of Yugoslavia, 'I don't like to speak it as Serbia, Croatia, this bullshit, it's all Yugoslav ... Serbian, Bosnian, Croatian, is same language ... We speak Yugoslav. When it comes some of this people who is no speak our language, we speak English' (Igor, interview, March 12, 2011). The obvious point here is that while we might now accord a level of bilingualism in 'Yugoslav' and English, his 'monolingualism' prior to learning English is very dependent on how we count languages. He rejects the break up of Serbo-Croatian into separate languages, and insists that he speaks Yugoslav. The reasons for such a stance might be anything from nostalgic nationalism to contemporary pragmatism, but the implications are clear: Monolingualism is not so transparent or discernible a condition. It is on these contested grounds that Busch and Schick (2007) have argued not only for the need to 'overcome the monolingual habitus in education' (p. 230) but also to show how mono- and multilingual myths in such contexts may be usefully undone. On this basic level, then, the question of whether one is monolingual or not is dependent on particular language ideologies.

Brigitta Busch (2012a) takes such arguments further, however, suggesting that 'Niemand is einsprachig' (no one is monolingual). Reinvigorating Gumperz's (1964) notion of the speech repertoire (see also the discussion outlined previously), which is not dependent on accounting for different languages as numerable entities but rather on the idea of a toolkit or arsenal of linguistic resources, Busch argues that instead of accounting for language varieties, or first, second and third languages, we need to ask how speech varieties serve to construct a sense of belonging or difference and how such constructions are experienced in terms of linguistic inclusion or exclusion (our translation, p. 8). The experience of starting school, for example, can render one's speech out of place, give one a feeling of being out of place (*ein Gefühl von Out-of-Place-Sein*), of being deplaced, of finding oneself with the wrong language in the wrong place (p. 16). Language, Busch goes on to argue, is a bodily (*leiblich*) and emotional relation of power and belonging.

In this exploration of the ways in which our language practices render us part or not part of different speech communities, Busch also takes up Derrida's (1996) key text on the monolingualism of the Other (*le monolinguisme de l'autre*). Derrida was born into an Algerian Jewish family (El-Biar, Jacques Derrida's birthplace, is along the coast from Tipaza (Tipasa) where Nabil, from *Petit Paris,* grew up) with French citizenship and thus, as he explains, French became his only language (Arabic and Berber were scarcely present in his upbringing, he points out, and Ladino – the old Judaeo-Spanish lingua franca based on varieties of Spanish, Hebrew, Turkish and much more – was no longer a language of the family). In her exploration of what she calls the 'postmonolingual condition', Yildiz (2012) discusses writers such as Kafka (as does Kramsch, 2008, from a related perspective), arguing that his adoption of the language of assimilation, German, is akin to Derrida's understanding of his own relation to French, the monolingualism of the Other (Evans, 2012; McNamara, 2012). These examples of writers such as Kafka or Celan, or of an Algerian Jew speaking French, should not, as Derrida (2005) reminds us, be taken as exceptional cases, but rather, as Bakhtin and many others have argued, as the general condition of language.

What Derrida questions here is a sense of ownership and belonging, the idea that our so-called mother tongue is something we own, we possess; rather, he suggests, echoing Bakhtin (1981; 1986) in another way, it is always someone else's – 'The monolingual of whom I speak speaks a language of which he is deprived. The French language is not his' (1998, p. 60): 'Je n'ai qu'une langue, ce n'est pas la mienne' (I have only one language; it is not my own). Our general argument, then, following Busch (2012a; 2013), is that one cannot be monolingual: The idea of monolingualism is an unfortunate historical myth that grew up in an age of nations and monocultures. Noting that it is 'monolingualism, not multilingualism, that is the result of a relatively recent, albeit highly successful, development', Yildiz (2012, p. 3) points out that 'monolingualism is much more than a simple quantitative term designating the presence of just one language'. Rather, it has become 'a key structuring principle that organizes the entire range of modern social life, from the construction of individuals and their proper subjectivities to the formation of disciplines and institutions, as well as imagined collectives such as cultures and nations' (p. 3). Monolingualism, then, is one of the founding principles of modernity, a set of beliefs about language that have ordered much of the world as we know it; and like many such myths, it is not easily overcome.

The way forward here, therefore, is not to critique monolingualism in favour of multilingualism, but to understand the discursive history of enumerative approaches to language (Makoni & Pennycook, 2007). As Canagarajah (2013) puts it, 'If languages are always in contact and communication always involves a negotiation of mobile codes, we have to ask if the term monolingual has anything more than an academic and ideological significance' (p. 8). To the extent that the critique of the monolingual mindset expands our understanding of the ordinariness of multilingualism, it can assist in undermining the discursive construction of the exceptionality of diverse language resources; but if it also, by assuming the real condition of monolingualism, contributes to the myth of language enumerability, it also falls prey to the linguistic ideologies it needs to supersede. Once we take on board Yildiz's (2012) contention that 'mother tongues' are not so much seamless wholes but rather aggregates of many elements, relations, belongings, attachments and identifications that may include multiple linguistic resources; if we accept Busch's (2012a; 2013) argument that the question is one of belonging, and only someone who has never experienced feelings of belonging and not belonging in different situations could be monolingual; and if we accept a Bakhtinian perspective on the heteroglossia of language (Pietikäinen, 2013), then the possibility of monolingualism becomes increasingly suspect.

Metrolingualism is not therefore dependent on the enumeration of language resources. Language practices constantly echo other language practices. Yiddish, it might be argued, is still spoken through English, German and, as Zuckerman explains, through Hebrew: 'Almost all "revivalists" … were native Yiddish-speakers who wanted to speak Hebrew, with Semitic grammar and pronunciation, like Arabs. Not only were they European but their revivalist campaign was inspired by European—e.g. Bulgarian—nationalism' (Zuckerman, 2009, p. 43). Modern Israeli (Hebrew) is, argues Zuckerman, relexified Yiddish. Although some practices of speaking languages through others (speaking other languages through English, for example; see Canagarajah, 2013; Pennycook, 2008) are premised on notions of bi- or multi-lingualism, this need not be so. A bit of 'Yugoslav' during the construction site lunchtime may be as metrolingual as Muhibb's '*tnanan* dollar', Talib's 'Zu::chi::ni::' or Nabil's 'Sorry **Chefterrine**. Sorry *gomen nasai* '. When we talk of metrolingualism, then, we are not necessarily talking of 'language mixing' or 'multilingualism'. We may equally be referring to what may be seen by others as 'monolingualism', which can no longer be conceived as a narrow capacity to speak only one language. Metrolingualism is neither monolingualism nor multilingualism; it has to do with the dynamic interrelationship between language practices and urban space.

Research notes and emergent themes

This book is based on extensive research in a variety of urban contexts in Sydney and Tokyo. The approach taken (which will be discussed further at different points in each chapter) may be classified, if such classifications are useful, as multisite linguistic ethnography. Our work is allied in a number of ways to the linguistic ethnography framework developed by Creese and Blackledge (Blackledge & Creese, 2010; Creese, 2008; Creese & Blackledge, 2011) and others (Maybin & Tusting, 2011; Rampton, 2007), which draws on the anthropological insights of linguistic anthropology but starts above all with language as its focus. The social meanings of participants have to be grasped ethnographically, as Rampton (2007) reminds us, and thus to understand the local language practices of participants we need both ethnography and close linguistic analysis.

Although we share some of the interests (daily multilingual language use in city space) captured by the idea of 'glottography' (Ehlich, 2011) – the mapping of languages as 'used by the actants in certain space segments (and the specifics of their domain) of the interaction space called city' (Redder, 2013, p. 264) – our aim is not to map language functions but to capture language practices. Like Li Wei's (2011) understanding of 'Moment Analysis', we do not seek either to map languages and functions or to describe language use according to assumed patterns of regularity. The analysis of multilingual practices 'requires a paradigm shift, away from frequency and regularity oriented, pattern-seeking approaches to a focus on spontaneous, impromptu, and momentary actions and performances of the individual' (Li Wei, 2011, p. 1224). This is not to say that such language use is random, indiscriminate or haphazard, but rather to suggest that 'original, momentary actions, or innovative moments, become patterns by being recognized, adopted and repeated by the other individuals' (p. 1224). It is the emergent and sedimented regularities of metrolingual practices that provide coherence, not assumed regularities in terms of functions and activities.

In line with Heller's (2011) 'critical ethnographic sociolinguistics', we are trying to study contextually (ethnographically) the social use of language (sociolinguistics) with an eye to understanding relations of social differentiation and inequality (critical). Like Heller, we are interested in

> what actors do with linguistic resources that circulate through social spaces and social networks, both in terms of how mobilizing linguistic resources is part of other forms of social action, and in terms of how that contributes to the construction of linguistic ideologies.
>
> (p. 49)

And like Blommaert and Dong (2010), we see ethnography here as a counter-hegemonic project, an attempt in constructing a discourse on social uses of language and social dimensions of meaningful behaviour which differs strongly from established norms and expectations, indeed takes the concrete functioning of these norms and expectations as starting points for questioning them, in other words it takes them as problems rather than as facts.

(pp. 10–11)

Or as Higgins and Coen (2000) put it, this is a form of *ethnographic praxis* (p. 15), aimed not only at description but also at change.

Just as globalization from below cannot be understood through the data gathering and statistical analyses that may inform an understanding of globalization from above, so multilingualism from below cannot be usefully understood through a perspective of linguistic accounting. In order to understand the use and flow of copied sports shoes and mobile phones from China to Cairo, Hong Kong to Kenya, or the clothes shipped from Hong Kong to the Philippines, or the Chinese CDs copied in Mexico, and the cash that changes hands along the routes such goods take across borders, we need ethnographies of everyday market practices, not international financial analysis. 'Ethnography is absolutely essential to grasp globalization from below because only through looking at the particulars of how its different parts work in different areas can it be made sense of' (Mathews & Vega, 2012, p. 6). Likewise, in order to grasp the linguistic interactions that accompany such trade, and the more general field of multilingualism from below, we need ethnographies of local language practices in markets, shops, streets, suburbs, construction sites and more.

The data are drawn from a project conducted over several years looking at local language practices as people get along metrolinguistically, shaping and remaking the linguistic landscape of restaurants, cafés, kitchens, market places, construction sites, shops and small businesses[3]. Although such a spread of multisite ethnographic investigation renders the time spent in each necessarily at the shorter end of desirable exploration, our repeated visits, follow-ups and continued engagement nonetheless allowed us a reasonable sense of ethnographic capture (Jeffrey & Toman, 2004). The goal of this project is to shed light on the ways in which multilingualism from below operates in the urban environment. It also ties, therefore, to Blackledge and Creese's (2010) understanding of 'ethnography of multilingualism', which reveals 'how language practices are connected to the very real conditions of people's lives' (p. 18).

Given that the linguistic ethnographic background has been well covered elsewhere (Blackledge & Creese, 2010; Blommaert & Dong, 2010), we have decided not to devote a major chunk of this book to a reiteration of research orientations. We will instead introduce particular research practices in shorter sections in each chapter: 'Ethnography as process' (Chapter 2), 'Languages and the unexpected' (Chapter 3), 'Researching language, mobility and practices in place' (Chapter 4), 'Research and stories' (Chapter 5), 'Multitasking and participatory research' (Chapter 6), 'Researching networks' (Chapter 7) and 'Writing it all together' (Chapter 8). Originally conceived around the different ethnographic sites (restaurants, cafés, kitchens, market places, construction sites, shops and small businesses), this book has instead developed around the emergent research themes. Rather than looking at different research sites in each chapter, therefore, we will instead be exploring themes that emerged during the research process, such as multitasking, linguistic affiliations, rhythms and mobility, spatial repertoires, conviviality, commensality, layers and metrolingua francas.

This chapter has introduced metrolingual multitasking (which will be taken up further at several points) and everyday multilingualism. In the following chapters we take up and develop these themes further through a focus on the linguistic and culinary networks that Joseph points to, and the ways in which workers become affiliated along linguistic and ethnic lines (Chapter 2). We will look in particular at Chinese market gardens and construction sites, the shared linguistic resources of some trades and also the ways in which these ethnic and linguistic affiliations are constructed. The idea of rhythms and mobility in the city (hinted at in the opening of this chapter), the linguistic implications of different temporal and spatial dispositions, will be explored in greater depth in Chapter 3, with a focus on a variety of small businesses and cafés. Kitchens and restaurants become part of the focus in Chapter 4, where we pay particular attention to the idea of spatial repertoires and of space and place more broadly.

In Chapter 5 we look at the tension between the convivial and the contested city: As Joseph comments, 'there's always a jokes about languages, where we pick all the bad words and naughty words. We throw at each other ... but not in a nasty way, just ah, a friendly thing'. While we find many examples in our data of very positive views of multilingualism and multiculturalism, these also often convey quite fixed and static images of others. Chapter 6 returns to the question of food and commensality. Here we look at different contexts of eating and talking together, talk about food and talk over food. The different layers, spaces and signs of the city are the central focus of Chapter 7 as we develop our exploration of particular suburbs, and the ways in which these become historically layered. In the final chapter we return to the markets where this chapter started and explore the relation between the spatial repertoires of such places and the *metrolingua francas* that emerge amid these complex communications. We conclude with a brief discussion of some policy and pedagogical implications of the arguments in the book.

Notes

1   This can be dangerous work, too: During our period of research at this market, at 5:20 am on June 26, 2012, forklift driver Lilipe Manuoliku Hehea was killed when his forklift turned over in one of the loading areas.

2   The choice of orthography and transcription style posed a major challenge in this research, nowhere more so than in texts using Japanese. In this extract (1.4), for example, we used *rōmaji* (Roman script in italics) in order not to increase the perceived difference between Japanese and other languages that would arise from using Japanese scripts (*kanji* or *hiragana*) and to avoid the pitfalls of using *katakana* (the Japanese

script for non-Japanese words). Elsewhere, however, we have used Japanese scripts, particularly in interviews. For further discussion, see research section of Chapter 3.

3   Most of the data in this book comes from the research project *Metrolingual language practices in four urban sites: Talking in the city,* an Australian Research Council (ARC) Discovery Project (DP110101014), chief investigators Alastair Pennycook and Emi Otsuji, with project manager Astrid Lorange.

2 Constructing affiliations and growing foreign vegetables

Gwai Lou Coi: growing foreign vegetables

Down at the 'Chinese end' of the Produce Market discussed in the previous chapter, old Uncle Tony fills us in on some of the history of the Sydney markets, having himself started work in the old Haymarket in 1938, before moving to the Produce Market in the 1970s. Unlike the Chinese-dominated market of today (see Chapter 8), Haymarket then was 'Italian. Italian. Italian. After Italian, the Maltese' (Uncle Tony, interview, September 21, 2012). Here Uncle Tony charts one of those slow patterns of change from the earlier Italian role in the fruit and vegetable businesses to the Maltese, and the fact that such markets have nearly always had such mixes. He recalls that they used to sell to small businesses who sold their goods from a horse and cart: 'They bought from Haymarket in their little, little, horse cart – one horse with a cart – and all the fruit in the back, you know.'

As Uncle Tony maps this history of ethnic patterns of migration and involvement in fruit and vegetable growing and selling, we are reminded of Joseph's remarks (Chapter 1) about the linguistic and ethnic affiliations – 'they do lingo in their own language' – that bring people together to buy similar fruit and vegetables from each other (and see Chapter 7 for the Japanese cucumber network). Eighty per cent of market gardeners in the Sydney Basin, as James (2008) notes, are from non-English-speaking backgrounds. Alongside the Chinese are Lebanese, Italian, Maltese, Vietnamese and Cambodian, and these clearly link along trading lines from market gardens to markets, shops and restaurants. Thus these gardens are connected through large social and linguistic networks across these local regions, with many of these ties, for the Chinese and Lebanese (but less for the Cambodians and Vietnamese because of their migration via refugee camps) linking to families, regions and neighbouring villages in China and Lebanon (James, 2008).

Looking at the market gardens in Kyeemagh and La Perouse around Botany Bay in Sydney, one might imagine oneself in a different place and time. The old wooden workers' cottages, brick chimneys rising above rusting corrugated iron roofs, broken fly screens on the doors and the corrugated iron dunnies (toilets) suggest old farms in the Australian outback. But the Cantonese radio program flowing through an open window; Chinese New Year sign above the door 安平入出 (from right to left, *chat yap peng on* in Cantonese; *chu ru ping an* in Putonghua: Safety to those

9. MF: 唐人菜就差唔多. (Chinese vegetables are similar.)
10. R: 唐人菜差唔多呀. (Chinese vegetables are similar to before.)
11. MF: 就鬼佬菜而家多...多...
    (we're growing more ... more ... Western vegetables now)
12. R: 鬼佬菜? 邊啲係鬼佬菜?
    (Western vegetable? what are Western vegetables?)
13. MF: Parsley,
14. FF: Parsley,
15. MF: Dill, thyme, mint,
16. R: Dill, thyme, mint,
17. MF: 即是嗰啲香...香...香菜. (Those ... her ... her ... herbs.)

Life is not easy for this couple. In the interview, they spoke colloquial, rural Cantonese[1] from the Gaoyao (高要) region of Guangdong (there is a long history of migration from Gaoyao district to Sydney; see Williams, 1999), with minimal English for some names of vegetables and numbers. They work almost every day, or whenever merchants come to pick up the vegetables, selling mainly to local grocers, as they don't have their own vehicle. When a merchant (of Bangladeshi background, who owns a local Asian grocery store) arrived to buy vegetables – he also walked directly into the fields to harvest bitter melon himself – communication was achieved with remarkably little use of any apparently shared linguistic code. Over the years, it seems, through their routinized buying and selling, they have established a way of communicating that operates across codes. While each speaks in a sense monolingually, their 'bilingual' interaction is another way in which metrolingual interactions may occur: getting things done without an obvious shared code (and see Chapter 8 for further discussion).

Despite the long history of Chinese involvement in market gardens, for this couple, resident in Australia for a little over 20 years, there remains an important contrast between Chinese (唐人菜) and Western vegetables (鬼佬菜) (lines 9 and 11). The term *gwai lou coi* (鬼佬菜) uses the common Cantonese for foreigner (or more literally 'ghost person' referring to white skinned foreigners, sometimes also translated as 'foreign devil'). The term, in common and informal use among Cantonese speakers, has been much discussed over the years as to whether it constitutes a derogatory or racist term (though foreigners in Hong Kong have also been known to use it to refer to themselves). Here, however, it is used to refer to the herbs this couple grow for the non-Chinese market (parsley, dill, mint, thyme), thus locating their worldview as if still in the soil of Guangdong, or at least within a Cantonese-oriented view of Australia. Abe san, who grows Japanese vegetables not far from here (see Chapter 7), even explains that he has developed 'Japanese soil' to grow his vegetables. Like the Japanese store and restaurant owners' (see Chapter 5 for convivial and contested city) use of the common term *gaijin* (meaning outside person, foreigner and similar in use to the term *gwai lou*), non-Chinese Australians and their vegetables remain forever the outsiders in this world. These *gwai lou* herbs may fetch better prices than the Chinese vegetables;

---

who leave or enter); Chinese calendars on the wall; blackened rice pots and woks in the dark kitchens; vegetables being washed in the large concrete trough; and conical straw hats of the workers pushing wheelbarrows and digging the rows of vegetables by hand (see Image 2.1); all suggest rural China. And yet the housing estates nudging the edges of these vegetable strips; the red kangaroo on a Qantas aircraft tailfin moving beyond one of the hedges; the Korean Air Boeing 747 coming in low overhead and the stacks of shipping containers further down the road remind us that this is neither rural Australia nor rural China: This is only a few kilometres from the centre of Sydney, and a busy transport and industrial hub.

Such market gardens have a significant history in relation to cities and languages, and are intertwined with a city such as Sydney. From the first arrival of European colonists (the First Fleet in 1788), these new settlers have struggled to bring forth food from this unfamiliar territory: convicts were granted land to grow their own crops in an effort to ward off starvation. Chinese started arriving in Australia in the early-nineteenth century to work as cooks, carpenters, farm labourers or in other forms of manual work, a small part of the wider Chinese diaspora that flowed from harsh conditions in southern China through southeast Asia and across the Pacific. The end of convict transportation also created a need for labour on the expanding agricultural properties in the colony, and over 3,000 indentured labourers were brought from China in the 1840s (Wilton, 2004). It was the possibilities opening up in the goldfields in the 1850s, however, that brought larger numbers, though following violent conflicts between Chinese and non-Chinese workers legislation was put in place to restrict Chinese labour.

Image 2.1 Chinese market gardens.

Chinese immigrants started working as market gardeners in the middle of the nineteenth century, as they moved into various occupations – from small businesses, such as general stores (often run by families and groups of Chinese) to fishing and market gardening. By the end of the nineteenth century there were, according to the locally produced *Tung Wah News* (東華新報), about 5,000 Chinese market gardeners in New South Wales (of whom about 2,000 were around Sydney), making up about two thirds of all market gardeners in the state (Willliams, n.d. para 5). For both expanding cities such as Sydney, as well as rural pastoral and mining concerns, Chinese market gardens came to play a significant role in the provision of fresh produce (McGowan, 2005). As with the general stores, market gardens provided an independent means of making a livelihood that also similarly relied on cooperative organization, low wages and family or clan control over the business. These market gardens were almost invariably on the edges and outskirts of towns, a result of the marginal and discriminatory position of Chinese workers in Australia, as well as the availability of cheap land and water.

About 30 per cent of the Chinese population in NSW around the turn of the nineteenth century were involved in market gardening, some in the rural areas, but the largest concentration was in the marsh land around Botany Bay. The market gardens at La Perouse (named after the French navigator who landed there a few days after the first fleet arrived from England in 1788), dating back to the early days of European settlement in the first decades of the nineteenth century, had been gradually taken over by Chinese gardeners in the middle of the same century. Yet these peripheries, like the sandy soil round Botany Bay, are no longer on the edge of the city. The gardens at Kyeemagh are now squeezed between the airport and suburban housing, while the gardens at La Perouse are under threat from container terminals and, more directly (the subject of an ongoing dispute), an expanding cemetery, itself a diverse and spreading multilingual and multifaith space. The Chinese thus became an integral part of the market network, as both buyers and sellers. The current Chinatown in Sydney sits alongside the old Belmore and Haymarket areas (the first of which has in recent years been developing into a 'Thai Town'), where some of the early cattle, hay and fruit and vegetable markets had been established in the mid-nineteenth century to replace the more ad hoc markets across the growing city.

While the Chinese population decreased and market gardens were shrinking, particularly as the White Australia Policy came into being in 1901 (Fitzgerald, 2007), and newer groups of migrants moved into the markets, most notably the Italians, this balance has shifted again in the last part of the twentieth century. Now the role of Chinese market gardeners needs to be set against the contemporary background of a growing and increasingly affluent Chinese population, changing food tastes in multicultural Sydney, and the changing politics of the real and symbolic economies around Chinese linguistic landscapes (Leeman & Modan, 2009). While the old Chinese-run gardens, dating back to the nineteenth century, used to supply the Chinatown shops and restaurants around Haymarket in central Sydney, much of their business has now moved to the expanding suburb of

Hurstville to the south. In the 1960s, Australians of Italian and Greek background started settling in the quiet suburb of Hurstville, some 16km south of central Sydney. Former Yugoslavian migrants followed, but the substantial growth came in the 1990s, with increased migration from Hong Kong and then China. Now, according to the 2011 Australian Bureau of Statistics (ABS, 2011), almost 70 per cent of Hurstville residents were born overseas, with over a third being of Chinese backgrounds. English is the sole home language of less than a quarter of the population, and now these peripheral gardens are squeezed between the airport, container terminals and housing estates; where once they loaded their fruit and vegetables onto carts for sale in the centrally located Haymarket, now their produce is carried off in white vans to the shops and restaurants to the south.

An elderly couple working one of these gardens moved to Australia from Baitu (白土镇) in Guangdong, he in the early 1990s, she some years later. He worked for various market gardeners; she worked as a nanny for a Chinese family (for $150 a week), before being employed briefly as a dishwasher in a Chinese restaurant. Eventually they started their own vegetable garden, living in the small, dilapidated cottage by the gardens and working long hours. Both around 60 years old, they are finding the work hard and are suffering from various ailments from their long working history (she shows us the patches she wears to ease her arthritis). They grow a variety of Chinese vegetables including *ku gua* or bitter melon, *een choy* (Chinese spinach), *bok choy* (Chinese cabbage), *dong gua* (winter melon), taro, *choy sum* (Chinese flowering cabbage), *Shanghai bok choi* (Shanghai cabbage), *gai lan* (Chinese broccoli) and spring onions. The demand for Chinese vegetables has stayed more or less the same over the last decade, but so has the price, and they struggle to make a living. As the wife puts it, after many years hard work, they have nothing to show for it (乜嘢都冇).

Excerpt 2.1 (FF: female farmer, MF: male farmer, R: researcher)

Chinese (Cantonese): characters

1. FF: 而家做農民, 以前啲菜又係差唔多嗰個單價, 嗰啲芥蘭而家又係!
   (the price of vegetables is nearly the same as before, the price of the gai lan is the same)
2. R: 係呀? 一直都一樣呀, 都幾呀年囉喎!
   (Really? The same as before, it's been some 20 years already!)
3. FF: 係上海白升咗啲 .
   (Except for shanghai bok choy, which has gone up a bit.)
4. MF: 廿呀幾年囉. (Some 20 years already.)
5. R: 以前係種乜嘢菜呀? 即係會唔會多啲…多啲其他…黎巴嫩呀,
   (What kind of vegetables did you grow before? Are you growing more … other types … like Lebanese,)
6. FF: 而家多 … 而家好賣. (We grow more now … it sells better now.)
7. MF: 而家多 … Parsley 呀. (We grow more now … like parsley.)
8. R: 係呀, 我都中意食 … 即係而家同以前有乜嘢唔同呀…種嘅菜?
   (yeah, I like it too … So what's the difference between now and before … the sort of vegetables you grow?)

they may be vegetables carefully grown from the soil they tend; but they remain forever foreign, vegetables from elsewhere.

Businesses such as this market garden, with its Chinese workers and vegetables, can survive amid urban growth, but depend on a growing Chinese market, a wider network of Asian and other stores, and an ability to provide for wider markets. It is quite possible to live and work in a city such as Sydney with minimal knowledge of English, and in such contexts, languages such as Cantonese operate as what Block (2007) has called *niche lingua francas* (we will return to this idea later in Chapter 8). Goldstein (1996) similarly found that Portuguese served as a common language not only among the Portuguese factory workers in Toronto that she studied, but also across a wider community and among workers of other language backgrounds (typically Spanish and Italian). These ethnolinguistic networks and their niche lingua francas, which, depending on the language and network, may be quite extensive, enable a range of businesses, restaurants and cultural activities to operate across the city.

Metrolingualism, the rural and the urban

These market gardens and their *gwai lou coi* raise another question: the relation between urban and rural. As the bucolic scenes in these market gardens next to the airport suggest, a rural/urban divide may not capture the far more complex dynamics of space and mobility. We are trying to understand how the organization of the city – economies, markets, movements, affiliations – is linked to the organization of language – its values, mixtures, mobilities and connections. When we look at 'the micro-publics of social contact and encounter which provide us with an understanding of ethnicity, and other identities too, as a mobile and incomplete process' (Watson, 2006, p. 18), it is clear that language is so often involved. It is not that every micro-exchange in public space involves language – there are bodies, signs, gestures, exchanges of money and much more at play here – but a great deal does involve a range of linguistic resources. Thus, 'language is directly implicated in the construction of social and spatial division, manifest in language ghettoes, enclaves and networks' (p. 146).

The focus on *urban* multilingualism is aimed at capturing the dynamics of change and location that are central to city life. Our focus on the city is about the intensity of diversity that occurs as people are brought together in urban spaces. All cities, we might say, are multilingual; it is perhaps a definitional characteristic of the city. This is not to suggest that towns, villages or hamlets may not be contexts of diversity, but rather that diversity is more commonly intensified in larger spaces. We are interested in the intersections of traffic, people, goods and languages, and the particular rhythms and spaces these movements bring about. A major focus of our work, for example, is on market places (see Chapters 1 and 8), on these centres of commercial, social and cultural interaction where people from different places come together to buy and sell, talk, eat and be entertained. Such places have been a driving place of human interaction and development, bringing people together into larger and more specialized urban occupations, but they also occur across the range of towns, villages, squares, ports and cities. There are many strong parallels between the multilingual contexts that we focus on in cities and the studies of dynamic change, multivocality and local language practices within a wider focus on globalization in 'peripheral' Sámi, Irish, Corsican and Welsh language contexts (Coupland, 2012; Moriarty & Pietikäinen, 2011; Pietikäinen, 2012).

Our interest is in those particularities of the city – size, diversity, rhythms, mobilities, contestations, convivialities – that render it distinct. By focusing on the dynamic diversity of Sydney's metrolingualism, for example, we by no means wish to detract attention from the multilingualism that has long been part of Australia before European and other migrants arrived. Indigenous Australian life has long been marked by complex chains of multilingual communication (Evans, 2010). As Kral (2012) explains in her study of literacy practices of the Ngaanyatjarra, these are a people who have 'incorporated extraordinary change' (p. 261) into their way of life in their 'remote' location in the Western Desert. While the English or other European countryside may be overlaid with pastoral images of tradition and lack of change, this is not how many non-urban regions are understood. Australia's 'countryside', for example, is also its 'outback': hot, harsh, dry and multilingual.

The non-urban, therefore, is not constructed here as some static, immobile, timeless, traditional place, the antipathy of the dynamic urban space. Just as Raymond Williams (1973) warned against the romantic juxtaposition of an idyllic, rural, unchanging countryside with the grimy and polluted industrial city (ignoring, among other things, the organization and conditions of rural labour), so, in different times and within different orientations to cosmopolitan, hybrid cityscapes, we want to avoid an idealization of urban metrolingual landscapes set against the assumed narrowness of rural living. The rural and urban are problematically juxtaposed, and our focus on urban environments is not intended to suggest that there exists some opposing rural environment where difference does not occur.

Our focus is on that particular context of diversification, the city. This is about the movement of people to and within cities (to work, to live, to visit relatives) and the complex and shifting relationships in vibrant urban spaces, where people mix, talk, write on walls, commute, create new vernaculars, intermingle, talk on mobiles, eat at restaurants, grab a quick snack of sushi rolls, borrow from each others' languages, communicate across social and cultural divides, vote, sleep on park benches, buy clothes, shop for shoes, sell newspapers, sing, ride in taxis, cross busy streets, live and work in and across communities, ride bikes, attend religious services, study, drink coffee, dream. This is not so much about how people mobilize their langauge as an individual capacity, but rather about how urban spaces are produced through activities that are part of this long history. This is the changing, shifting world of the urban landscape, where languages are blended, sorted, created, used for new purposes, taken up, tossed aside, learned and renewed.

who leave or enter); Chinese calendars on the wall; blackened rice pots and woks in the dark kitchens; vegetables being washed in the large concrete trough; and conical straw hats of the workers pushing wheelbarrows and digging the rows of vegetables by hand (see Image 2.1); all suggest rural China. And yet the housing estates nudging the edges of these vegetable strips; the red kangaroo on a Qantas aircraft tailfin moving beyond one of the hedges; the Korean Air Boeing 747 coming in low overhead and the stacks of shipping containers further down the road remind us that this is neither rural Australia nor rural China: This is only a few kilometres from the centre of Sydney, and a busy transport and industrial hub.

Such market gardens have a significant history in relation to cities and languages, and are intertwined with a city such as Sydney. From the first arrival of European colonists (the First Fleet in 1788), these new settlers have struggled to bring forth food from this unfamiliar territory: convicts were granted land to grow their own crops in an effort to ward off starvation. Chinese started arriving in Australia in the early-nineteenth century to work as cooks, carpenters, farm labourers or in other forms of manual work, a small part of the wider Chinese diaspora that flowed from harsh conditions in southern China through southeast Asia and across the Pacific. The end of convict transportation also created a need for labour on the expanding agricultural properties in the colony, and over 3,000 indentured labourers were brought from China in the 1840s (Wilton, 2004). It was the possibilities opening up in the goldfields in the 1850s, however, that brought larger numbers, though following violent conflicts between Chinese and non-Chinese workers legislation was put in place to restrict Chinese labour.

Image 2.1 Chinese market gardens.

Chinese immigrants started working as market gardeners in the middle of the nineteenth century, as they moved into various occupations – from small businesses, such as general stores (often run by families and groups of Chinese) to fishing and market gardening. By the end of the nineteenth century there were, according to the locally produced *Tung Wah News* (東華新報), about 5,000 Chinese market gardeners in New South Wales (of whom about 2,000 were around Sydney), making up about two thirds of all market gardeners in the state (Willliams, n.d. para 5). For both expanding cities such as Sydney, as well as rural pastoral and mining concerns, Chinese market gardens came to play a significant role in the provision of fresh produce (McGowan, 2005). As with the general stores, market gardens provided an independent means of making a livelihood that also similarly relied on cooperative organization, low wages and family or clan control over the business. These market gardens were almost invariably on the edges and outskirts of towns, a result of the marginal and discriminatory position of Chinese workers in Australia, as well as the availability of cheap land and water.

About 30 per cent of the Chinese population in NSW around the turn of the nineteenth century were involved in market gardening, some in the rural areas, but the largest concentration was in the marsh land around Botany Bay. The market gardens at La Perouse (named after the French navigator who landed there a few days after the first fleet arrived from England in 1788), dating back to the early days of European settlement in the first decades of the nineteenth century, had been gradually taken over by Chinese gardeners in the middle of the same century. Yet these peripheries, like the sandy soil round Botany Bay, are no longer on the edge of the city. The gardens at Kyeemagh are now squeezed between the airport and suburban housing, while the gardens at La Perouse are under threat from container terminals and, more directly (the subject of an ongoing dispute), an expanding cemetery, itself a diverse and spreading multilingual and multifaith space. The Chinese thus became an integral part of the market network, as both buyers and sellers. The current Chinatown in Sydney sits alongside the old Belmore and Haymarket areas (the first of which has in recent years been developing into a 'Thai Town'), where some of the early cattle, hay and fruit and vegetable markets had been established in the mid-nineteenth century to replace the more ad hoc markets across the growing city.

While the Chinese population decreased and market gardens were shrinking, particularly as the White Australia Policy came into being in 1901 (Fitzgerald, 2007), and newer groups of migrants moved into the markets, most notably the Italians, this balance has shifted again in the last part of the twentieth century. Now the role of Chinese market gardeners needs to be set against the contemporary background of a growing and increasingly affluent Chinese population, changing food tastes in multicultural Sydney, and the changing politics of the real and symbolic economies around Chinese linguistic landscapes (Leeman & Modan, 2009). While the old Chinese-run gardens, dating back to the nineteenth century, used to supply the Chinatown shops and restaurants around Haymarket in central Sydney, much of their business has now moved to the expanding suburb of

Hurstville to the south. In the 1960s, Australians of Italian and Greek background started settling in the quiet suburb of Hurstville, some 16km south of central Sydney. Former Yugoslavian migrants followed, but the substantial growth came in the 1990s, with increased migration from Hong Kong and then China. Now, according to the 2011 Australian Bureau of Statistics (ABS, 2011), almost 70 per cent of Hurstville residents were born overseas, with over a third being of Chinese backgrounds. English is the sole home language of less than a quarter of the population, and now these peripheral gardens are squeezed between the airport, container terminals and housing estates; where once they loaded their fruit and vegetables onto carts for sale in the centrally located Haymarket, now their produce is carried off in white vans to the shops and restaurants to the south.

An elderly couple working one of these gardens moved to Australia from Baitu (白土镇) in Guangdong, he in the early 1990s, she some years later. He worked for various market gardeners; she worked as a nanny for a Chinese family (for $150 a week), before being employed briefly as a dishwasher in a Chinese restaurant. Eventually they started their own vegetable garden, living in the small, dilapidated cottage by the gardens and working long hours. Both around 60 years old, they are finding the work hard and are suffering from various ailments from their long working history (she shows us the patches she wears to ease her arthritis). They grow a variety of Chinese vegetables including *ku gua* or bitter melon, *een choy* (Chinese spinach), *bok choy* (Chinese cabbage), *dong gua* (winter melon), taro, *choy sum* (Chinese flowering cabbage), *Shanghai bok choi* (Shanghai cabbage), *gai lan* (Chinese broccoli) and spring onions. The demand for Chinese vegetables has stayed more or less the same over the last decade, but so has the price, and they struggle to make a living. As the wife puts it, after many years hard work, they have nothing to show for it (乜嘢都冇).

Excerpt 2.1 (FF: female farmer, MF: male farmer, R: researcher)
Chinese (Cantonese): characters
1. FF: 而家做農民, 以前啲菜又係差唔多嗰個單價, 嗰啲芥蘭而家又係!
    (the price of vegetables is nearly the same as before, the price of the gai lan is the same)
2. R: 係呀? 一直都一樣呀, 都幾呀年囉喎!
    (Really? The same as before, it's been some 20 years already!)
3. FF: 係上海白升咗啲.
    (Except for shanghai bok choy, which has gone up a bit.)
4. MF: 廿呀幾年囉. (Some 20 years already.)
5. R: 以前係種乜嘢菜呀? 即係會唔會多啲…多啲其他…黎巴嫩呀,
    (What kind of vegetables did you grow before? Are you growing more … other types … like Lebanese,)
6. FF: 而家多 … 而家好賣. (We grow more now … it sells better now.)
7. MF: 而家多 … Parsley 呀. (We grow more now … like parsley.)
8. R: 係呀, 我都中意食 … 即係而家同以前有乜嘢唔同呀…種嘅菜?
    (yeah, I like it too … So what's the difference between now and before … the sort of vegetables you grow?)

9.   MF: 唐人菜就差唔多. (Chinese vegetables are similar.)
10. R: 唐人菜差唔多呀. (Chinese vegetables are similar to before.)
11. MF: 就鬼佬菜而家多…多…
     (we're growing more … more … Western vegetables now)
12. R: 鬼佬菜? 邊啲係鬼佬菜?
     (Western vegetable? what are Western vegetables?)
13. MF: Parsley,
14. FF: Parsley,
15. MF: Dill, thyme, mint,
16. R: Dill, thyme, mint,
17. MF: 即是嗰啲香…香…香菜. (Those … her … her … herbs.)

Life is not easy for this couple. In the interview, they spoke colloquial, rural Cantonese[1] from the Gaoyao (高要) region of Guangdong (there is a long history of migration from Gaoyao district to Sydney; see Williams, 1999), with minimal English for some names of vegetables and numbers. They work almost every day, or whenever merchants come to pick up the vegetables, selling mainly to local grocers, as they don't have their own vehicle. When a merchant (of Bangladeshi background, who owns a local Asian grocery store) arrived to buy vegetables – he also walked directly into the fields to harvest bitter melon himself – communication was achieved with remarkably little use of any apparently shared linguistic code. Over the years, it seems, through their routinized buying and selling, they have established a way of communicating that operates across codes. While each speaks in a sense monolingually, their 'bilingual' interaction is another way in which metrolingual interactions may occur: getting things done without an obvious shared code (and see Chapter 8 for further discussion).

Despite the long history of Chinese involvement in market gardens, for this couple, resident in Australia for a little over 20 years, there remains an important contrast between Chinese (唐人菜) and Western vegetables (鬼佬菜) (lines 9 and 11). The term *gwai lou coi* (鬼佬菜) uses the common Cantonese for foreigner (or more literally 'ghost person' referring to white skinned foreigners, sometimes also translated as 'foreign devil'). The term, in common and informal use among Cantonese speakers, has been much discussed over the years as to whether it constitutes a derogatory or racist term (though foreigners in Hong Kong have also been known to use it to refer to themselves). Here, however, it is used to refer to the herbs this couple grow for the non-Chinese market (parsley, dill, mint, thyme), thus locating their worldview as if still in the soil of Guangdong, or at least within a Cantonese-oriented view of Australia. Abe san, who grows Japanese vegetables not far from here (see Chapter 7), even explains that he has developed 'Japanese soil' to grow his vegetables. Like the Japanese store and restaurant owners' (see Chapter 5 for convivial and contested city) use of the common term *gaijin* (meaning outside person, foreigner and similar in use to the term *gwai lou*), non-Chinese Australians and their vegetables remain forever the outsiders in this world. These *gwai lou* herbs may fetch better prices than the Chinese vegetables;

they may be vegetables carefully grown from the soil they tend; but they remain forever foreign, vegetables from elsewhere.

Businesses such as this market garden, with its Chinese workers and vegetables, can survive amid urban growth, but depend on a growing Chinese market, a wider network of Asian and other stores, and an ability to provide for wider markets. It is quite possible to live and work in a city such as Sydney with minimal knowledge of English, and in such contexts, languages such as Cantonese operate as what Block (2007) has called *niche lingua francas* (we will return to this idea later in Chapter 8). Goldstein (1996) similarly found that Portuguese served as a common language not only among the Portuguese factory workers in Toronto that she studied, but also across a wider community and among workers of other language backgrounds (typically Spanish and Italian). These ethnolinguistic networks and their niche lingua francas, which, depending on the language and network, may be quite extensive, enable a range of businesses, restaurants and cultural activities to operate across the city.

Metrolingualism, the rural and the urban

These market gardens and their *gwai lou coi* raise another question: the relation between urban and rural. As the bucolic scenes in these market gardens next to the airport suggest, a rural/urban divide may not capture the far more complex dynamics of space and mobility. We are trying to understand how the organization of the city – economies, markets, movements, affiliations – is linked to the organization of language – its values, mixtures, mobilities and connections. When we look at 'the micro-publics of social contact and encounter which provide us with an understanding of ethnicity, and other identities too, as a mobile and incomplete process' (Watson, 2006, p. 18), it is clear that language is so often involved. It is not that every micro-exchange in public space involves language – there are bodies, signs, gestures, exchanges of money and much more at play here – but a great deal does involve a range of linguistic resources. Thus, 'language is directly implicated in the construction of social and spatial division, manifest in language ghettoes, enclaves and networks' (p. 146).

The focus on *urban* multilingualism is aimed at capturing the dynamics of change and location that are central to city life. Our focus on the city is about the intensity of diversity that occurs as people are brought together in urban spaces. All cities, we might say, are multilingual; it is perhaps a definitional characteristic of the city. This is not to suggest that towns, villages or hamlets may not be contexts of diversity, but rather that diversity is more commonly intensified in larger spaces. We are interested in the intersections of traffic, people, goods and languages, and the particular rhythms and spaces these movements bring about. A major focus of our work, for example, is on market places (see Chapters 1 and 8), on these centres of commercial, social and cultural interaction where people from different places come together to buy and sell, talk, eat and be entertained. Such places have been a driving place of human interaction and development, bringing people together into larger and more specialized urban occupations, but they also occur across the range of towns, villages, squares, ports and cities. There are many strong parallels between the multilingual contexts that we focus on in cities and the studies of dynamic change, multivocality and local language practices within a wider focus on globalization in 'peripheral' Sámi, Irish, Corsican and Welsh language contexts (Coupland, 2012; Moriarty & Pietikäinen, 2011; Pietikäinen, 2012).

Our interest is in those particularities of the city – size, diversity, rhythms, mobilities, contestations, convivialities – that render it distinct. By focusing on the dynamic diversity of Sydney's metrolingualism, for example, we by no means wish to detract attention from the multilingualism that has long been part of Australia before European and other migrants arrived. Indigenous Australian life has long been marked by complex chains of multilingual communication (Evans, 2010). As Kral (2012) explains in her study of literacy practices of the Ngaanyatjarra, these are a people who have 'incorporated extraordinary change' (p. 261) into their way of life in their 'remote' location in the Western Desert. While the English or other European countryside may be overlaid with pastoral images of tradition and lack of change, this is not how many non-urban regions are understood. Australia's 'countryside', for example, is also its 'outback': hot, harsh, dry and multilingual.

The non-urban, therefore, is not constructed here as some static, immobile, timeless, traditional place, the antipathy of the dynamic urban space. Just as Raymond Williams (1973) warned against the romantic juxtaposition of an idyllic, rural, unchanging countryside with the grimy and polluted industrial city (ignoring, among other things, the organization and conditions of rural labour), so, in different times and within different orientations to cosmopolitan, hybrid cityscapes, we want to avoid an idealization of urban metrolingual landscapes set against the assumed narrowness of rural living. The rural and urban are problematically juxtaposed, and our focus on urban environments is not intended to suggest that there exists some opposing rural environment where difference does not occur.

Our focus is on that particular context of diversification, the city. This is about the movement of people to and within cities (to work, to live, to visit relatives) and the complex and shifting relationships in vibrant urban spaces, where people mix, talk, write on walls, commute, create new vernaculars, intermingle, talk on mobiles, eat at restaurants, grab a quick snack of sushi rolls, borrow from each others' languages, communicate across social and cultural divides, vote, sleep on park benches, buy clothes, shop for shoes, sell newspapers, sing, ride in taxis, cross busy streets, live and work in and across communities, ride bikes, attend religious services, study, drink coffee, dream. This is not so much about how people mobilize their langauge as an individual capacity, but rather about how urban spaces are produced through activities that are part of this long history. This is the changing, shifting world of the urban landscape, where languages are blended, sorted, created, used for new purposes, taken up, tossed aside, learned and renewed.

Looking at the pioneering sociolinguistic work of Labov (1966) and Trudgill (1974), it is noticeable that they have relatively little to say about the social, physical and cultural spaces of the respective cities – New York and Norwich – in which their studies occur. But these two cities, in their relation to their environments and in comparison to each other (an old cathedral city in rural Norfolk that thrived around the wool trade in pre-industrial Britain but by the late-twentieth century was a quiet, regional market town, compared with the vast metropolis crammed onto Manhattan Island, a city of immigration) are both very particular as cities and in the deep differences between them. While Labov's (1972) classic work *Language in the inner city: Studies in the Black English vernacular* rightly holds a position as a foundational study in sociolinguistics that changed ways in which language is understood – particularly with respect to showing 'the logic of nonstandard English' or that Black English vernacular had to be understood in terms of what it did do rather than what it did not (that is, in terms of its difference rather than deficit) – it is also noticeable that the city itself plays a very minor role.

For Labov, the focus is on 'black English vernacular', that

> relatively uniform dialect spoken by the majority of black youth in most parts of the United States today, especially in the inner city areas of New York, Boston, Detroit, Philadelphia, Washington, Cleveland, Chicago, St. Louis, San Francisco, Los Angeles, and other urban centres.

> (p. xiii)

The focus then is centrally on the social dialect spoken across urban centres. Although the actual studies move from the generic 'children in the urban ghetto areas' (p. 203) to far more specific accounts of 'major adolescent groups that dominated the tenement areas from 110th Street to 118th Street between Sixth and Eighth Avenues' (p. 243), this urban context remains for most of the analysis a contextual background. The streets, the buildings, the shops, the movement of people through this environment receive little or no comment.

If we follow this trajectory of sociolinguistic work in the city to studies 30 years later, an ethnographic turn (rather than interviews and speech sampling) becomes much more evident. Rampton's (2006) classic sociolinguistic work on language use among young adolescents focuses, like much recent work on multilingualism, on educational contexts. García (2009) and Blackledge and Creese (2010), for example, draw on various types of educational contexts for much of their discussion of translanguaging. There are a number of reasons for this, including the educational focus of the authors and the fact that classrooms, although difficult spaces to conduct research, are nonetheless bounded research spaces where interactions are often usefully regulated. The educational contexts of these studies are also largely urban ones – New York in García's case and Birmingham (along with other British cities) for Blackledge and Creese. Although interested most significantly in the informal heritage school settings that are the focus of their study, Blackledge and Creese locate their work in the wider spatiotemporal context: 'It is a hot, sunny Sunday afternoon in June 2006, and three researchers ... arrive at a small, converted terraced house owned by a Muslim community organisation' (2010, p. 1).

Other than such moments, however, the city remains in the background, the organizing space that gives rise to the need for 'heritage' classes in Bangla, Turkish, Cantonese, Gujarati and Mandarin. Rampton's work, which draws more closely on the urban sociolinguistic tradition of Labov, locates the study in an urban school. Like Labov, the city operates here largely as a spatial organizer of social class and ethnicity. Cosmopolitan or global cities, Rampton (2006) reminds us, 'serve as centres of finance, transport and communication, and as such, they are both highly diverse and highly stratified. In London, ethnic diversity is particularly pronounced, and wealth and income differentials are also sharper than anywhere else in the UK' (p. 7). On the one hand, a global city such as London is 'a home for cosmopolitan elites, professional and business people, while on the other, there are large numbers of people working in low-skilled, low paid jobs, often in a substantial hidden economy' (p. 7). The city, and the schools it contains, then, is a place in late modernity where class relations are played out in sociolinguistic interactions. The city, however, remains something of a shadow, a place where labour is distributed, where people settle and live, a backdrop to the dynamics of schooling.

A slightly different approach is found in Alim's (2004) work. Like Labov, he is interested in Black American vernacular English, and like Rampton, in aspects of styleshifting, schools and a broader ethnographic account of language use. But in this study of 'styleshifting in a Black American speech community', we are taken much further into the ethnographic present of urban language and space:

> So, we sittin outside Mickey D's havin this convo and a White couple come walkin by – and right when I was about to ask a follow-up question about White people in Shadyside, too. They bout to hop in their shiny, black Volvo, so I held up my question, like, 'hold on.' You know, not wantin to be rude, you know what I'm saying?
>
> (p. 121)

Now we are in the city, sitting down, talking, outside a McDonald's restaurant (sittin outside Mickey D's havin this convo), and the styleshifting that is the focus of the study is in the very text we are reading. There is a much clearer relationship between people and place; and the shiny, black Volvo matters.

A central location of connection for Alim in this study of the language practices around Haven High school in Sunnyside was a local barber shop, which 'served multiple purposes for me. Not only was I gettin a tight fade every week (gotta stay sharp), but I was immersing myself in the community to which my students belonged' (p. 80). This barber shop was one of the few Black-owned businesses in Sunnyside,

> and serving a predominantly Black American clientele made it one of the few Black-owned public spaces in the city. It's a small shop, but it does the job

you know. All the barbers line they walls up with pictures of they wives, brothers, sisters, aunts, cousins, nephews, nieces and friends.

(pp. 84–5)

This comes much closer to our own approach to space in the city. The pictures matter, who owns the space matters, the haircut matters (a tight fade). Language is bound up with all of this – it does not just happen against an urban backdrop, it is part of the city, the barber shop, the market garden, the networks of buying and selling.

We need therefore ways of understanding cities as particular social, cultural and spatial arrangements. This is some of the work that we want the idea of metrolingualism to do, to make the idea of the city salient, to address questions of space and its dynamic relation to language, to suggest that the meaning of the city is highly dependent on the languages of the city, and that the languages of the city are deeply bound up with the urban spaces in which they occur. Space (place, location, context) is not a backcloth on which events and language are projected through time. Rather, language practices are activities that produce time and space. The invocation of the *everyday* (see Chapter 1) – practices are very much part of the focus on everyday activities – suggests not only the temporality of frequency, of things that occur over and over in a mundane way, but also an everyday locality: our everyday activities are always in places that become part of the process. It is this spatial turn, in relation to the city in particular, that forms a crucial part of work on metrolingualism. 'Recapturing the geography of places involved in globalization' Sassen (2005, p. 32) reminds us, 'allows us to recapture people, workers, communities, and more specifically, the many different work cultures, besides the corporate culture, involved in the work of globalization.'

We need an understanding of cities – the global city, the local city, the historical city, the diverse city, the city as space and place – in order to understand language in the city, and we need to understand language in the city – its mobility, mixing, shifting and changing – in order to understand the city. Languages in the city are about place and mobility, about conviviality and resistance, creativity and conformity. There are many ways in which language and the city intertwine. We have already pointed to (and partially critiqued) the ways in which we can map linguistic demographies of who speaks what language where. Here however we want to point to a deeper set of relations. As Simon (2012) puts it, we need to focus not only on the visual life of the city but also on 'the audible surface of languages, each city's signature blend of dialects and accents' since this is

an equally crucial element of urban reality. Just as 'seeing' the buildings and streets of an urban aggregation is crucial to understanding its history, its organization into neighbourhoods, its systems of circulation, so 'hearing' introduces the hearer into layers of social, economic and cultural complexity.

(p. 1)

This has several corollaries: Metrolingualism as a practice is not confined to the city; it is intended as a broad, descriptive category for understanding language and the city, rather than a term of cosmopolitan idealism; and part of our project is not only to rethink language through the lens of metrolingualism but also to rethink the city. While characterized by the kinds of language use commonly found in the contemporary city, the kinds of everyday mutlingualism that interest us may also occur in contexts of mobility and 'peripheral multilingualism'. Unlike currently popular notions such as superdiversity (Blommaert, 2010; 2013a) – driven largely by an interest in the increasing diversity in European cities as a result of immigration – metrolingualism focuses on the ordinariness of historical and diverse ways in which people get by with their linguistic and non-linguistic resources. The city, which brings together people with a particular intensity, and has very particular organizations of private and public space, rhythms of movement, organizations of employment and locations of social interaction, is often the archetypical locus of such interaction, but is not the only place where it occurs.

'People are basically from everywhere': ethnicity and language at work

Vukasin, a supervisor of a group of house painters of Bosnian Serbian background,[2] who moved to Australia in 1993 with his wife and an eight-month-old baby on a refugee visa, explained the trades he works with:

> We are using lots of contractors, right, you saw this Malaysian people doing the tiling for us. So on the other job we've got Korean people doing the tiling for us. And a guy that's going to come tomorrow here, carpenter, his background is Greek, I think. So, you know, everywhere. People are basically from everywhere.
>
> (Vukasin, interview, November 14, 2011)

People are basically from everywhere. But these links – Malaysian Chinese tilers, Italian concreters, Serbian painters – occur again and again across Sydney. This presents a very particular image of the multicultural workplace that needs both explanation and exploration. These characterizations of ethnicity and work suggest at the very least that these are indeed the terms in which people view themselves and others: Korean tilers over there, Serbian painters here, Fijian scaffolders here, Lebanese excavating crews over there. We shall complicate this picture later in the chapter but clearly these are part of the relations of fixity and fluidity that inform many understandings of language and culture (see Chapter 5). If we wish to take seriously the linguistic and cultural ideologies of these workers, then we need to deal with the terms in which they define themselves and others.

These lines of affiliation have played an important role in how many of these workers got into the trades they are in. As Vukasin explains his own history, he left Bosnia during the war, and came to Australia: 'Yeah, I started in the building trade, basically, yeah. And after two and a half years I started working for this company. So it's more than fifteen years, actually, that I work for this company.' This was not because of a background in the industry or a particular interest, but

> some people that we would meet in the school when we were learning English. OK, and most of those people are again from the same background and most of them at the time they were working in building industry. That's how, that's how you start.
>
> (Vukasin, interview, November 14, 2011)

Construction sites in Sydney are frequently bound up with these ethnic affiliations, often with the troubled history of the Balkans lurking behind the work of the painters and plasterers. Here Vukasin's own linguistic trajectory intervenes as he explains why he is able to talk with workers of Macedonian background painting the fence: 'I was in the army for a year, we had compulsory army back then, and when I was in the army, I was in Macedonia. So I could speak – I could understand really well and I could speak quite well, at the time.' Igor, a contracted construction worker who is persistent in identifying himself as Yugoslav (see Chapter 1) is also a victim of the Bosnian war and left

> because I want to go too far of my country. To going too far of my country, to can't back. Because no like anymore going back. Because my father is died there, my mother is die, my sister is die. My sister is now being thirty-one, but everybody die in the war. Yeah, I no want to going back.
>
> (Igor, interview, December 3, 2011)

Zlatan, another worker of Bosnian Serbian background working in the construction industry, has, on the other hand, a trajectory quite different from Vukasin's and Igor's: he had been on holiday in Montenegro when he met a Croatian Australian (she had moved to Australia as an infant, but speaks Serbian). They married and moved to Australia, where 'I met with people from my country, and ask for job or something on the building because the easiest way for me, if I working in a building, because English is not good' (Zlatan, interview, February 14, 2012). Tomo, the safety officer on another construction site, is of Croatian background, part of a fairly substantial migration in the 1960s and 1970s. His father had come in 1969 and 'he worked on construction. He met somebody and they got him a job. OK. And stayed there' (Tomo, interview, May 13, 2013). Because 'there was a lot of Croatians in construction in Croatia, they went into concreting and the form working. And carpentry. So you'll find form workers and stuff like that are Croatian'. Tomo himself had left school in Australia and worked in various jobs before his father suggested he join him in construction work, and from there he had moved up to become a safety officer. His background as a form worker gives him credibility with the workers when he deals with them from a safety point of view:

I say to them, 'I've been on the tools, I know what it's like to put my boots on at five in the morning and work under the sun, the heat, and the conditions'. I say 'Guys, I'm not here to work against ya'.

Tomo's linguistic background is helpful too:

Being of a Croatian background, having Serbians working there, I'm never worried. I tell them I'm Croatian, but when they do their induction, their forms, I help them. And when I speak their language, they say 'oh, cool, I wasn't sure about this question because English is my second language'.

Similar language issues were raised by another construction site supervisor, Len, of Lebanese background. Seven of the eight workers on site at the time (excavation work) were Arabic speakers of Iraqi and Lebanese backgrounds (the other worker, of Afghani background, had also learned some Arabic): 'I speak to them – it's easier sometimes 'cause they don't understand what I'm saying to them. So I speak to them in Arabic' (Len, interview, September, 23, 2012). Since the interview was held during Ramadan, he also explained how he accommodated the religious (fasting) as well as the linguistic needs of his workers.

Elsewhere on the much larger site where Tomo works, he explains there are

Italians, predominately ... the Italians are known for concreting. Um, gyprocking gyprocking and plastering, that was the Croatians in the late '80s, mid '90s, now it's moved into ... the Bosnians have come through. During, or after, the civil war over there, a lot of the Serbians came through, they're predominately on gyprocking or formwork.

(Tomo, interview, May 13, 2013)

When new migrants come to Sydney, he explains, 'whatever the majority of the community is doing, whether they meet at social functions or whatever, they will find work there through someone'. Even if they lack experience, they can get into the industry as labourers, before they 'jump on the tools and then next thing, two years later they're a capable tradesperson'. Vukasin, for example, had run 'a little shop back in Bosnia until the war broke out' and had tried his hand at running one in Sydney before he got into the construction business.

On this particular site, Tomo explains, about half the form workers (carpenters constructing the moulds for concrete) are from a Portuguese[3] background, with another third identifying as Balkan (Croatian, Serbian, Bosnian, Macedonian); the concreters themselves are half Italian, with another third of Middle Eastern background, while the contractor operating the excavation equipment is of Lebanese background and employs almost all workers of Middle Eastern background. Some of the trades such as plumbers and electricians are more Anglo-Celtic based. This pattern is always changing – part of the rhythms of the city (see Chapter 3) – as the work on the constructions site changes: 'I might have eight

Arabic excavating crew, they'll be finished in about a week or two. And I might get more steel fixers coming on, and stuff like that.'

He explains these connections along several lines: As already noted, this is in part a result of social connections; if one part of the industry is populated by people of a particular background, this is often perpetuated over considerable periods of time. If companies are owned by people of a particular background, this also increases this trend, sometimes creating a niche ethnic industry, such as Vietnamese manicurists. There are also, as he suggests cautiously, certain physical characteristics that may help certain trades, noting the Pacific Islanders working in scaffolding: 'Pacific Islanders generally do … some of them have branched into concrete, they tend to do the more physical work. Not trying to stereotype them, but generally you'll find that those type of people'. Phillip, the foreman at another construction site (ABC) puts it this way: 'Now, when that goes down you'll start to see me dig holes, big holes, in the basin. When that … when those holes are dug, shortly thereafter will be the steel-fixers. You're going to have a big Maori … *hey bro* … you're going to get a big Maori influx' (Phillip, interview, October 31, 2012). As he continues, 'from there you'll see a little bit of concrete, but they're Italian guys, usually. But then what'll happen is the form-workers will come on. Then you'll see a *big* mix, massive cross-section of nationalities and communications'.

These construction site overviews are supported more broadly by studies of the construction industry in Australia, where 'Italian-Australians dominate concreting trades, Croatian-Australians specialize in carpentry trades, Korean-Australians are concentrated in tiling trades, and those of Southern Islander origin in scaffolding and the Irish in labouring, etc' (Loosemore, Phua, Dunn & Ozguc, 2010, p. 179). This study reported that aside from English the most commonly spoken languages on construction sites were Mandarin, Cantonese, Croatian, Portuguese, Spanish, Serbian, Arabic and Bosnian. While there was a reportedly high level of interaction among groups, both because of the necessity for 'subbies' (subcontractors) to work together and through social contexts such as lunch, the degree of mixing across work lines remains limited, in part because of the temporal and physical organization of eating spaces. As Igor, another worker of Bosnian-Serbian background in the construction industry explained, it was often the case that communication between groups was mediated by a small number of more fluent English speakers; referring to the Chinese Malaysian tilers: 'You know all these guys here, which one is work tiling? Only one is speak English. Only one speak, all the rest not speak English' (Igor, interview, December, 3, 2011). We will return to the complexity of lunchtime conversations on construction sites in Chapter 6.

Ethnic business and ethnolinguistic repertoires

While it is clear, then, that ethnic and linguistic affiliations play an important role in the kind of work people find, or the places they buy and sell goods, we need to complicate this picture. Joseph's comments in the previous chapter about the relations between buyers and sellers along linguistic lines – 'whether they Eastern Asia or South Asia or whatever, they come in they do lingo in their own language' – also point in two significant directions: the metrolingual networks that criss-cross the city, from markets, to shops, to restaurants and homes, and the historical background that links ethnic minorities to particular products. To this picture, which might suggest fairly stable linguistic and cultural groupings, we need to add dimensions of temporality (these groupings change over time), mobility (people move in and around the city) and repertoires (people draw on ethnic repertoires as part of these processes of affiliation).

As has already become clear from the previous discussion, people of different backgrounds do not work in particular trades because they particularly want to, or are somehow predisposed to do so through culture, history or experience. Some of the early writing on urban growth in the Chicago School tradition tended more towards a match between race, ethnicity and employment, with Burgess (1924) commenting for example that

> The immigrant from rural communities in Europe and America seldom brings with him economic skill of any great value in our industrial, commercial, or professional life. Yet interesting occupational selection has taken place by nationality, explainable more by racial temperament or circumstance than by old-world economic background as Irish policeman, Greek ice-cream parlors, Chinese laundries, Negro porters, Belgian janitors, etc.
>
> (p. 92)

More recent commentators on ethnicity and small business have been at pains to distance themselves from these racial and ethnocultural explanations and instead to emphasize patterns of migration and settlement, and the channelling of workers into particular fields. Panayiotopoulos (2010) emphasizes the need to understand culture in its everyday manifestation rather than as a predefining set of characteristics. Avoiding 'ethnocultural views' whereby ethnicity defines culture, he argues that:

> It is in the culture of everyday life, work and day-to-day learned experiences of conventions and norms which govern the sociability and daily transactions that define us as humans, that the ethnicity of 'being' is itself shaped and re-shaped.
>
> (p. 190)

This form of 'multiculturalism from below', then, views ethnocultural practices as emergent from the conditions of everyday life and work rather than as preconditions for it.

The development of ethnic small businesses can therefore best be understood within the particular economic, class, gendered, temporal and spatial conditions that bring about particular constellations of work and ethnicity: What economic conditions, processes of migration, forms of gendered work, prejudice and discriminations lead these people to take up this work in this place? People migrate towards certain forms of work through processes of 'ethnic channelling', where work is available to people of assumed shared backgrounds. These 'ethnic networks' have long played a major role in the 'channelling of immigrants and internal migrants into sectors where co-ethnics and co-nationals were concentrated' (Panayiotopoulos, 2010, p. 12). Thus, as had happened for Russian-Jewish women in nineteenth-century New York, twentieth-century London saw 'the vast majority of Greek and Turkish Cypriot women channelled into the clothing industry as either indoor machinists or as homeworkers' (p. 13). Different areas of work are thus commonly gendered – garment, domestic and health workers being typical examples – and also dominated by certain linguistic and cultural groups, though these may shift over time: Women may still be working on the sewing machines but now they may be Vietnamese rather than Russian Jewish, Chinese rather than Greek Cypriot.

The Vietnamese nail care business, 'an ethnic labor market niche in manicuring' (Eckstein & Nguyen, 2011, p. 666), is another example of gendered ethnic employment, created by offering inexpensive nail care to people of various class and ethnic backgrounds who had never before been able to afford such treatment. Once established, these businesses then provided low-paid work for new Vietnamese migrants – with limited training and linguistic requirements – that also helped increase the business. For Lim, working at a Vietnamese manicurist in Marrickville, this work nonetheless presents a positive change from her fomer life in Vietnam: 'I just cooking in Vietnam. I didn't do anything. In the family, I just cooking at home. Like, um, housewife [laughs]' (Interview, 20 November, 2012). After initially doing 'labour work' in Australia, she eventually talked to other Vietnamese in the manicure business, took a TAFE (Technical and Further Education) course and found work in this shop. This work she finds pleasantly sociable: 'this job I get a lot of friend. Lots of friends. Because when you like, come in you see and talking and ... friendly, very nice.'

Into the mix of cultural and linguistic connections, therefore, comes the role of small enterprise business – shops and restaurants being common examples. To understand such patterns of work – that, for example, over 25 per cent of Bangladeshi men in the UK work as cooks or waiters (Panayiotopoulos, 2010) – and the particular implications for language use, we need to look at several related factors. One such factor is skilled or unskilled labour: For those with limited skills (at least as far as employment markets are concerned) – and language plays an important role here – unskilled labour markets offer the most obvious chances of employment, often requiring limited skills in dominant languages. As the work opportunities available to the Chinese market gardeners outlined previously showed (underpaid work in restaurant kitchens or as a nanny; hard toil in the market gardens), and as Igor's comments suggest (only the foreman of a group of workers may be able to use English more broadly), linguistic networks may provide work, but one is often dependent on other linguistic mediators.

Areas of a city thus start to develop around certain communities, sometimes because the work is nearby (though cheap housing and poorly paid work may also entail considerable travel) and, often because in a cyclical process, small enterprises – restaurants, take-aways, grocery stores, DVD outlets, and so on – and later places of worship, become established, and people therefore move there. Typically such businesses rely on family labour, are based in working class communities, have indistinct divisions of labour (ownership, management and production are elided), are relatively small-scale and low-productivity outfits, are conducted along traditional paternalistic and personal network lines and maintain close links between the business, the clientele and other local and similar ethnic and linguistic businesses (Panayiotopoulos, 2010). Eventually, such areas may start to develop and even to market themselves as 'ethnic precincts',

> places in the city that combine both private and public spaces and where the cultural and symbolic economy gain prominence shaped by the interaction of producers (ethnic entrepreneurs), consumers and the critical infrastructure (regulators, community leaders, critics, place-marketers).
>
> (Collins & Kunz, 2009, p. 40)

The growth of such ethnic business and ethnic enclaves have often played 'a key role in reviving industrial, warehousing, and retailing districts of the central city' (Lin, 2011, p. 34) after older businesses have relocated to suburban locations. The ethnic precinct can also, as Lin (2011) reminds us, become the 'ethnic theme park' (p. 14). A sense of place and cultural heritage can 'help to sustain local communities and cultures' but can also 'be easily appropriated by global capitalism for promoting urban redevelopment' (p. 16).

During this project, we had the chance to study one such emergent precinct. From a train station in north Sydney, an alley runs between the station and a residential street. Since the 1980s it has been inaccessible by car, and in the last few years it has been repaved, fitted with benches, and beautified with transplanted pepper trees. For more than a century, the avenue has been the site of various and diverse small businesses (see Chapter 7): milliners, butchers, pharmacists, solicitors, greengrocers, milk bars, lolly shops and laundromats, to name a few, have over the years shared and changed the space. Today, it is home to a sushi restaurant, a ramen restaurant, two Japanese grocery stores, a Japanese second-hand bookshop, a café, a Thai restaurant, a gym and a Japanese pottery studio. A Korean barbeque restaurant is currently under construction. This was by no means a planned development but instead developed as one Japanese business opened in this slightly dodgy alley – it had a bad reputation and was considered very much the wrong side of the tracks, a place to hurry through on the way home – and over time others followed. It is now a markedly Japanese space, and indeed, is a destination for Japanese people living in the greater Sydney region (see Chapters 3 and 5).

Such precincts thus change over time. In the Sydney suburb of Marrickville, Greek, Turkish, Lebanese and Vietnamese family businesses sit shoulder to shoulder, from beauty salons and bakeries to solicitors and travel agents (see Chapter 7 for layers of multilingual signs on the street), reflecting the changing population of the suburb. As a waitress of Turkish background in her early twenties explained, 'when my grandparents first migrated they actually migrated to Marrickville. And so there's a lot of Turk ... Turkish people and Greek people. They've migrated around this area and stayed there'; though now, with the Vietnamese nail salon and bakery, the pattern of the suburb is changing, altering the patterns of who works and lives there. As Lin (2011) notes, the largest Koreatown in the USA, in Los Angeles, may be primarily Korean, but Koreans themselves only make up less than 15 per cent of the population, which is primarily Hispanic. Likewise, Leichardt in Sydney, which is known for its Italian flavours, is no longer a majority residential area for those of Italian background. More generally, this becomes part of the complex *layering* of the city (see Chapter 7) – visible in the different signs on buildings – the ways in which different sites carry the histories of different enterprises.

Businesses themselves may also be taken over. As Radice (2009) notes on a small business in Montreal,

It is hard to put an ethnic label on the bagel shop run by a Sikh family on Sherbrooke Street that also sells home-made Indian curries. The same goes for the 24-hour St-Viateur Bagel Shop, whose Italian owner first started work there as a teenager on the night shift in 1962, learning Yiddish on the way.

(p. 147)

On another street, Radice describes a Chinese immigrant-owned small supermarket with an Italian name, employing a Greek-speaking man in the deli counter, a cashier related to the original Italian owners and a young Black student. Since the district is ethnically diverse, the shop reflects a diversity of products. As we shall see later in Chapter 4, there is nothing strange about a Greek-run pizzeria in Sydney. As soon as we walk into a Lebanese owned shop in Marrickville, we see Greek on the tins of olives and olive oil; Turkish on the fresh bread and semolina; Chinese and Vietnamese on the rice bags and spice boxes. There are also sauerkraut and gherkins, Indian spices and Ethiopian coffee.

Under current conditions of globalization, such migratory patterns may be quite organized, with Vietnamese manicure salons linked transnationally (Eckstein & Nguyen, 2011) or 'labor brokerage states' such as the Philippines organizing its export of labour as an overt economic strategy, with clear linguistic implications. In the Philippines, workers are turned into 'globally marketable, made-to-order and profitable migrant labor for particular niches in the global labor market' (Lorente, 2011, p. 201). These workers are supposed to have 'translocally valid language resources' (p. 201), which include workplace communication skills, English and the languages of their target destination (Cantonese for Hong Kong, Arabic for the Middle East, and so on). For the domestic workers, as carers of middle-class children, it is their English that is often the most important linguistic commodity. And yet, although Filipino workers form large ethnic networks within the various countries where they work – nowhere more obvious than on Sundays in Hong Kong when the workers gather in the centre of the city – their transitory migratory work, their residence in the apartments of their employers, means their spatial representation in the city is less than that of permanent settlers.

At one level, the labels and identifications we have seen – Chinese market gardeners, Serbian painters and plasterers, Lebanese fruit and vegetable sellers – clearly identify certain lines of affiliation; and yet, they also conceal layers of diversity. As we have already noted with the Serbian (or 'Yugoslav') workers, the practical affiliations they make around language and work may override other possible regional differences, so that a Croatian safety officer helps Serbian workers fill out forms, and Bosnian, Serbian and Macedonian differences are put aside. In the context of the 'Lebanese' end of Flemington Market (see previous chapter), we can also observe this 'Lebanese-ness' is maintained in part by a range of Arabic (and other language) speakers. The brothers employ workers of Turkish, Pakistani, Moroccan, Sudanese-Egyptian, Somalian and Filipino backgrounds, so that within the broader descriptions of the market, these workers become part of the 'Lebanese' contingent. These affiliations (they lingo in Lebanese and broken English, as Joseph puts it) do not describe the varied interactions or the ways in which being Lebanese is here supported by a range of Arabic-related and other workers. As we shall see in later chapters, the broad labels of 'Chinese' or 'Cantonese' conceal a host of differences.

This therefore needs to be seen as a constant process of construction, of a making of work ethnicities through both daily interactions and external labelings. Ethnocultural and linguistic patterns are as much the emergent properties of forms of work and interaction as they are the preconditions for work. As Benor (2010) argues, in order to overcome the contradictions of talking about 'ethnolects' (ways of speaking marked by ethnicity) when these varieties are also marked by great diversity, it is more useful to talk in terms of *ethnolinguistic repertoires*: fluid sets of 'linguistic resources that members of an ethnic group may use variably as they index their ethnic identities' (p. 160). This idea links with our discussion elsewhere of repertoires (see Chapters 1 and 4), and the importance of seeing such repertoires of cultural and linguistic resources in relation to places of work.

Likewise, when we view metrolingual practices from this performative perspective, we can see on the one hand that these ethnic labels are the sedimented effects of repeated strategic action (whether filling out forms at immigration or heading to the Serbian Club to look for work) and on the other that the linguistic and cultural interactions that actually take place are far more diverse than these labels allow (Otsuji, 2010). The linguistic and ethnic affiliations that bring people together to buy similar fruit and vegetables from each other operate as networks that include linguistic, cultural and culinary associations that work as a different layer – both ideologically and in practice – from the layers of mixed language use that operate in the everyday exchanges through which such networks may be realized. The language use that goes on within and across these affiliations remains metrolingual. While on the one hand we need to take seriously the ethnic and linguistic labels that people employ, we also need to view these as part of the ethnolinguistic and spatial repertoires, the fluid sets of linguistic and cultural resources people draw on to index their identities as part of the city.

Ethnography as process

Five in the morning on a Friday in September, 2012. Sitting in one of the Produce Market cafés having an early coffee and planning our morning's research. We record some of our own conversations as part of our ethnographic work. A smart phone on the table, rather than one of the digital recording devices we're using in the research, does this easily enough. This is one of those mornings when it's good that the three core research team members – Astrid Lorange, Emi Otsuji, Alastair Pennycook – are all together. One reason of course is because we need to plan how we're going to go about recording this morning: there are important minor issues we need to work out, such as the essential presence of a man to fix the lapel mics to the T-shirts of these Lebanese-Muslim men. More importantly, however, these moments of sitting and talking in research contexts are often the space where we generate ideas. When we drove down to the market gardens the previous week, it was the discussions in the car, the discussions as we walked along the edge of the rows of vegetables that were almost as important as the interviews with the gardeners.

This is about ethnography as process. As Blommaert and Dong (2010) note, ethnography has to accord 'great importance to the history of what is commonly seen as "data": the whole process of gathering and moulding knowledge is part of that knowledge; knowledge construction *is* knowledge, *the process is the product*' (p. 10; emphasis in original). Importantly too this is about a team of ethnographers, walking and talking together, recording our own discussions in situ, sleepy, in need of coffee, but feeling the business of the market. It is also about the shifting nature of the research teams, as different people join for specific parts of the project. It was crucial on our second visit to the market gardens that we brought Jo along – not just because she speaks Cantonese, Mandarin and English (an earlier visit had rather floundered with our inadequate knowledge of Cantonese beyond a few greetings and comments), but also because she knew where these market gardeners were from in Guangdong and how they lived their lives (she herself had grown up both in Guangdong and then in the next suburb to this one in Sydney); her parents had worked those long hours in factories and the kitchens of restaurants, and she knew what they were talking about.

These shifting multilingual research teams were constantly providing us with unexpected insights into our data. Describing certain sounds – 'A joj! Ohh, Mmm' – in one of the construction site lunchtime recordings as 'sounds of satiation', we asked our translator/transcriber, Smiljana, what she meant by this. She replied: 'yeah it's funny how sounds of satiation are culture specific! I was taken back to the days I spent as a child, in summer, sitting outside the country house, with my dad and uncles after a roast pig lunch, full and tired from the heat.' Ahhh, that sound. This comment, apart from its delightful poetic specificity, raised for us too the extraordinary role our co-workers played in the construction of this text, as they explained, interpreted, translated, explained again. Each of these people, for obvious reasons, shared some of the background of the people we had recorded and interviewed. Jo knew the Chinese market gardens, and like others of our research assistants was often pushing us to explain why we were fascinated by certain types of language use which were so ordinary, everyday, mundane.

Just as we have emphasized the everydayness of this multilingualism, so this was reinforced by our research assistants: 'What's the big deal? That's how people speak.' Our translator of Arabic could fill us in on the many subtleties of Lebanese Australian English and Arabic, and when we were pushing to use Arabic for our transcriptions, she dissuaded us, explaining her generation, like the people we recorded, rarely use it; and anyway, it would never work for this colloquial language in the workplace. Smiljana helped us see that Drago's Serbian was young and hip, not like the more stilted Serbian of some of the older workers. With the transcriptions and translations came comments as paratexts, providing not just information but questions about what counts as data and what is 'noteworthy' or 'intriguing'. And after all, each of us is as much an ingredient of the urban space, with our own personal and ethnic trajectories, as any other.

We will discuss in later chapters some of the particular insights we gained from our shifting multilingual research teams, as well as the complexities of working with metrolingual data. Here it is the process of research we wish to draw attention to. Ethnographic research is not only about the gathering of data in specific contexts, the note-taking, the recording, the questioning, the observing; nor is it only about the writing, the attempts to capture what is going on, to describe the bustle of the market, the hectic work in the restaurant or kitchen, the interactions over lunch in a construction site. It is also about the conversations, the developing understandings as we sit and talk about the market gardens, watch the conical hats in the fields and the planes flying overhead and try to make sense of all this. The diversity of these research teams matters therefore, as we talk and bring our own reflections on these many places and people and languages.

Notes

1   Transcribing spoken Cantonese is a task with many problems and limits: Not only are there few established conventions, but the status of written Cantonese is also contested. Our representation of this spoken interaction captures some of the colloquial nature of their speech but not enough of the dialectal variation. Our thanks to Angel Lin for advice (and see Lin, 2009).

2   In the process of writing up this research we have constantly faced issues associated with ethnic and language labeling. As with our reluctance to use various linguistic labels, common ethnic descriptions do not sit easily with our approach to diversity, even if participants use them themselves. Trajectories of countries/space and people are always complex and the seeming fixity in labeling someone as 'Chinese', 'Serbian' and so on is always an uncomfortable compomise with the need to provide indications of their history and background. We have used various moderating descriptors, such as 'second-generation Lebanese Australian', or 'a worker of Serbian background', or simply describing the life history of the individual, but remain aware of the problems these terms also bring.

3   The categories used here are those supplied by this worker, and are based both on his knowledge of the worksite and the health and safety forms they fill out.

3 Mobility, rhythms and the city

Catching a train in Sydney

The train leaves Chatswood station. A woman in her early thirties sits down, talking on her mobile. '對對！' (right right!), she affirms to her interlocutor. English is mixed in with her Mandarin Chinese: 'Otherwise 我就覺得他就去找 someone better 好了, 是吧?' (Otherwise, I feel like he can just go find someone better, right?). Other English words and phrases such as 'weird', 'turn around' and 'you are right' are interspersed through the predominantly Chinese conversation. Like Hurstville to the south (see Chapter 2) or Ashfield to the west, Chatswood is one of the growing new 'Chinese suburbs' of the city, where a range of linguistic resources, including English and varieties of Chinese, are deployed. These mobile resources – on a phone on a train to an interlocutor also presumably comfortable with these mixed resources – are common in the transport networks across the city.

Behind the woman, an elderly man of South Asian appearance is reading an English newspaper while a young Asian woman next to him is texting, apparently in Japanese. Three young men with large backpacks are sitting at the other end of the carriage speaking in English, though two of them occasionally switch to Dutch when talking to each other. The train slows down and approaches the next station. A few Japanese-speaking people, including the young woman who was texting, are getting ready to get off the train. The train halts, the doors open and people leave. The station is adjacent to a little pedestrian lane known as the 'Japanese alley', with sushi, ramen and grocery shops (see Chapter 2). The train departs again and new passengers take seats in the carriage: a Middle Eastern couple (there is a Lebanese mosque near the station) and a Caucasian man in his fifties in a business suit. This is the mobile landscape of the train at 11 a.m. on a Thursday morning in Spring 2013, as it passes quietly through the northern suburbs of Sydney.

'One only needs to catch a bus in Sydney or a tram in Melbourne', suggests Lasagabaster (2010), 'to realise how multilingual and multicultural Australia's everyday life is' (p. 187). Block (2006) also starts his account of a multilingual city (London) with a bus journey. He is travelling on a bus from Finchley, North London, to Bloomsbury, central London, and talking to his partner in Catalan (they moved from Barcelona to London ten years before). A man sitting behind them is talking on his mobile in Spanish; two rows in front teenagers are talking in Russian. As the journey goes on he hears Greek, Gujarati and Arabic, and there are varieties of English, with their London influences, Jamaican influences and ubiquitous 'innit?' (p. vii). This, then, is one of our points of departure: Urban journeys in and through diversity. We are interested in these language mobilities across the city as workers, shoppers, consumers, travel with their linguistic companions and linguistic others to and from work, to and from different suburbs, at different times and speeds. This is about the linguistic consequences of the rhythms of the city.

There is another way in which this is a departure point for us: As Lasagabaster goes on to recount, the 2006 census of Australia confirms this impression of diversity 'and records 16.8% of the population speaking a language other than English (LOTE) at home, but this proportion is much higher in Sydney (31.4%) and Melbourne (27.9%).' More recent data based on the 2011 census (Sydney's Melting Pot of Language, 2014) suggest that close to 40 per cent of people in Sydney now speak a language other than English at home. While such data give us one window on diversity, this is not the approach we have been taking. We might for example have noted that according to the 2011 census of Australia, of the 21,194 inhabitants of Chatswood, about 41 per cent speak only English at home, while 59 per cent speak other languages at home, the most common being Mandarin Chinese (14 per cent), Cantonese (13 per cent), Korean (8 per cent), and Japanese (3 per cent). In the first place, as Lasagabaster notes,

> these statistics are an underestimation, as they do not include those who have no one to speak their own language to at home (because they live on their own, for example) and those who speak LOTEs on a regular basis in other social spheres (parents, other relatives, neighbours or friends).
>
> (p. 187)

Such figures are not only an underestimation, however: they are also a particularly static representation of diversity, with little space for mobility, change, travel, commuting, shifting patterns of people and languages as people come and go.

Approaches to multilingualism that seek numerical accounts of languages in cities – what we might call linguistic mapping or 'demolinguistic representation' (Daveluy, 2011, p. 156) – provide us with some potentially useful data about linguistic diversity but make very particular assumptions about languages and multilingualism. In their *Multilingual Cities Project* (looking at various European cities), Extra and Yağmur (2008; 2011) are able to conclude that 'the proportion of pupils in whose homes other languages were used next to or instead of the mainstream language ranged per city between one third and more than a half' (2011, p. 1182). These languages include Arabic, Turkish, Kurdish, Chinese, Polish, Vietnamese, Berber and Urdu. Thus they are able to show (cf. also Barni & Extra, 2008; Martinovic, 2011) that children across Europe commonly alternate between more than one language depending on context and interlocutor and that children appear to be growing up speaking both the language of their parents and the national language (with no apparent detrimental effects).

While such numerical representations may enable minority groups to claim better linguistic and educational rights (or become part of the panoptical gaze of the state, leading to attempts to overcome the problem of diversity by greater state intervention though schooling), they provide us with a very particular snapshot of diversity: They are premised very obviously on the common assumption that languages can be counted, that people's multilingualism can be numerically accounted for, and that proficiency and frequency of use can also be reliably and accurately measured. As Moore, Pietikäinen and Blommaert (2010) put it, '"speakerhood" and "language-hood" are matters whose complexity poorly suits them for numerical representations' since such counting 'inevitably draws attention away from the speech-community dynamics of language contact and change' and obscures 'the complex pragmatic and metapragmatic dimensions of actual language-in-use' (p. 2). The use of such numerical accounts thus diverts focus away from 'detailed considerations of the actual linguistic and communicative resources that people have and deploy in social life'. Following Moore *et al.* (2010), then, we have likewise shifted our analytical gaze 'away from abstract "languages" and "speakers" to practices and actual resources' (p. 2).

This is more therefore than just a question of method and analysis, or the tired debate around qualitative and quantitative research approaches; rather, it has to do with more profound questions about how we understand language. Language mapping, as Makoni and Pennycook (2007) note, has deep origins in colonial projects of fixity, in 'nineteenth-century notions in which languages are tied to specific geographical localities and speaker national identities' (Makoni & Makoni, 2010, p. 260). A map may work quite well for a tract of land (though not unproblematically so) but languages are rather different entities: more fluid, more mobile, much harder to pin down. Where in a linguistic map of Africa is the local 'taxilingua culture' (Makoni & Makoni, 2010, p. 269) of the minibus/taxi, its exterior emblazoned with signs, Kwaito music blaring on the inside and a mix of languages negotiating back and forth between the workers getting a ride back to the township?

Not only are the language ideologies of researchers important here, but also those of the research participants. In lunchtime conversations on a Sydney construction site (see also Chapters 2, 5 and 6), one comment that occurred a number of times among the workers of Bosnian Serbian heritage was that despite the differences constructed among the languages of the former Yugoslavia (see Busch & Schick, 2007), there were no grounds to enumerate them separately: 'I'm using English, Serbian, Croatian, and Bosnian. But those three languages is the same, you know, grammar is the same, just couple of words is different' (Damijan, interview, December 3, 2011). Zlatan, another worker of Bosnian-Serbian background, similarly counts his linguistic repertoire as two languages, English and Serbian, since 'Serbian, Bosnian, and Croatian, that's similar' (Zlatan, interview, February 14, 2012). Zlatan's remark comes in the context of a discussion with Nemia, his co-worker from Fiji, who has just asserted that he speaks 'different language, maybe sixty language?' Nemia explains, 'We have different language. Like, my village, we have different language, other village is a different language, other village is a different language. But all the language … all the village … I can speak the language' (Nemia, interview, February 14, 2012). In response to Zlatan's downgrading of his own repertoire to two, Nemia rethinks his count: 'Yeah, I've got one, two, three, four, five, six … seven, maybe ten, twenty?' Nemia's shifting account of his multilingualism points on the one hand to the popular tendency to count languages but on the other hand to great flexibility about what that number might be and what might count as a language. Zlatan simply comments, 'He is polyglot'.

On another occasion, Drago (of Serbian background; moved to Australia a year and a half before) explains that he understands Macedonian because he used to live and work in Macedonia as a bricklayer, and his girlfriend's mother is Macedonian. But he downplays this diversity, which now includes Bulgarian: 'And we're close. Next to Serbia is Macedonia. And we lived in Macedonia. And Bulgarian same … All this is similar … Bosnian, Serbian, Croatian, Bulgarian, Macedonian' (lunchtime discussion, July 8, 2012). In the earlier conversation, Nemia meanwhile returns to a discussion of the different languages in Fiji but Marko, a worker of Serbian background (he moved to Australia at the age of ten) in charge of the site, decides that these are not languages: 'Dialect, or different language?' Now Nemia is unsure: 'Different … but … yeah. Similar similar.' Marko turns teacher: 'Probably different dialect. Like north of Serbia and south of Serbia … oh, very different. I have to go "What? What?" for them, for me, to understand them.' Drago confirms: 'Same happen in Macedonia. Small country, lot of different dialects.' Nemia does not seem convinced by this: 'But the words the same?', but the conversation moves on and this struggle over language enumeration and languages and dialects gets lost in the general lunchtime banter.

These discussions suggest that with Marko, Drago and Zlatan counting down their numerical multilingualism ('all this is similar') while Nemia counts his up ('maybe sixty') before downgrading to 'maybe ten, twenty?', and with the indeterminacy of whether languages should be seen as national entities or village entities, whether speaking the same language should entail mutual comprehensibility or whether we should talk in terms of dialects or languages, self reporting on languages is interesting qualitatively, but problematic quantitatively. Numerical representation of languages and their speakers through synchronic snapshots of reported language use is a peculiar and often limiting approach to understanding diversity. Not only does it potentially present a fixed notion of languages as 'neatly-bounded, abstract, autonomous grammatical systems (each of which corresponds to a neatly-bounded "worldview")' (Moore, Pietikäinen & Blommaert, 2010, p. 2), but it also suggests an equally fixed notion of what bilingualism or multilingualism entail. Any putative relations between language and thought are not usefully understood in terms of abstract mappings of languages, cultures and cognition, but rather need to be understood in terms of the everyday contexts of language learning, meaning, status, education, literacy, interlocutors, families and much more. This is not just a question of distinctions between high and low, elite and folk bilingualism (de Mejía, 2002; Skutnabb-Kangas, 1981) but rather that the notions of bi- or multilingualism cannot be used as if they refer to the same thing by dint of a plurality of languages being learned: There are many and different multilingualisms.

As outlined in Chapter 1, we are interested in this book in *multilingualism from below*, in the everyday diversity of public places, on public transport, in city squares, in restaurants, shops and construction sites, as people make do, get by, rub up against each other with whatever linguistic (and non-linguistic) resources they can muster. As we argue further in Chapter 4, we are also interested not only in individual accounts of personal trajectories, but also the use of languages in particular places. Metrolingualism therefore takes up the challenge of understanding everyday multilingualism not through the demolinguistic enumeration of mappable multilingualism but rather through the study of local language practices. Metrolingualism focuses on everyday multilingualism (practices and experiences) and the interrelationships between language, mobility and urban space. Metrolingualism is a way of understanding language in the city that is neither reliant on linguistic categories as commonly defined nor on notions of community or territory. Metrolingualism takes up that challenge of everyday multilingualism on Sydney trains and Tokyo restaurants, but does not pursue its explanations of diversity in the enumeration of speakers or languages. We are interested instead in the local language practices in kitchens, shops, markets, parks, streets, as people move and get by metrolinguistically, shaping and remaking the linguistic landscape as they do so.

The breathing city

As trains and buses move through the city, they also take on different linguistic patterns according to suburbs and different work patterns. With the particular hours of the construction industry (start early morning, finish mid-afternoon) and the particular linguistic and ethnic affiliations of sectors of that industry (see Chapter 2), the 3:30 going south from Redfern, with a range of new construction projects in progress, takes on a character of its own:

> If I catch the 3:30 train out of here ... 'cause I live in Campbelltown ... and if I catch that 3:30 train, the train is packed. It is packed full of the tradies[1] from the city. And they are loud! And they're form-workers. They are very, very loud. And they talk about, they talk about ... 'cause it gets broken up into English and their language, and they generally talk about what their rights are, and ... always about their right, you know, what they can achieve.

As the train heads south, Phillip, the foreman from ABC construction company notes, with 'eight carriages full of them', people get off and it quietens down, with different languages dominating as different people leave the train for different suburbs. Then, 'around Holsworthy the noise actually settles down and then the conversation becomes very easy to listen to. Not that I listen to it, I'm asleep, but ... yeah' (Phillip, interview, October 31, 2012).

'In any space', Edensor indicates (2011, p. 191), 'the activities and interactions of numerous social actors intersect, as suburbanites, young, old, shopkeepers, dog-walkers, the religious and the festive, drug addicts, schoolchildren, shoppers, workers, traffic wardens and students collectively constitute space through their rhythmic and arhythmic practices'. Cities are rhythmic: Shops open and shut, commuters drive in and out of the city, public transport takes people to and fro. Such rhythms are not linked only to the daily commute of the office worker , those cars, trains, buses ferrying people to work for a nine o'clock start, and back again after five. Other workers and parts of the city have different schedules. Markets and garbage collectors and delivery workers may start early. While a market in the city centre only gets going after 9 a.m., many of the products have already been bought and transported much earlier in the morning from the Produce Market, which bustles in the pre-dawn dark, the café full, the buyers walking the aisles of vegetables and fruit, and the sellers busy and sweating.

Construction workers, who often travel not only to work, but also with work – traversing the city to different construction sites – start early and leave early. A plasterer may travel from one outer suburb to another to be picked up by a co-worker and then drive to a site where they work an early shift before relocating to another site in the afternoon. Vukasin, who supervises multiple sites, travels across Sydney every day to keep in touch with the progress of work sites, often using morning tea or lunch time to visit. These work rhythms and mobilities have linguistic consequences. As Mac Giolla Chríost (2007) notes, language is 'central to the sense of place, the rhythms, the mobility, the fixity, the connection and disconnection that variously define social life in the city' (p. 146). In the basement car park of a construction site near Redfern station on the edge of central Sydney (the same station from where Phillip, working at another site, takes his 3:30 train going south), the workers change their participation patterns and manipulate their linguistic repertoires amid the traffic of people and phone calls.

Mobile phones play an important role for both social and work calls, connecting the different workers across multiple sites, and keeping them in contact when they are working: During an interview Zlatan reports having recently spoken with Igor, a co-worker from another site: 'Actually I talked yesterday with Igor. I called him, you know. They working in Bondi now. Bondi Junction or Bondi Beach, I'm not sure.' They often make phone calls during lunch break. Thus, the languages of the basement fluctuate from almost none (minimal talk amid the noise of construction) to a mixture of English, Serbian (between Vukasin and Marko on the phone or between Marko and Drago at the lunch table) and Fijian (frequent phone conversations by Nemia with a Fijian friend). These resources change with the mobility and rhythms of the space (the time of day, the day's work schedule, the arrival of equipment and materials), objects (mobile phones, the food they eat), material arrangements (the space set aside for lunch breaks, the state of construction work, the location of the site) and people (who is in the space).

In Excerpt 3.2 Vukasin arrives, interrupting a lunch time conversation between Marko (of Serbian background who is in charge of the site), Drago (also of Serbian background) and Temo (a new worker who started only a few days ago: second generation Fijian Tongan, born and raised in Australia) and Nemia (of Fijian background), about the Serbian tennis player Novak Djokovic.

Excerpt 3.1 (M: Marko, D: Drago, V: Vukasin)

1. M: Novak Djokovic … Now. But when he started he was a lot younger. Here's Vukasin [noticing Vukasin's car entering the basement of the building]. Twenty five now? When he started … like you say, 18, 19, when he first popped up. Yep.
2. D: Career prize money. Thirty-eight millions.
3. M: Thirty-eight? In a period of five, six, seven, years maybe?
4. D: Ah:: I think [Drago is cut off by Marko greeting Vukasin, who walks into the basement]
5. M: Hello mister supervisor, how are you?

[Vukasin gives instructions. Conversation is mainly between Marko and Vukasin in English]

6. V: Alright. Tomorrow … render should be finished completely.
7. M: Completely. Yep.
8. V: And we should clean, clean unit.
9. M: Yep.
10. V: Ah take plastic off, clean everything.

In this excerpt, as Vukasin's arrival interrupts the lunchtime conversation, English is used between Vukasin and Marko so that instructions given by Vukasin to Marko can be indirectly passed on to other workers who are sharing the space, including those such as the recent addition to the team, Temo, who do not speak Serbian.

The people present in the space, the modes of conversation and time of day affect the diversity of language use, register and repertoire. When Marko and Drago talk, they often include Serbianized English resources, such as 'payslipa' (pay slips) in their Serbian; for example, Marko: 'Eto vidis ti si ima tri payslipa I sest ipo su zgrabili' (There you go, you see you've had three pay slips, and they grabbed six and a half). When, on a different day, Marko receives a call from Vukasin during lunch (Drago and Nemia are sitting silently eating), their conversation is in Serbian (although Marko claims that Vukasin speaks a different dialect from his) with some traces of English words, including terms such as 'a lot of'. Although still about work (the term *sika* is common among plasterers and related trades, and refers to the construction product manufacturing company Sika, and by analogy to its products, here to a kind of wall-filler), this conversation is less obviously directed to others (in contrast to Excerpt 3.1).

Excerpt 3.2 (V: Vukasin, M: Marko)
Serbian: *italic*; English: plain (translation in brackets)
1. V: *Bolje ga nemoj ubacivat nego, nego nabijo taj sik.* (Better not to throw it in, but, but, shove in that sik [sika].)
2. M: No *pa si video kolko mesta ima bas ima puno mesta.* (No, well did you see how much room there is there's heaps of room.)
3. V: *Da.* (Yes.)
4. M: *Bas ima* a lot of sika *ce otici ako ako onda ubacicemo jos taj* lintel *pa cemo napuniti.* (There's a lot of sika it'll get used up if, if then we'll throw in that lintel and we'll fill it up.)

As well as the long-term migratory mobilities that have brought these workers from the former Yugoslavia to this basement on a construction site in Sydney, the more local movements – from one site to another, Vukasin's visits to sites, calls on mobile phones, workers of different backgrounds turning up – bring in not only different layers of language to the basement (see Chapter 7 for more discussion on language layering) but are also constantly creating new linguistic mixtures.

This mobile landscape of workers and the linguistic landscapes of construction sites take on a different flavour when seen from the point of view of the owner of a café around the corner from ABC construction site (where Phillip supervises) and the building where Marko, Nemia, Drago and Temo are working. Lynda (Chinese background) used to work at the café before taking it over from the previous owner. Her kitchen staff are from 'Colombia, Chinese, Hong Kong, and plus, Bangladesh. And India. And India as well. So all cultures and mix' (for further discussion of kitchen staff, see Chapter 4). As a café owner, Lynda has an extensive knowledge of the mobility of people who live and work around the area, and particularly of how the construction industry works and the stages of construction sites of the area.

Excerpt 3.3 (L: Lynda, R: Researcher)
1. L: There's different groups, they finish different jobs. So I think we used to have some customers from that side [pointing east towards Surry Hills] but now this building has just finalised, and lots of people move in, so they are already finish this job. So now this job [ABC] has start, I would say … end of last year? and I don't really know about that group. But what I say from my customers, my:: uh:: how do you say? Different specialise in jobs, and yeah.
2. R: And then after a few weeks, sometimes they disappear?
3. L: Yeah yeah yeah that's right. And then they come back again in another few weeks and say Oh, I just finished another job in Parramatta. And they come back. So that's how it make people feel like they are closer, because you see every day, even 30 seconds, one minute. But we're still with each other, so there's similar things.

As she also noted, a recent absence had been the workers from the ABC site since many were not coming to her café during Ramadan. As Len (Lebanese background; supervisor before Phillip took over) explained, seven out of eight of his workers – of Lebanese, Iraqi and Afghani background (the eighth was a Christian Iraqi) – were fasting. 'I don't push too hard, but … We do what we have to do. I just tell them, I just … I just tell them that this is what I need done, and they try to meet it. You gotta understand that they're fasting, and that's the way it is' (Len, interview, July 23, 2012). For Lynda, like the workers who disappear for a while and then return, the temporary absence of workers from this construction site during Ramadan was another part of the rhythmic patterns of the city and its people.

Ramadan becomes one of those regular markers of city times and spaces. For Joseph (of Christian Lebanese background) at the Produce Market, it was one of those quiet times for his café.

Excerpt 3.4 (J: Joseph , R1: Researcher 1, R2: Researcher 2)
1. R1: I guess it's a change at the moment, during Ramadan? It's different now, for this month?
2. J: Let's move on from that subject! [laughs] It does. They go a little bit quiet. And they don't eat during the day.
3. R1: Are you open before,
4. J: I open from midnight.
5. R1: Oh!
6. R2: Midnight!
7. J: Midnight, yeah, I open. So between 12 o'clock … but they do, they have their home … their food at home … they have their *suhoor* or whatever they call it, their early breakfast. And they come back over here and they top up with something else. And about five o'clock they have trading, and trading slows down completely to the other ordinary, ordinary customers.

(Joseph, Interview, August 8, 2012)

Just as commuting 'sews places together and produces an itinerary shaped by time, as temporalities of movement are continually reinscribed on places and periods of travel en route' (Edensor, 2011, p. 192), so these repeated visits, disappearances and returns to cafés bring the city together. Here in Lynda's coffee shop, the mobility of diverse people as they come and go with the changing rhythms of the construction industry becomes part of the business for a while. In the morning, some Arabic-speaking workers who know little English bring in handwritten notes to order coffee while talking among themselves in Arabic. The café opens at 6:30 to serve the construction workers, 'plus we have another customers, regular customers from the station. So normally they come morning. These people stop coming, but normally before they come for coffee in the morning, 6:30. So that's the reason we keep open earlier' (Lynda, interview, February 28, 2013). Lynda's coffee shop has a different linguistic landscape at different times of the day. The rhythms of work, the ethnic connections to particular trades, the areas people live and the transport systems all contribute to the ways the city breathes languages in and out.

Ishikawa-san, who runs a small grocery shop in the Japanese alley (where the train paused at the beginning of this chapter), opens her shop around 11 a.m. and shuts around 9 p.m., aligning with the opening hours of the Japanese restaurants on the alley. The secondhand book shop next door and the grocery shop across the alley have similar trading hours so that they can share the same wave of customers (see Chapter 5 for conviviality of the space). During weekdays, it is often Japanese women who visit Ishikawa-san's grocery shop and have lunch at the Japanese ramen shop around 1 p.m.; school children (some of Japanese background, others not) dash into Ishikawa-san's shop around 3 p.m. after school to buy sweets and snacks. In the evening, the alley attracts people to have sushi and ramen after work. Saturday has a different landscape; the second-hand bookshop is busy wih Japanese kids checking comic books after Saturday Japanese language school while their parents are 'slurping' ramen across the alley. Meanwhile, the coffee shop run by young 'オージー: Ōji' ('Aussies') (see Chapter 5) keeps different hours ('Ōji style' as one of the Japanese owners called it), opening earlier and closing around 2 p.m.

On every first Saturday of the month – 'Lucky Saturday' according to the grocery shop owner, Mariko-san, across the alley from Ishikawa-san – sales products are displayed outside her shop. Both customers and other shops on the alley take advantage of 'Lucky Saturday': the whole alley is in full swing, attracting customers not only from various suburbs in Sydney but also from suburban cities and towns as far as Canberra. It is the day for customers to get Japanese-related things done: eat, speak, drink, shop and socialize around things Japanese, as well as enjoying coffee after their sushi, delivered from the coffee shop across the alley. This alley shifts its rhythms and languages during the day, across the week, and around the monthly Lucky Saturdays, with people synchronizing with each other and also with the rhythms of schools, weekends, churches and mosques, day care centres, gym times and trains.

Similarly, the complex where Joseph works in the Produce Market has a dynamic linguistic and cultural landscape that changes across a range of time frames – daily, weekly, yearly, or over longer time spans (Uncle Tony's 75 years in the markets gives him a special insight into the changing patterns of market workers, from Italians to Maltese, Lebanese to Chinese). The complex turns from a produce market into a weekend flea market selling leather jackets, shoes, wigs, Australian souvenirs and daily commodities on Fridays and then reverts to a produce market on Saturdays, attracting people of various backgrounds.

> You got Friday – we got Paddy's – comes from very common different nationalities. And Saturday we have more – I found out in the last two years, two to three years, there's a lot of foreign from Iraq, Afghanistan. A lot of refugees who arrived in Australia in the last five, six years.
>
> (Joseph, interview, August 8, 2012)

Although English remains a language of common communication, these shifting patterns of produce and people also inevitably bring about other language patterns.

> But in the last ten years I would say an Arabic of Lebanese background spoken is become very common in this area of the market because of the multiple numbers of them trading in this area. And um, it varies on a Saturday, it goes back to a different languages, more Italians and Greeks and so on. But the common, common language is, in numbers, is a second language after English, is, would be Arabic.
>
> (Joseph, interview, August 8, 2012)

As is the case of the Japanese alley, during the weekend people travel greater distances for shopping, to catch up with relatives and for a weekend away. According to Wafiq, who runs the Craving Coffee and Nuts shop in Marrickville, many people come to his shop from further afield especially at certain times.

> Thursday, Friday, Saturday. The Australian, you know, coming from Dee Why, that north shore areas. And they haven't got some sort of shops there, like this one. And they got, you know – as soon as they smell the coffee and the spices, they come inside the shop. They find a lot of different products from too many different countries. And they haven't got it up in their area.
>
> (Wafiq, interview, July 17, 2012)

As he goes on to explain, these 'Australians' (for further discussion of 'Aussies' and also his use of 'too many' see Chapter 5) are after foods such as '*ajvar*,[2] you know, the chilli. In the jar. Spices. We got too many different spices!'

Different ethnic precincts may also keep different hours. Chinese areas of a city typically start later and continue much later than others. Sunday opening hours radically changed city rhythms. Religious practices also bring large shifts of people, perhaps best signalled by the call of the *muezzin* from the the mosques' minarets for Friday afternoon prayers. Migration patterns (caused in part by wars and invasions), employment possibilities and ethnic affiliations mean that the Friday call to prayer summons taxi drivers from across the city to their various mosques. As Carolyn, one of our informants on the background to the Japanese alley, commented after we had talked to her, it should be easy to get a taxi because of the mosque on the other side of the station. On Saturdays Jewish populations have their inner city migrations, and on Sundays it's the Christians' turn. Sports events (an inner city stadium for a Saturday evening match or a suburban stadium for a Sunday afternoon), nightclubs, festivals in parks, all bring about a different set of spatial and temporal engagement with the city. As Edensor puts it, '(r)hythms may be linear or cyclical and operate at circadian weekly, monthly, seasonal, annual, lifetime, millennial and geological scales' (Edensor, 2011, p. 189).

Conceiving space-time not so much as knowing and representation but as doing and practice, (Crang, 2001, p. 193) helps view the city in terms of 'a becoming, through circulation, combination and recombination of people and things' (p. 190). Thus, as we problematize demolinguistic approaches to language mapping, we can see how the language resources used at 8 a.m. in one place may be very different from those at 3 p.m. as people commute, consume, talk on their mobiles or come together to eat, pray, work and shop. The urban, therefore, is the site of multiple colliding temporalities of practices (Crang, 2001, p. 189). These patterns of time and mobility as the city breathes and exhales linguistic resources happen over multiple time frames, from work schedules, to changing market days, from Ramadan to migration patterns. The city is an intense intersection of movements and practices from very local levels in kitchens and markets to wider levels of networks, from particular localities in suburbs to the wider context of migration.

Metrolingualism, space and mobility: 'chef, iedi efu iki kishu'

Our move to talk in terms of metrolingualism entails not only an intense focus on the city, but also a move away from terminology such as code-mixing and code-switching. Even if not initially conceived as such, these terms have become tied to a priori assumptions about language and belonging, about fixed codes that are then mixed together, that did not seem to fit well with the kinds of data we are dealing with. We have been far from alone in raising this concern (Bailey, 2007; Garcia, 2013, 2014; Heller, 2007), and indeed others had also been searching for new terminology beyond bilingualism, multilingualism, code-mixing and the like. 'What would language education look like', asks García (2007, p. xiii), 'if we no longer posited the existence of separate languages?' In their studies of mixed language use in Danish schools (Jørgensen, 2008a), similar questions arose for the researchers concerning the use of descriptions such as bi/multilingual. 'What if the participants do not orient to the juxtaposition of languages in terms of switching?' Møller (2008) asks. 'What if they instead orient to a linguistic norm where all available linguistic resources can be used to reach the goals of the speaker?' If this is the case, Møller argues, 'it is not adequate to categorise this conversation as bilingual or multilingual, or even as language mixing, because all these terms depend on the separatability of linguistic categories. I therefore suggest the term polylingual instead' (p. 218).

Common across these views is a focus on the use of available linguistic (and non-linguistic) resources (or *features* in Jørgensen's and Møller's terms) rather than the ability to speak one or more languages. There is also a largely shared view that we need to think in terms of *languaging* to capture the fact that 'human beings use language to change the world' (Jørgensen, 2008b, p.180). Li Wei (2011) likewise aligns his use of the term *translanguaging* with this understanding of an active process of achieving things through language. García and Li Wei (2014) explain translanguaging as

> an approach to the use of language, bilingualism and the education of
> bilinguals that considers the language practices of bilinguals not as two

autonomous language systems as has been traditionally the case, but as one linguistic repertoire with features that have been societally constructed as belonging to two separate languages.

(p. 2)

Canagarajah (2013) has argued along similar lines for a need to look at *translingual practices* where communication transcends both 'individual languages' and words, thus involving 'diverse semiotic resources and ecological affordances' (p. 6).

Clearly there are strong affinities between these polylingual and translingual approaches to language use and our own version of metrolingualism. Rather than the demolinguistic enumeration of mappable multilingualism or the language-to-language focus of translingualism and polylingualism, however, metrolingualism focuses on everyday language practices and their relations to urban space, on the ways in which the spaces and rhythms of the city operate in relation to language. In our search for a new sociolinguistics, new ways of thinking and new terminology that might better account for the data we were observing, we were struck by Maher's (2005) work on what he calls *metroethnicity*: 'a hybridised "street" ethnicity deployed by a cross-section of people with ethnic or mainstream backgrounds who are oriented towards cultural hybridity, cultural/ethnic tolerance and a multicultural lifestyle in friendships, music, the arts, eating and dress' (Maher, 2005, p. 83).

For Maher (2005; 2010), however, the idea of metroethnicities and metrolanguages remains tied to notions of style, choice and play, a focus that Coupland (2007) and Rampton (2009) read as a shallow form of ethnic identification in terms only of being *cool*. Thus while metroethnicity usefully 'rejects the logocentric metanarrative of traditional ethnicity' and 'sidesteps the bruised-n-battered ethnic bollard around which an ethnic group assembles in order to construct an internally validated description of itself' (Maher, 2010, p. 584), it might nonetheless be seen as overemphasizing the freedom to choose and to play with language and ethnicity in contexts where such choices are unlikely to be afforded (Rampton, 2009). While not rejecting the ludic possibilities of language play, metrolingualism takes seriously the everyday language practices of people in cities, which may be playful and convivial or divisive and contested (see Chapter 5).

Even when metrolingual practices are seen as playful linguistic acts, however, there may also be serious business afoot in the challenges to linguistic orthodoxies (retrolinguistic views of language). As we have argued elsewhere (Otsuji & Pennycook, 2014), just as the metrosexual may undermine gendered orthodoxies, albeit through superficial and fashion-oriented style options, so may style (Coupland, 2007) and the undoing of linguistic orthodoxies have important implications. As Coad (2008, p. 197) argues, there are good reasons to see metrosexuality as more profound than mere grooming: 'Metrosexuality tells us something about the relations between the sexes, about nonnormative sexualities, and about how gender and sexuality are used as interpretative tools to label individuals and as markers of self-identity.' Metrosexual males may look prettier and be more fragrant than their retrosexual brothers, but metrosexuality is part of more decisive changes in the realm of sexual politics; it influences how heterosexual males interact with homosexual males and it is in the process of replacing traditional categories of sexual orientation. Likewise, metrolingual practices, whether intentional stylizations or everyday linguistic practices, can unsettle linguistic orthodoxies and assumptions about language, identity and belonging.

Metrosexuality also therefore helps shed light on some of the problems with the notion of hybridity. To view it as a hybrid of the masculine and feminine would be to retain normative accounts of the constitution of such identities. Metrosexuality, however mild, sweet-smelling and fashionable, seems to question the stability of categorizations rather than blend them. Likewise, then, metrolingualism: To see metrolingualism as a hybrid mix of languages is to reinvoke those very categories of language we hope to avoid. On these grounds, therefore, we would argue that metrolingual practices are not hybrid in the sense that they combine pre-made languages into a new mix. Hybridity has been mobilized to oppose what are seen as essentialist accounts of culture and identity. Rather than people being assumed to adhere to ascribed identities (Japanese, chef, male, Muslim, Serbian, plasterer, waitress and so forth) whose characteristics are pregiven and known, hybridity has emphasized multiplicity and the diversity of mixed outcomes. This leads to the problem, however, that hybridity is always looking backwards, always invoking precisely those essential categories that it aims to supersede. Approaches to hybridity thus 'remain fixated on attacking an old form of power and propose a strategy of liberation that could be effective only on the old terrain' (Hardt & Negri, 2000, p. 146). Our understanding of metrolingualism seeks to avoid the potential traps of 'hybridity-talk' (Allatson, 2001; Hutnyk, 2000; 2005; Perera, 1994), where 'the notion of the "hybrid" can become as fixed a category as its essentialist nemesis' (Zuberi, 2001, pp. 239–240).

In order to show further how some of the connections between cities, people and language work, let us turn to a conversation held in the kitchen of a Mediterranean restaurant, カルタゴ (Karutago [Carthage]) in Tokyo. Named after the ancient city, now part of Tunis, capital of Tunisia (the Japanese approximates the Latin *Carthago*, which itself derives from the earlier Phoenecian name meaning 'new city'), the owner/chef intends this to invoke histories, tastes and mobilities. The complex trajectories of Carthage through Phoenician, Roman and Islamic influences have created a diverse linguistic, cultural and political space, where, like all port cities, people, languages, artefacts, politics, ideologies intersected, co-habitated and clashed. Having lived as an art student in a precinct of Paris with a large Tunisian population, he had opened the restaurant in search of *couscous,* the version he remembered from Paris.

The *couscous* available at the time (early '80s) in Tokyo was 'フランス人が やっているスパイスの効いていない上品なクスクスしか出てこなかった' (a sophisticated version of couscous without the kick of spice when the French make it). Together with his wife, who studied Spanish in Granada, where she gained a sense of the Mediterranean as an idea operating above the regional and state divides, he had decided to open a restaurant that encompasses the

'Mediterranean sea' connections, and thus *Carthage*. Akin to the chef's claim that '国々は密接に関わっている。国境は人間が引っ張ったもの。文化はグラジュエイションのよう' (Countries are closely intertwined. Borders are something people draw. Culture is a continuum), it is hard to draw not only cultural and culinary borders but also linguistic borders in this space.

Conveniently located five minutes' walk from Nakano station (five minutes on the main train line from Shinjuku in central Tokyo), the largest customer group of *Carthago* is Japanese, though they also boast French, Northern Africans, Middle Eastern and American customers. The Nakano area has diverse faces, old, new, conservative and alternative. Since the late 1980s, it has been associated with *Otaku* subculture, and attracts people from all over the world who are interested in Japanese animation and comic characters. France being one of the largest markets for Japanese comic books and animation, and the centre of Otaku culture in Europe (Sabre, 2013), it is not unexpected to find French people hanging around in the area. As the chef/owner of *Carthago* says, '近年、目に付くのは、アニメブームで日本語がとても上手な外国人のお客が急増したこと。アメリカ人でもフランス人でも、中東人も' (Recently, what I notice is the increase of foreign customers with very high command of Japanese due to the animation boom. That includes Americans, French and middle Easterners).

Mama (this is what Chef calls his wife),[3] who looks after the restaurant, joined him, adding 'ここにくるフランス人にもアニメオタクが多い。この間来たお客さんも、手塚治虫の漫画について、日本人と対等に議論していた' (We have many French customers who are Animation Otaku. The other day, one of our [French] customers was having a heated debate with Japanese about Osamu Tezuka's comic books). Chef and Mama agree that *couscous* for French is like curry rice for Japanese people, an everyday, casual, domesticated food (see Chapter 6). With these postcolonial and Mediterranean influences, the restaurant is frequented not only by those of Maghrebi (Algerian, Tunisian – including Nabil from *Petit Paris*) and Middle Eastern (Lebanese, Turkish, Egyptian, Iraqi and Israeli) background, but also by 'French' customers with 'home cooking' cravings. *Carthago* provides a culinary, ethnic and linguistic hotpot.

Excerpts 3.5 and 3.6 are conversations between Chef and Mama. The recorder was left on the counter between the kitchen and the little cove hidden from the dining floor, adjacent to the toilet and smoking area. Mama was hurrying between the floor and the kitchen counter to place orders, report the floor situation (to coordinate the timing of preparing and serving food), to pick up and bring back dishes. Sometimes a customer comes and sits at the smoking table and talks to Chef and Mama. With two people running the entire restaurant, there is constant multitasking, not unlike Nabil in *Petit Paris* (Chapter 1). The linguistic repertoire in *Carthago* is diverse. They use Turkish for table numbers, the number of people and the number of dishes ordered. *Kişi* is a counter for people and *tane* is a counter for the number of dishes. The name of the dishes are in Arabic, Turkish and French but they also sometimes contract the names. For example, *Patlican Mousaka* (eggplant Mousaka) is shortened to *pamusaka*. French is used for *couscous* dishes such as *couscous poulet* (chicken couscous) or *couscous poisson* (fish couscous). According to Mama, however, while the chef prefers to use 'poisson' (pronounced po-ah-son) she prefers to use the Arabic word *samak* to refer to fish.

Excerpt 3.5 (C: Chef, M: Mama)

Japanese: plain in Rōmaji (Romanized Japanese script); French with Japanese pronunication:[4] *italics*; Turkish with Japanese pronunication: **bold**; (translation in brackets)

1. C: Mama,
2. M: hai. (yes.)
3. C: etto, *poason*, (erm, fish,)
4. M: po:: po:: ahh *poason*. hai … shitsurē shimashita. (fi::fi:: ahh fish. yes … I beg your pardon.)

[noise]

5. M: *poason*. (fish.)
6. C: **iede** wa hayai to omounde, (I think table 7 is quick so,)
7. M: hai. (yes.)
8. C: *kusukusu* desu. (here's the couscous.)
9. M: hai … *chefu*, sore wa **iki** desu ka? (Yes … chef, is that for table 2?)
10. C: hai. (Yes.)

Although a knowledge of English, Japanese, Turkish and French may help in understanding the code-like language used between the chef and Mama at the kitchen counter in excerpt 3.5 – the use of Turkish **iede** or **iki** to refer to tables 7 and 2 – for example, the historical trajectories that have led to this use, the sedimented practices that have established its use over time and the highly context-dependent use of terms render it hard to follow without insider information (we are indebted to Mama for her help with this). Furthermore, it is hard to put a language label – Japanese, French, or Arabic – on such words as 'poisson', 'iede' (spelled as Yedi in Turkish) and 'kusukusu' with Japanized pronunciation.

Excerpt 3.6 (C: Chef, M: Mama)

Japanese: plain in Rōmaji (Romanized Japanese script); Turkish (with Japanese pronunciation): **bold**; English (with Japanese pronunciation): ***bold italics***; French (with Japanese pronunication): *italics* (translation in brackets)

1. M: goma wa doko ni? ichiban shita? (Where is the sesame? At the bottom?)
2. Hai … **susamu** ga mienai. (Yes … I cannot find the sesame.)
3. M: **beshi** ikimasu. (I'll go to table 5.)

[mama returns from the floor]

4. M: *chefu*, **uchi** onegaishimasu. (chef, table 3 please.)
5. C: hai. (yes.)
6. M: ato, **Harisa** chōdai … ***ōru raito***. Kore *ōkē*? (And also can you give me Harissa … all right. Is this okay?)
7. C: mm.

[Mama goes to the floor for four and a half minutes and returns]
8.   M: *chefu*, **iedi** *efu* **iki kishu**. (chef, table 7, no reservation, two people)

In lines 1 and 2, Mama is looking for sesame, first using the Japanese word 'goma' and then the Japanized Turkish word '**susamu**' (the Turkish 'susam' with the common Japanese 'u' added after the consonant) later in the same utterance. After finding the sesame container, Mama picks up the dish and brings it out to table 5, '**beshi**' (bes) and returns to the counter in line 4. She asks the chef to start preparing food for table 3, '**uchi**' (üç). Here again linguistic identifications in the transcription are a challenge. The same issue was raised in Chapter 1 when we briefly touched on the concerns of labelling linguistic resources such as *carpaccio* in *Petit Paris* with common language identifications. While the Turkish word 'bes' (5) and 'üç' (3) are pronounced as '**beshi**' and '**uchi**' by Mama with a consonant-vowel pattern, they originate from the Turkish words for numbers 5 and 3 respectively. In line 6 Mama asks for Tunisian sauce, Harissa.

She continues '*ōru raito*' and 'Kore *ōkē*?' to ask if the food is ready to go. '*ōru raito*' (alright) and '*ōkē*?' (OK) are well adapted expressions in everyday Japanese language life. After approximately four and a half minutes of silence, Mama returns from the floor to the kitchen counter in line 8 to report to the chef that two new customers without a reservation have sat down at table 7 ('*chefu*, **iedi** *efu* **iki kishu**'): 'chefu (chef), **iedi** (yedi: 7) *efu* (Japanese way of pronouncing F stands for 'Free' in English and means 'no reservation' in their *Carthago* jargon) **iki kishu (iki kişi: two people)**'. While we can possibly say that various linguistic codes were embedded in the Japanese syntactical system, it is still hard to determine which language it is spoken in. This resonates with Nabil calling on the floor at *Petit Paris* in Chapter 1, '**pain** (bread) two people and two people *onegaishimasu* (please). **Encore une assiette. De pain.** (One more plate. Bread)'.

According to Mama, these linguistic features in *Carthago* are a sedimented product of both their and the restaurant's life trajectories. Chef and Mama used to work for a Turkish restaurant before they opened *Carthago* and the use of Turkish in *Carthago* is inherited from the experience of that time. In the Japanese food industry, in order to be discrete about the freshness of ingredients, it is common to use the Japanese word '兄' (Ani), referring to an older brother and thus food that is not so fresh. In the Turkish restaurant where they worked before, the Japanese custom was adapted via the Turkish word 'abi' (elder brother) and the 'secret code' was carried over to *Carthago*. Here the term 'abi', a Turkish variant of a very specific Japanese register referring to food that is losing its freshness, is neither exactly Japanese nor Turkish, but a sedimented linguistic resource that has become part of the spatial repertoire of Carthago. Thus expressions such as 'kokoni aru **samuk** docchi ga **abi**?' (Of these fish – Arabic **samuk** – here, which one is older – Turkish **abi**?) result from their working histories and life trajectories. These sedimented practices, however, are not static, with the Arabic word 'Ajnabi' – introduced earlier by a waitress who had been studying Arabic – replacing the Turkish word 'yabancı' (foreigner) since the latter sounds uncomfortably like '野蛮人' (yabanjin; barbarian in Japanese).

This example of language use in *Carthago* raises several points for our discussion of metrolingualism. As discussed in the previous chapter, it is not necessarily the case that this could not happen in non-urban settings but rather that the intensification of diversity of the city (from the French and middle-Eastern customers drawn there through their interest in Japanese cartoons to the addition of Arabic terminology from a waitress who had been studying Arabic) makes all this more possible. The rhythms and spaces of the city – the patterns of shops opening and closing, of workers and customers having lunch and dinner – are also part of this. Important too are the trajectories of the chef and Mama via Paris (where he picked up a taste for couscous) and then a Turkish restaurant in Tokyo, from whence derives their use of Turkish. Their choice of *Carthago* – a great trading port and mixing pot of the Mediterranean – adds a further layer to this complexity. These trajectories and mobility contribute to the linguistic patterns of the restaurant but also trigger the mobility of other people to come by train to the restaurant after visiting Japanese animation shops. The restaurant also attracts others such as Nabil, whose Maghrebi background links this restaurant, couscous, French and *Carthago* together.

For Canut,

> Language mixing, linguistic overlap, and plural linguistic practices are all part of daily life and do not for the most part evoke any special type of metadiscourse, they are simply a reality: moreover, speakers are always baffled by the importance researchers give to the topic.
>
> (2009, p. 87)

Metrolingualism, thus, is not a term of exotic, exceptional, extraordinary language mixing. It is, by contrast, a description of everyday urban language use, of multilingualism from below. Thus, when Mama says '*chefu*, **iedi** *efu* **iki kishu**', what is interesting is the sedimented language resources at use in the everyday rather than an enumeration, exoticization or hybridization of languages. For Mama, their use of this type of language is the most economical way of communication between them. Nabil's '*Pizza mo* two minutes coming' (see Chapter 4) or his Maghrebi-accented 'Voilà. Bon appétit!' is not so much unexpected as it is emergent everyday language in the city.

Metrolingualism is about language in the city. It is certainly grounded in forms of style – these are often active choices in stylistic identification – but it does not render notions of linguistic choice central: Metrolingual practices, like Canagarajah's (2013) translingual practices, are as much about getting things done, about everyday language use, about multilingualism from below, as they are matters of choice. Hence, like Canut (2009) we make language practices central to our thinking since this allows us to steer a path between the overdetermination of social structure (what we do is but a reflex of the social, political or economic order), the overdetermination of linguistic structure (language is determined by rules) and the overemphasis on agency (we freely choose between our social and linguistic options). Above all, metrolingualism takes up the challenges posed by metroethnicity, polylingualism and translingualism, and focuses attention on the relations between everyday language practices and urban space.

Research: languages and the unexpected

One of the obvious challenges of recording data in markets, restaurants, shops and construction sites (putting aside for a moment issues of access, noise and ethics) is that you never quite know what you will find. When we started working on the recordings from *Carthago*, while our observations had alerted us to the diversity at play, we had not expected this mixture of linguistic resources from Turkish, Arabic, French, Japanese and English. Languages turn up in unexpected places (Pennycook, 2012a). Unlike relatively safe places such as institutions where we think we know what the languages will be, the open doors of markets, shops, kitchens and restaurants mean languages can wander in and out. Research in heritage language classes (Blackledge & Creese, 2010) may have found fascinating language uses, combinations and forms of resistance, but the researchers almost always have a reasonable chance of knowing what languages they are likely to be dealing with. Rampton's (2006) discussion of the use of *Deutsch* is an example of the unexpected but nonetheless a containable one. For us, throwing ourselves into the uncontained language environments of markets, shops, streets, workplaces, always threw up the unexpected.

In the Chinese markets (see Chapter 8), for example, we thought we would deal with Cantonese, some Mandarin and English. Immediately, however, it turned out to be more complex: It wasn't just Cantonese of course, but also Hokkien and other Chinese languages (we're still not sure about some) but nor was Cantonese just Cantonese – there were Malaysian, Vietnamese and Indonesian Chinese, whose Cantonese was different, and who, depending on who they were talking to, might also mix in other languages. Meanwhile in the market, other languages constantly drifted by – Russian, Spanish, Korean, Thai. Having done little more than identify these languages, we know if we delved further, each will be more complex: the Spanish is South American Spanish, the Russian is not just Russian but a particular variety.

Just when we thought we'd worked out the languages of the *Patris* kitchen (see Chapter 4) and got hold of a Nepalese transcriber, she got back to us and explained that in one section, they are speaking Hindi (though one of them with a Nepalese accent). Of course, not so surprising when we know that an Indian cook also works there and that the Nepalese cook, Nischal, speaks Hindi (related anyway to Nepalese). We just hadn't expected it. Not only was identifying and transcribing the impossible mixtures of language hard (as in the examples from *Carthago*, where Japanese versions of Turkish numbers were used to refer to different tables), but we also found that even when we pulled together multilingual teams of transcribers, they didn't always agree on what was going on.

A case in point occurred when we were working on the *Petit Paris* data, for which we needed not only transcribers and translators that understood French, Japanese and English, but also teams that could work together to collaboratively explain what was going on by sending transcripts back and forth with track changes and comments. Thus, we would have someone who spoke French and English working together with someone who spoke Japanese and English. Even then, it wasn't always clear, an example being the following exchange from *Petit Paris* (see Chapter 4).

Excerpt 3.7 (Na: Nabil, C: Customer)
French: **bold**; Japanese: *italics*; English: plain (translation in brackets)
1.   Na: Sorry *Sumimasen, Gomennasai.* **hein**? *Chotto:: Chotto* Small place
      dakara., kokowa na, (sorry, excuse me, sorry. It's a bi::t bit small space
      so,)
2.   C: *Daijoobu de::su.* (That's O::K)
[With customer table B]
3.   Na: **Voilà.**

The first transcription had Nabil saying 'Chotto Small place dakara: Hola'. The
Spanish 'Hola' seemed unlikely here (it does turn up in the *Patris* kitchen,
however, in the next chapter), although both transcribers knew some Spanish and
Nabil was known to drop in a few Spanish terms now and again. After further
discussion, two possibilities emerged: French 'voilà' (here it is) and Japanese
'koko wa na' (here). Speakers of each language tended to favour the other
(Japanese speakers thought it was French; French speakers thought it was
Japanese), and speakers of both languages tended to go back and forth. When we
gathered a group of Japanese and French speakers around the computer one day to
try to resolve this – bringing multiple linguistic resources and trajectories together
to work out particular sections of metrolingual data – most (but not all) Japanese
speakers didn't like the strange Japanese 'koko wa na'. Most French speakers,
however, were also not convinced by 'voilà'. In the end, the 'kokowanas' won the
argument. It will probably never really be quite resolved, but some time later, Emi
returned to *Petit Paris* to confirm some details with Nabil. She emailed Alastair
from the counter at *Petit Paris*, convinced it should be 'voilà' and not 'kokowa na'
(she had never been convinced in the initial debate). Alastair, in Paris at the time,
played the recording to a young Parisian acquaintance, who noted the particularity
of Nabil's Maghrebi accent, and the intonation on his other uses of 'voilà'. In the
latest version of the transcript, we've been hedging our bets with both.
   Returning to talk with our participants was of course another useful way we
could unravel some of the resources (Mama from *Carthago* sent us instructions on
how to decode the 'Carthagonese'). On another occasion, when Marko from
Renewal construction company offered chips to Nemia, the Fijian worker, during
lunch (see Chapter 6), it was initially transcribed as 'Gura, have some chips, bro'
by the transcriber of Serbian background. She had drawn attention to the hip
Belgrade accent of one participant, the Serbianized English accent on 'OK', the
sound of satiation when Marko said 'A joj!' when he was eating chips (see
research notes in Chapter 2), but this term stumped her. A year and a half after the
recording was made, Emi managed to reach Marko's mobile (he was on holiday
in the outback with his family), who explained that it was 'Ula', used to address
his Fijian workmates. Some further investigation indicated this was his version of
the Fijian address term 'Bula'. Meanwhile, tracking down songs in different
languages (from Serbian, to French, to Nepalese) has involved trying to reproduce
melodies to research assistants elsewhere. And yet, just as Pennycook (2012a)
argues that we need to question our assumptions of unexpectedness – why

shouldn't Turkish turn up in *Carthago*? – and not only expect the unexpected but also unexpect the expected, so we and our research assistants came to view more possibilities at any moment than we had imagined as trajectories of people, objects and places intersect and produce their own metrolingual repertoires.

Equally demanding with this kind of data is the question of transcription. Apart from the basic difficulty of transcribing data from noisy environments (if you think classrooms are hard, try markets and kitchens), the next question of how to transcribe loomed large. Beyond the obvious concerns about transcription conventions and the choices around how closely to describe (intonation, pauses, overlaps and so on), the two most challenging questions were how to deal with the different languages involved and how to represent different pronunciations. Since 'transcription is an act of interpretation and representation, it is also an act of power' (Bucholtz, 2000, p. 1463). As Bucholtz advises, we cannot overcome these problems by standardizing our conventions, but rather need to acknowledge the problem, to note the 'inherent instability of our transcripts' (ibid). This becomes more complex when dealing with multilingual data, and the use of a range of scripts. Indeed, alongside the discussions we had about whether something was 'voilà' or not was the hard question of how to write it.

Our initial transcriptions of *Petit Paris* and *Carthage* were in Roman script – partly a result of having teams of researchers working together who needed to be able to read each other's transcripts. But since other transcripts (of interviews of small business holders in Sydney) had been transcribed using Japanese scripts, why not these? We had also opted for Chinese (Cantonese) characters in other sections (originally Cantonese with jyutping transliteration, which we later dropped – see Chapter 8). On the other hand we had not opted for Arabic in the produce market: like Chinese, it can create a distance from the spoken text, and since it is written from right to left, and neither our transcriber or many of the people we worked with seemed to use it, we opted again for Roman script. Likewise Serbian, which we chose not to write in cyrillic script, in part because this might have created the kind of boundaries around Serbian that our participants seemed reluctant to maintain.

But the Japanese contexts of research presented particularly difficult decisions. Were we using Japanese scripts when the speakers were Japanese (see for example interviews with people in the Japanese alley) and Roman script when they were not (a potentially disrciminatory transcription practice)? The *Carthago* transcripts, however, spoken by people of Japanese background, also seemed to work better in Roman script. We tried versions of the transcripts in *kanji, hiragana* and *katakana* (the script for borrowed words in Japanese), but this presented a range of other problems. Should carpaccio (カルパッチョ) and even 'sorry' and possibly 'voilà' be in *katakana,* thereby rendering them 'foreign' words spoken in Japanese? Should poisson/ poason above be in *katakana* (this was a good candidate) as well as the Turkish terms in Carthago?

The problems here are caused by the use of written scripts for transcription (phonetic scripts don't help a wider readership either) and the particular ways in which Japanese scripts operate. Japanese and Roman scripts are not equivalent:

Roman script can be used for a variety of languages: although sometimes conflated with 'English', Roman script is not language-specific, whereas Japanese scripts create a divide between what is deemed properly Japanese (kanji and hiragana) and what is not (katakana). In some cases Japanese scripts worked: When shop owners in the Japanese alley, for example, spoke of 'Aussies', we had originally transcribed this in Roman script, but later changed to katakana 'オージー (Ōji) to suggest a common borrowing into Japanese in this context (and an interesting parallel with the use of terms for Japanese and Chinese: ジャパニーズ [Japanīzu], チャイニーズ [Chainīzu] rather than the Japanese terms – see Chapter 5). Using Japanese scripts helped present 'Japaneseness', but we also had to deal with the dual effects of katakana: On the one hand having a separate script for borrowing makes borrowing easier – thus we could easily incorporate various terms into Japanese – but on the other hand it keeps them as distinctly non-Japanese.

Thus by using Roman script for utterances such as '*chefu*, **iedi *efu* iki kishu'** while still having to deal with the difficult questions as to whether we wanted to identify items as French, Turkish or English, we could avoid the distinction between Japanese and non-Japanese. Our final option for 'Turkish (with Japanese pronunciation)' in **bold** is by no means ideal, but seemed the best compromise. Such transcriptions present a series of hard questions. To use non-Roman scripts presents an important 'otherness' to transcription but can pose many other difficulties. But to opt for Roman scripts runs the risk of presenting this as somehow more transparent. All transcripts, as Bucholtz (2000) makes clear, are partial interpretations with many implications. We also struggled with our use of **bold**, *italics* and so on to distinguish languages, but ultimately, though problematic because of the kinds of identification it assumes, this helped highlight not so much the divisions between languages or the kinds of 'borrowings' that occurred, but rather the ways our participants used a wide variety of linguistic resources. But all such transcripts have to be seen as temporary, unstable and problematic pointers towards a very different spoken world that they strive to recreate.

Notes

1   'Tradies' is common slang for tradesmen (and women), that is, workers such as electricians, plumbers and so on. Form workers (see Chapter 2) are the construction workers who build the wooden structures prior to concreting.
2   *ajvar* is an originally Turkish food that is best known in Serbian cooking.
3   We have generally used the naming practices of the participants in the research. Thus, we have maintained this use of 'Mama' and 'Chef' as used by the owners of this restaurant, but have elsewhere used names such as 'Ishikawa-san' to refer to the shop owner (not her real name, but reproducing the type of naming practice where 'san' is used by others as an honorific).
4   When non-Japanese words are adapted into Japanese, vowels are frequently inserted after consonants to match the Japanese phonetic system (CV). Also consonants that do not exist in Japanese such as 'Y' or 'V', will often be modified to 'I' or 'B'.

4   Kitchen talk and spatial repertoires

At one restaurant in an area of Sydney known for Latin American shops and restaurants, the owner of a restaurant explains that since a large part of the clientele, particularly at lunch time, are either Colombian like herself, or at least Spanish-speaking from other Latin American countries, Spanish is used 'a hundred per cent' in the restaurant.

Excerpt 4.1 (RC: Restaurant owner, R: Researcher)
1. RC: A hundred per cent.
2. R: A hundred per cent?
3. RC: Yeah, a hundred per cent.
4. R: So all the staff are Spanish-speakers,
5. RC: No, no. Ah, the staff is from Indonesia. So we speak English, yeah. But they understand everything all our menu's in Spanish and you tell them, like, to do this in Spanish dish, and they do it. They're very good.
6. R: Right, so they've actually picked up quite a lot of Spanish? Interesting, interesting. So in the restaurant then you would have ... you speak English to the Indonesian staff, and then they speak Indonesian to each other, and then you speak Spanish to the Spanish-speakers... Right. So there's always the three.
7. RC: Yes yes.

In the short space of this interview, this 100 per cent Spanish-speaking restaurant shifted to one using Spanish as the main language of interaction between staff and clientele, English and Spanish as the languages of mediation in the restaurant (the Indonesian staff had picked up some Spanish terms for dishes, numbers and so on) and Indonesian (though we were unable in this context to ascertain more clearly what layers of Indonesian languages might lie behind this term) as the language of interaction in the kitchen.

A similar shift occurred in a discussion with the owner of the sushi restaurant in the Japanese alley. After suggesting that most of his kitchen staff were Japanese (キッチンは、まあ、日本人がほとんどなんですけど), the owner then acknowledged greater diversity in his staff (Chinese and Koreans), suggesting that as a result English was a common language of the kitchen.

Excerpt 4.2 (S: Sushi restaurant owner, R: Interviewer)
1. S: チャイニーズの子とコリアンの子も働いてるんで、
   (Chinese and Korean are also working so,)
2. R: うん. (yup.)
3. S: で, その子たちがいる時は大体英語になっちゃうんですよね.
   (so, when they are around, it becomes mostly English.)

As the owner reflects further on language use in the kitchen, however, he observes that the Korean workers learn Japanese (or at least 'half Japanese') very quickly (日本語を半分覚えるんですよ, すぐ) and that the language of the kitchen is really therefore a 'mix' of languages (ほんとにミックスになります).

Excerpt 4.3 (S: Sushi restaurant owner, R: Interviewer)
1. S:　もう日本語が飛び交ってるから, …だから, 日本語と英語とコリアンとなんか混ざった, なんか, (Japanese is flying around, so Japanese, English and Korean are somewhat mixed,)
2. R: ええ,　おもしろい. (right interesting.)
3. S: [Laughs]すごい言葉になってます. [Laughs] (It has become an extreme language.)

Commenting on a Frederick County (Maryland, USA) board of commissioners' decision to make English the official language of a fast-growing and increasingly diverse place (rising Hispanic and Asian populations had decreased the percentage of White residents from 88 per cent in 2000, to 78 per cent by 2010, causing alarm among the White population), Dvorak (2012, np) points out why English is important:

> Imagine Trung Huynh's kitchen at the Lucky Corner restaurant in downtown Frederick if everybody spoke his native language. Cooking and serving the carmelized pork pots, pho bowls and lotus salad orders would be nothing but a mess of confusion. 'I've got Pakistani, Indian, Vietnamese, Spanish. Nobody could do their jobs if we didn't all speak English,' said Huynh, who came to America when he was 11.

Leaving aside the strange business of making English the official language of a Maryland county, of interest to us here are the observation of diversity in this kitchen, which is very much like several of the kitchens we observed, including Lynda's account of the kitchen staff at Hungry Café near the construction sites (Chapter 3): 'Colombia, Chinese, Hong Kong, and plus, Bangladesh. And India. And India as well. So all cultures and mix.'

The central question here is what language resources are necessary to get the cooking done. Let us first of all imagine that indeed everyone spoke their 'native language'. There is of course no particular problem with this, but if there was no one else to speak to, this might not occur so often and might not matter very much. As we shall see later in this chapter, these first languages nonetheless do seem to play an interesting and occasional mediating role as cooks sing and talk during their work. But by and large, everyone speaking their first and only their first language would present us with a rather Babel-like and possibly dysfunctional kitchen. This does not, on the other hand, suggest that everyone need speak English (or French, or Spanish or Japanese, or whatever language operates more broadly in each context). Most of these workers have complex work and language trajectories, having picked up bits of other languages (and usually very functional bits) as they work their way through different kitchens.

Kitchens and restaurants can operate quite well multilingually, and it is these complex metrolingual practices that are of particular interest to us in this book. The argument that we all need to share one language in order to get by needs to be seen as a very particular language ideology that assumes that linguistic diversity can only be overcome through a shared language. As Harris (2009) observes, there is no need to postulate that two speakers 'must both know the same language in order to engage in verbal communication' (p. 74). Rather, they need to know 'how to integrate their own semiological activities with those of their interlocutor' (p. 75). Such workplaces function with the use of a diverse and mixed set of resources (we do not need to 'overcome' linguistic diversity), rather than a namable language as a shared code. As we saw from both the 'one hundred percent' Spanish restaurant and the 'mostly English' sushi restaurant, there are always other languages lurking below the surface of any apparent monolingual context. It is quite possible for different languages to work around each other in kitchens and restaurants, and we should be careful not to assume that the varied backgrounds of kitchen staff need to be compensated for by monoglossic language policies.

When Mama places an order for the chef in *Carthago* in Tokyo (see Chapter 3), by saying '*chefu*, **iedi efu iki kishu** (chef, table 7, no reservation, two people)' or '*chefu*, **beshi** *tēburue* ni tsuika de **shishi kebabu** ga **biru-tane** desu (Chef, for table 5, one additional shish kebab)' drawing on various linguistic resources (applying Turkish terms such as numbers and counters within Japanese syntactic structure), she does this both for practical reasons (a private code among staff can be useful) but also because it is their sedimented practice deriving from their linguistic trajectories, including a Turkish restaurant in Tokyo they used to work for. So while the first languages of kitchen workers may, like their culinary repertoires, need to find a place amid the wider repertoires of the restaurant, the resources picked up from trajectories through other kitchens and workplaces will provide a wider set of possibilities. Communication in kitchens, as we shall see, is in any case a fairly multimodal affair, with all sorts of objects and artefacts, gestures, singing and foods playing a role. So of course some shared knowledge of a language such as English, French, Spanish, Japanese, Cantonese, Swahili, Urdu, Hindi, Italian and so on, helps and is not uncommon, but in the metrolingual multitasking environment of such kitchens, there is far more at stake than the need for one shared language.

Discussion of 'kitchen language' also needs to be seen in a wider context where the term has often been used pejoratively to describe vernacular or mixed language use. Pavlenko and Malt (2011) note that the language of people of Russian background who have grown up in the USA with limited Russian input may be derided as 'Kitchen Russian'. The reasons for the kitchen being associated with vernacular language use appear to reside primarily in the context of class and colonial divides between kitchen staff (of different class and ethnic backgrounds) and their employers. Indeed Fanagalo, a Zulu-based pidgin used across parts of southern Africa, has also been referred to as 'kitchen kaffir' – a pejorative term for the language used by Black kitchen staff in interaction with Europeans (see Mesthrie, 1989). In the context of the labour market, wages, skills and visas that bring people of many backgrounds to kitchens, we should note the history of derogatory assumptions about the language of those who work there.

The pizzeria: 'it's all part of the Greek culture'

The inner-city Sydney pizzeria *Patris*[1], owned by a second-generation Greek migrant, reverberates with a wide range of languages, with Italian only playing a very occasional role. Unlike the Tokyo restaurants *Petit Paris, Maison Bretonne* or *Carthage* where the 'reproduction' or 'relocation' of their culinary and cultural practices play a major part in their management philosophy (i.e., Paris Bistro, Rustic Breton home and exotic Mediterranean space, see Chapter 6), *Patris* pizzeria carries its Greek name – both a common Greek name and the name of one of the ships that brought Greek migrants to Australia – as a different sort of badge of mobility and relocation. Apart from the food and some artefacts such as *Chinotto* bottles used as chandeliers, association with Italy may be hard to make. Unlike *Petit Paris* where there is also a 'branding' effect (with the symbolic capital of French playing an important role) on the restaurant floor (which may be very different from the kitchen), here Italian does not have a strong presence.

As a second-generation Greek migrant, the owner, Dexter, inherited the business from his father who initially bought the pizzeria. In response to our question regarding the rationale behind the choice of an Italian rather than Greek restaurant, Dexter answers, 'Well ... Ah it's all part of the Greek culture. Greeks are running, they run ... they've diversified into many different businesses in different locations'. While this dissociation of ethnic business from one's own ethnic background is similar, for example, to the Indian-run Bagel shop in Montreal mentioned in Chapter 2, the association here is not arbitrary: 'it's all part of the Greek culture' to run a pizzeria. The Greek migrant tradition of running and owning cafés and restaurants had little to do originally with Greek food (this was a later trend). Rather it had to do with running a small business where the food was often Anglo-Australian or American-inspired (Janiszewski & Alexakis, 2003). Pizzerias, furthermore, are also part of a larger circuit of transnational foods: pizzas were developed by immigrant Italians in North America, from where 'the pizza effect' then contributed to the popularity of pizzas in Italy and elsewhere.

For Dexter: 'Yeah, look. we're very ... we do very basic simple Italian food, pizza, pizza and pasta ... and it's been successful.' A pizzeria should not in any case be confused with an Italian restaurant, but neither should we expect an Italian restaurant to be run 'in Italian'. *Patris* is better described as a *metroethnic* and *metrolingual* casual dining space.

Restaurants, like other small businesses, may be tied to particular ethnic and linguistic formations and patterns of migration. As discussed in Chapter 2, such businesses typically rely on familial, linguistic and ethnic ties, and are run around traditional links and networks, maintaining close links with other local, and similarly run shops, restaurants and small-scale enterprises (Panayiotopoulos, 2010). Changing patterns of migration, ownership and labour markets generally start to disrupt such organizations of labour and language, however, so that even with the establishment of 'ethnic precincts' (Collins & Kunz, 2009) and 'ethnic niches' (Eckstein & Nguyen, 2011), the backgrounds of staff may vary considerably. The need in some restaurants for a 'front' language (linking food and language and often the clientele), coupled with the complexities of the labour market, visas and part-time serving staff often leads to hidden linguistic complexities behind the façade of ethnicity. As we will argue, furthermore, assumptions that there might be clearly delineated functional roles for languages, as Kropp Dakubu's (2009) critique of triglossic models of urban language functions suggests, may also fail to capture the dynamics of such spaces.

Patris is located in a relatively affluent residential suburb with cafés, restaurants, boutiques, galleries and bars. It is situated close to the intersection of several streets, with a Japanese restaurant and an old Victorian style pub (built in the late 19th century) across the street and an upmarket chain grocery shop next door. While the demography of the area is Anglo dominant, inside *Patris* is ethnically, linguistically and culturally diverse, with members of staff being variously identified as Polish (Kristyan, Aleksy and Tomek), Greek (Dexter and Simon), Nepalese (Nischal), Indian (Jaidev), French (Jean), Thai (Betty) and Anglo-Australian (Mark), the majority of whom are either immigrants or on working or student visas. Such identifications, of course, have to be used cautiously, since these workers are generally only at one stage of far more complex cultural and linguistic trajectories. Betty, who is in her forties and migrated to Australia at the age of 13, for example, explained how she uses Teochow to her mother (of Chinese background), Thai to her sister and friends (they grew up in Thailand), English at various work places and with other friends and also speaks Lao (her nanny in Thailand was from Laos) and Vietnamese (which she picked up at school after moving to Australia).

Betty's linguistic repertoire at this point of her life trajectory thus very obviously complicates an easy identification as 'Thai'. The question we are interested in here, however, is the relation between these individual repertoires, i.e., the totality of linguistic resources sedimented in the individual, and the repertoires of the restaurant, i.e., the totality of linguistic resources available and potentially mobilized in the restaurant. The Nepalese cook, Nischal, who speaks Nepalese,

Bangla and 'a bit of Gujarati, Punjabi ... definitely a lot of Indian' as well as English, explains some of his more recent linguistic repertoire from interacting with other restaurant workers: 'Actually I can speak a bit of Czech and Slovak also. Because of the work mostly, words ... ' So what, we asked, was the language used mainly in the kitchen, English?

Excerpt 4.4 (N: Nischal, R: Researcher)
1. N: Polish.
2. R: Polish?
3. N: Polish. Not much English going on in here.
4. R: Really? OK, that's not what the brothers said. The brothers said you all spoke English!
5. N: Well maybe that brother [points to one of them] said because he has Colombian girlfriend who doesn't speak Polish.
6. R: Right, right, right. So you reckon it's mostly ... When you're in the kitchen it's mostly Polish?
7. N: Polish.

This exchange was revealing since it countered the view expressed earlier by the other two cooks, Polish brothers Aleksy and Krzysztof, who said they used mainly English unless talking to each other. When we questioned Nischal further on whether he used Polish, he replied, 'A little bit. But I don't need to speak, I just work. They're the ones speaking'. This points to the obvious but by no means trivial point that in environments such as this, work may be fairly minimally dependent on language. The kitchen is a place of activity and shared expertise, where there may be limited need for verbal communication.

More importantly, Nischal's suggestion both that Polish is the language of the kitchen and that it's the others who do most of the speaking points to the way that Polish is part of the spatial repertoire of this kitchen, which includes not only Polish and English, but also the intermittent use of other languages including names of artefacts, food and ingredients such as *formaggio* and *moussaka* as well as the use of non-linguistic resources and shared cooking practices. As we have already seen, this observation applies to other contexts of our research, such as markets and construction sites, where a mixed, multilingual workforce achieves its tasks through a range of practices, from linguistic mediation to mixed language use, and from knowledge of construction practices to physical demonstration. Our own data recorded in the kitchen confirmed this pattern, with a great deal of cooking and other activity interspersed with comments, swearing, singing and joking in either Polish, English or Hindi.

As Nischal continued to describe his linguistic repertoire, it turned out that his knowledge of Polish predated his work with the brothers in this particular kitchen: 'I had Polish friends before them as well.' Asked how good Nischal's Polish was, another Polish worker, Tomek, present in the restaurant told us, 'It's very good. For first study it's very good'. Recapping part of an earlier discussion where they had gently argued about the percentage of Polish he understood (and where his earlier claim to understand 40 per cent of the Polish used was negotiated down to 25 per cent), Nischal conceded, 'OK, 25. If he says 25, it's 25, because he would know better than me. It's his language, so ... Yeah, but I speak only, like, 3 to 5 per cent'. While the readiness of these workers to discuss and negotiate their language use in such percentage terms is in itself intriguing (as part of popular discourse or local language ideologies), such comments – as with the 100 per cent Spanish restaurant discussed previously – of course do little to capture the nature of actual linguistic interactions.

As we try to get a handle on the individual and spatial repertoires of this restaurant, several complexities thus become apparent. When people talk about their language use, they may mean all sorts of things by their naming of languages, their descriptions of what they speak with whom or their use of percentages. This is not to suggest that they are unreliable linguistic informants so much as to acknowledge that these accounts of individual repertoires are a product not only of diverse life trajectories but also of particular perspectives on language. Like the discussions over lunch in the construction site (Chapter 3) about Bosnian, Serbian, Macedonian and Fijian languages, the views of the speakers themselves matter. We need to be able to accommodate a view that both Nischal's opinion that Polish is the language of the kitchen and Aleksy and Krzysztof's that it is English may be right.

Not only is it the case that people in busy metrolingual workplaces (where only limited amounts of language use may be required) may find it unimportant in what language interactions occur, but it may also be true in a sense that one person's Polish is another person's English. Just as Walter (1988) suggests that the original *lingua franca* worked because of its 'particular quality that each user thought that it was the other's language' (p. 216, our translation), so perhaps it is not so much about 'which language' is being used but what things are getting done with what language use. Languaging, i.e., the behaviour that 'language users employ whatever linguistic features are at their disposal with the intention of achieving their communicative aim' (Jørgensen, 2008a, p. 169), supersedes the recognition (or particularity) of languages. In this sense, it is not so much about which language is required to get cooking, digging the ground, dish washing or vegetable bartering done, but how different language resources and tasks interact.

This also points to the fact that languages are only one part of a multimodal, multitasking environment, and may have more or less relevance at many particular points in the action. Restaurant staff are also often located temporarily in such places as part of a much wider trajectory and part of their everyday life. So while it may be useful to try to capture these individual linguistic repertoires at a particular point in time, we also have to appreciate that people are not containers of linguistic resources, but rather are able to achieve these resourceful communications (Pennycook, 2012a) interactively. Thus Nischal's use of Polish, Spanish, English and Hindi, which we introduce in the next section, emerged locally through specific interactions rather than being resources he brought to and from these sites. We need therefore to see these individual repertoires in relation to the linguistic repertoire of the workspace, which is constantly changing with the flux of the metrolingual multitasking that is common in busy work environments. It is thus always temporarily (the ebb and flow of the restaurant) and spatially (the floor plan and location of the restaurant) realized.

Kitchen repertoires

On the day from which this data is drawn, a new French cook is making pizza dough next to the entrance. Behind him is a cashier and gelato counter. Opposite the gelato counter and next to the door to the enclosed kitchen is a pizza oven, the territory of Krzysztof, who is in charge of baking, cutting and serving pizza. Jaidev and Betty are busy attending to customers while Dexter and his Greek friend, Simon, who is also helping out as floor staff, are casually chatting in the bar area in Greek. On this particular day, Nischal and Aleksy are in the kitchen, a place where both social and professional activities are mixed together. The following brief exchange happens near the kitchen door when Jaidev approaches Nischal.

> **Excerpt 4.5 (J: Jaidev, N: Nischal)**
> Hindi: *italics*; English: plain (translations in brackets)
> [The conversation refers to cigarettes]
> 1.   J: *Acha ye* last *pada hua hai*? (OK this is the last one?)
> 2.   N: It's alright … it's all yours.
> 3.   J: *Haa? Hey tere pas dusara*? (You sure? You got any more?)
> 4.   N: I'll buy.

In excerpt 4.5, Jaidev's questions in Hindi (incorporating the word 'last') receive responses from Nischal in English. Jaidev's use of informal register for '*Haa? Hey tere pas dusara?*' (You got any more?) in line 3 suggests not only a casual relation between them but also that Jaidev assumes Nischal is capable of understanding or engaging in informal colloquial conversation in Hindi. While Nischal's English responses here confirm both his knowledge of Indian languages (Hindi and Nepalese are in any case close) and the possibility that this capacity may be more receptive than productive, a later conversation about Indian festivals occurs almost entirely in Hindi. Here, then, at this intersection between the restaurant floor and the kitchen, the spatial repertoire of the kitchen expands to include Hindi as Jaidev and Nischal interact over a cigarette.

A few seconds later, Aleksy calls out to Krzysztof in Polish and then starts talking to himself in a sing-song voice while he works.

> **Excerpt 4.6 (A: Aleksy)**
> Polish: *italics* (translation in brackets)
> 1.   A: *Pozniej? Rece tak?* (Later? Hands this?)
> [Aleksy is calling out to Krzysztof, who is inaudible]
> 2.   A: *Ich kurwa mać. Trzeba raz dać.* (Fuck them. Gotta do it again.)
> [Here Aleksy is talking to himself in slang and a sing-song voice]

This kind of interaction – here Polish slang (another aspect of multilingualism from below is the use of such language), words called out that only make sense when accompanied by actions, singing and talking to oneself while working – is relatively common in such workplaces. This provides another role for Polish resources in getting things done: self-directed talk as part of this spatial repertoire.

For the next 15 minutes (apart from some faint verbal interactions further away) there is only the noisy silence of the kitchen: the sounds of kitchen utensils, chopping ingredients, food frying, taps running, footsteps. This is followed by a 16-minute period with a variety of interactions:

1   (00:00–01:52) Aleksy orders bulk items from the grocery supplier over the phone, assisted by Nischal.
2   (06:24–06:30) Nischal starts singing Beyoncé's 'Single ladies' after Betty in the background calls out 'I'm single'.
3   (10:35–11:48) Aleksy receives a phone call from his Colombian girlfriend and leaves the kitchen. Betty still speaking in the background.
4   (11:56–12:12) Aleksy returns and starts a conversation in Polish with Krzysztof about garlic for cooking.
5   (16:18–16:33) Nischal teases Aleksy about his Spanish and then discusses the lamb dish he is preparing.

Although this list suggests a fairly ordered sequence, interactions and activities overlap: from continuing cooking activities (Nischal is experimenting with a lamb dish, which he discusses with Aleksy in the final series of exchanges, which follows on from a previous interaction in Polish between Aleksy and Krzysztof about garlic) to the phone calls going out (Aleksy ordering food over the phone) and coming in (his girlfriend), as well as Betty's voice from outside triggering Nischal to sing Beyoncé's 'Single ladies', the kitchen is a place of 'articulated moments' of 'a particular constellation of social relations, meeting and weaving together at a particular locus' (Massey, 2005, p. 28).

In sequence 2, Nischal sings 'Single ladies' to tease Betty who was recently divorced from her Anglo-Australian husband. As much as the kitchen is the professional space where people get things done, it is also one intersection among many between people's embodied and social lives. People's life trajectories, stories and everyday concerns are part of this kitchen just as this kitchen is part of those lives. Betty's divorce and Aleksy's girlfriend are, in a sense, absent but present in the space. Our data recorded in the kitchen was interspersed with comments, phone calls, swearing, singing and joking, and all can be counted as a part of the metrolingual multitasking and spatial repertoires. Nischal sometimes sings alone (or to the food) in English or in Nepalese and at other times he sings for or with others. The next excerpt is an example of how singing becomes part of the spatial repertoire of the kitchen.

Excerpt 4.7 (B: Betty, N: Nischal, A: Aleksy)
[Betty enters singing Kylie Minogue's 'I just can't get you out of my head'.
Nischal responds by singing Beyoncé's 'Single ladies' again.]
1. N: [initially mimicking Betty, singing generic, non-linguistic song 'wa wa
    wa wa' and then going into Beyoncé] 'I'm a single lady! I'm a single lady.'
2. A: 'I'm a single lady! I'm a single lady.'
3. B: 'All the single lady! All the single lady.'
[laughter]
4. N: Now you damage the young boy. [referring to Aleksy].
5. B: 'If you like what you see put the rings on it! If you like what you see
    put the rings on it! Uh uh uh uh uh uh … ' [laughs]

In line 2, Nischal picks up Betty's singing mood and transforms the song to
'Single ladies' to tease Betty, which Aleksy also picks up. 'Single ladies' was the
theme music for Betty at the particular time in the restaurant (we witnessed playful
sing-along sessions of 'Single ladies' in the recordings a number of times). In line
5, Betty twisted the song and created her own chorus version: 'If you like what
you see put the rings on it!' Here language play involves not only throwing
different languages back and forth but also creating niche, insider jokes and music.
This niche practice connects people's everyday life, music and language resources,
which in turn constitute the spatial repertoire.

Singing occurred in a number of our research sites, a feature of workplaces
where silence is not expected (unlike, say, offices) and work may be at least
temporarily solitary. Pierre, from Réunion, one of the staff at *Petit Paris*, also
turned out to be a 'singing chef'. His singing in English and French became part of
the wider spatial repertoire (it is an open kitchen) and a topic of discussion with
one of the regular customers seated at the counter. Similarly, at one of the
construction sites, Marko, a construction worker of Serbian background, was
singing a modern Serbian pop song and a traditional Gypsy song on separate
occasions when waiting for other workers to join him for lunch. These seemingly
monological (non-interactive) moments as people sing to themselves while waiting
or working thus become part of the potential spatial repertoire as they get taken up
and taken over by others, either through talk about music, taking up the song or
responding with another song. These resources in people's personal repertoires
may remain just that, but are always also part of the potential spatial repertoire.
People, food, language and music interact with a diversity of potential outcomes.

The call to the supplier involving Aleksy (on the phone) and Nischal (reading
the list of items to order) – the first part of the sequence described previously – is
another example of overlapping activities and language that we would call
metrolingual multitasking (even though there is little obvious use of languages
other than English in the exchange, except perhaps *mozzarella*).

Excerpt 4.8 (A: Aleksy, N: Nischal)
1. A: Hey how are you?
2. N: Six ham,

3. A: I'm OK. Yeah of course. Can I get, ah:: Six halfs of ham,
4. N: Six halfs … 12 *mozzarella,*

It is the collaborative achievement and overlapping activities that interests us here: Nischal, for example, reads out 'six ham' while Aleksy is still engaged in the social activity of greeting and responding on the phone. Having finished the necessary social interaction, Aleksy rewords Nischal's 'six ham' to 'six halfs of ham', which Nischal then repeats before moving on to '12 *mozzarella*'. Here the repertoire is very much kitchen- and cooking-oriented, though as we see from a number of the events in the sequence, the repertoire of the kitchen is by no means confined to such talk.

It is not surprising in this pizza restaurant that certain Italian terms occur: Aleksy orders '12 *mozzarella*'. While it is unclear how to classify such terms (like Nabil's use of *carpaccio* in Chapter 1, it is hard to know – and largely unimportant – whether this should count as an Italian resource), we can nonetheless see how the fact that this is, after all, a pizza restaurant will have linguistic implications for the kitchen repertoire. In an exchange between Nischal, Krzysztof and Aleksy that occurs some 30 minutes after the phone order, Krzysztof trips up in his search for the English word for cheese, via Italian rather than Polish.

Excerpt 4.9 (N: Nischal, K: Krzysztof, A: Aleksy)
Italian: *italics*; English: plain
1. N: No … the *mozzarella*. And a whole bag of potatoes. I'll cut it.
2. K: I'll bring *formaggio … formaggi …* Whatever whatever it is!
3. A: Cheese.
4. K: Yes.
5. N: Cheese well that's what it is.

Here the Italianness of the pizza restaurant intervenes in their linguistic negotiations, as Krzysztof, perhaps picking up on Nischal's mention of *mozzarella*, searches for their shared resource for talking about cheese. It is not of course Polish that is intervening here but the Italian *formaggio*, which is a well-established 'ingredient' of the repertoire of the space.

Aleksy's Columbian girlfriend (whose lack of Polish, according to Nischal, may be the cause of Aleksy's view that the cooks spoke English rather than Polish together), meanwhile, has broadened the spatial repertoire of the kitchen, with the occasional use of Spanish. Aleksy leaves the kitchen to take the phonecall but Nischal, who has overheard the initial interaction, draws attention to it later when Aleksy returns.

Excerpt 4.10 (N: Nischal, A: Aleksy)
Spanish: *italics*; English: plain (translation in brackets)
1. N: *Hola.* (Hello.)
2. A: *Hola.* (Hello.)

3.   N: *Hola, como estas*? (Hello, how are you?) So you can speak, like, really good Spanish now?
4.   A: Yeah of course.
5.   N: How good? Can you scream in Spanish in the night?
6.   A: I ... of course I can.

This sort of light (male) banter across languages does not imply particular competence in Spanish, but for the moment (cf. Li Wei, 2011) certain available and increasingly sedimented (until Aleksy and his girlfriend split up some months later) Spanish resources have become part of the spatial repertoire of the kitchen.

These different linguistic resources are only one part of the multimodal, multitasking environment and the larger set of resources now available as part of the repertoire of this kitchen. As people come and go, asking for cigarettes, calling their boyfriend, singing, ordering bulk supplies, different linguistic resources become available in this place. Just as it is difficult to decide when the use of a particular linguistic item becomes part of an individual repertoire, so it is also hard to name the moment where an available resource starts to become sedimented as part of the spatial repertoire of a particular place. What is clear, however, is that when we look at a kitchen such as this – a spatiotemporal hub criss-crossed by trajectories of people (cooks, floor staff, phone calls), artefacts (knives, sieves, plates) and food (ingredients, cooking, finished items) – we can observe the ways in which activities, linguistic resources and space interact to produce new configurations of language use that are not best understood by looking at language-to-language relations (trans, poly, pluri, multi), functional domains (this language for this purpose) or individual repertoires (personal accounts of linguistic resources) but need to be viewed in relation to multiple tasks and available resources.

Spatial repertoires: 'Pizza mo two minutes coming'

As much as *formaggio* was part of the spatial repertoire in the Sydney pizzeria, pizza, black olives, anchovies as well as the *denpyō* (food order sheet) placed by the open kitchen are equally constituents of the spatial repertoire in *Petit Paris* in Tokyo. Excerpt 4.11 is a typical example of the spatial repertoires of *Petit Paris* on a busy evening.

Excerpt 4.11 (Na: Nabil, C: Customer)
French: **bold**; Japanese: *italics*; Italian: ***bold italics***
English: plain (translation in brackets)
(With customer table A)
1.   Na: Sorry *Sumimasen, Gomennasai.* **hein**? *Chotto:: Chotto* Small place *dakara, kokowa na.*
     (sorry, excuse me, sorry. It's a bi::t bit small space so, this place is.)
2.   C: *Daijōbu de::su.* (That's O::K.)

(With customer table B)

3. Na: **Voilà.** *Yasai to* anchovy *kuro* olive sauce. (Here it is. Vegetable and anchovy black olive sauce.)
4. C: *Ha ::i.* (Ye ::s.)
5. Na: **Bon appétit** ! (bon appetit/ enjoy your meal!)

(To chef)

6. Na: **Chef ... on peut faire marcher le** *carpaccio***, hein, j'ai mis une ligne, mais on peut l'envoyer. De la six.**
    (Chef ... we can get the carpaccio going, I put a line, but we can send it out. From six.)

(To customer table C)

7. Na: *Hai. Daijōbu daijōbu daijōbu.* (Yes OK OK OK.)

(To Stéphane)

8. Na: *Hai* **Deux assiettes s'il vous plaît** ! (Yes Two plates please !)

(Customer table C)

9. Na: *Dōzo.* ***Pizza*** *mo* two minutes coming. (Here you are. The pizza will also be here in two minutes.)

In line 1, Nabil is squeezing past table A, carrying food to table B, apologizing in English and Japanese (sorry, *sumimasen*) for the small space (*Chotto* small place *dakara*). There, between French flourishes (**voilà, bon appétit**), he announces the dish of vegetables with anchovy and black olive sauce (*Yasai to* anchovy *kuro* olive sauce). He then turns around and gives instructions in French to the chef about the timing of cooking and serving food (on the *denpyō* [food order sheet] on the wall where they manage orders, drawing a line between the names of the dishes to control the timing of serving food; hence his reference to the line) (see Image 4.1). He then confirms to another customer in Japanese that everything is under control: '*Hai. Daijōbu daijōbu daijōbu*' (yes, OK, OK, OK). In line 8, Nabil confirms a request (hai) before asking Stéphane (floor staff) for two more plates (**Deux assiettes s'il vous plaît**). As he serves a dish to the customers in line 9 (Dōzo), he confirms that their pizza is also (*mo*) on its way (***Pizza*** *mo* two minutes coming).

Here, then, we see a prime example of what we have been terming metrolingual multitasking, where Nabil's everyday multilingualism is on the one hand a mixture of written and spoken linguistic resources drawn mainly from English, French, Japanese and occasional Arabic (Nabil talks with his brother on the phone), and on the other hand an interaction between these resources and the everyday practices (managing and serving in this restaurant), the objects that are also part of the action (lines drawn on the *denpyō*, the plates, the vegetable dish, the pizza) and the other resources that then make up the transient spatial repertoires of the different parts of this restaurant. It is not only the linguistically mixed '*Yasai to* anchovy *kuro* olive *sauce*' that adds to the *Petit Paris* potage, but also the dish itself of vegetables with an anchovy and black olive sauce that becomes part of this mix.

Image 4.1 The *denpyō* (food orders) at *Petit Paris*.

The complexity of the repertoires of *Petit Paris* suggests that easy ascription of language labels or code-switching metaphors cannot account well for what is going on here. It is difficult to find an obvious label for many terms – 'small place', 'olive', 'anchovy', 'sauce', 'pizza', 'bon appétit' – for a number of reasons. The food items have a certain linguistic mobility in themselves: It is unclear whether a term such as pizza is now better classified as existing across languages. It is also worth noting how the pizzas in these different places have different cultural and culinary meanings: *The Chicken Teriyaki, Marinara, Moroccan Lamb* and *El Diablo* pizzas in the Greek-owned pizzeria in Sydney sit very differently within the restaurant and the culinary landscape of the suburb and city from the *Pizza Margharita, La Flammenküche Alsacienne* and *La Pissaladière Niçoise* on the menu in the Algerian-French-owned bistro in Tokyo.

Nabil's grammar and pronunciation complicate the picture in terms of linguistic labels: The phrases '*Chotto:: Chotto* small place *dakara*' and '*Pizza mo* two minutes coming', with their English inserts into what seems to be Japanese syntax, might appear to be classifiable as code-mixing between Japanese and English, and yet the strangeness of 'small place' and 'two minutes' (with their Japanese echoes) make this less clear. The pronunciation of 'anchovy *kuro* olive sauce' also raises questions about what language this is in. 'Olive', for example, with its 'l' and 'v' somewhere between French/English pronunciation and the Japanese 'ri' and 'bu' (olive/ orību), or the 'su' ending at the end of sauce, leaves the status of such words ambiguous, and it is worth noting again that it is not so much a case of speaking in one language or the other that matters here so much as using linguistic resources to effectively accomplish tasks. After several years in Japan, word endings (such as the 'su' on the end of sauce) that may be more easily understood by his customers have become part of Nabil's repertoire.

This presents us with numerous transcription dilemmas (see Chapter 3), and we indeed have alternative transcripts of this section using 黒オリーブソース (*kuro orību sōsu*). The use of terms such as 'bon appétit' and 'voilà', furthermore, do not necessarily imply linguistic competence in French on the listeners' behalf, but rather draw on the linguistic capital and aesthetic/symbolic value (Leeman & Moden, 2009) of French and its place in the repertoires of the restaurant. We do not wish to draw a distinction here between examples of 'multilingual communication' involving these small restaurant-oriented terms (such as similar *ciao, grazie, prego* in an Italian restaurant) and 'genuine multilingual practice' (Redder, 2013, p. 278) involving more complex interactions. We are instead interested in the ways these many linguistic resources are mobilized in such spaces, and how food, drink and talk are so intertwined.

While some utterances are more easily aligned with particular languages, this identificatory orientation only takes us so far. Rather, we would suggest, Nabil's resources are part of the linguistic soup of *Petit Paris* and, like the ingredients of a good soup, may defy identification. Of at least equal interest from our point of view are the activities, use of space and artefacts and the wider repertoire that is part of *Petit Paris,* which makes it possible for all this to make sense. Thus, when Nabil says '*Dōzo. Pizza mo* two minutes coming' in his wine bazaar *Petit Paris,* the phrase encompasses not only bits of Japanese, English and possibly Italian, but more importantly space, time, objects and activities. It entails trajectories of both people and place: Nabil's passage from Tipaza in Algeria, various restaurants in Paris and Tokyo to his own *Petit Paris* 'wine bazaar', as well as the passage through time of *Petit Paris,* in Kagurazaka (神楽坂), and the traces of people and objects that have passed through this space.

To the picture of metrolingual multitasking – the interwoven activities and semiotic resources of busy workplaces – that we have been exploring over the first few chapters, therefore, we want to develop in greater depth what we have called *spatial repertoires*. Metrolingualism focuses on the one hand on everyday multilingualism – everyday practices and lived experience of diversity in specific locations – and on the other hand, on the interrelationships between language and urban space. Language, as Mac Giolla Chríost (2007) has noted, is fundamental to the meanings, uses and significance of space and place in the urban context. Likewise, the relation between language and space is central to the idea of metrolingualism. While it shares some similar ground to translanguaging and polylanguaging approaches in its attempt to get outside the framing of languages in terms of enumeration (multilingualism), metrolingualism focuses centrally on the relation between urban space (metro) and language practices. Rather than making the plurality of linguistic features (poly) or the movement between languages (trans) central to the analysis, metrolingualism links these linguistic insights to the relation with space.

The need to relate recent thinking about language use to concepts of space has been taken up in Li Wei's version of 'translanguaging space', which he understands as 'a space for the act of translanguaging as well as a space created through translanguaging' (2011, p. 1223). For Li Wei, translanguaging 'creates a social space for the multilingual language user', as different aspects of their personal history are brought together in their multilingual performances. Like related discussions of linguistic repertoires as the 'social and cultural itineraries followed by people' (Blommaert & Backus, 2013, p. 28), however, the focus here remains centrally on the relation between individuals and resources, on the 'resources individuals use to create their own space' (Li Wei, 2011, p. 1223) or how 'different resources enter into our subject's repertoire' (Blommaert & Backus, 2013, p. 26).

As Benor (2010, p. 161) notes, 'recent work on sociolinguistic style sees individuals as making use of a repertoire of sociolinguistic resources'. A focus on style, Rampton (2011) argues, has led to a focus on individual agency over social structure or other means of understanding the sociality of speech. In using concepts such as 'translanguaging' and 'repertoires', therefore, while necessarily eschewing outmoded ideas such as speech communities, there is a danger that the individual becomes the sole locus of the repertoire. Since community under conditions of superdiversity no longer operates as a useful category, Blommaert and Backus (2013) argue, the idea of repertoire is more usefully oriented towards the linguistic trajectory of the subject. Even though these accounts of the development of such linguistic repertoires may involve bodily (*leiblich*), emotional and historico-political dimensions of life trajectories (Busch, 2013), the social nature of the idea of repertoire – a concern for any social theory of language – that was originally part of Gumperz's (1964, p. 137) understanding of repertoire as 'the totality of linguistic forms regularly employed in the course of socially significant interaction' may be lost.

This tension between individuals and communities has long been a concern for sociolinguistics generally and ideas such as repertoires more specifically. Platt and Platt (1975, p. 35) distinguished between speech repertoire (community) and verbal repertoire (individual), arguing that a 'speech repertoire is the range of linguistic varieties which the speaker has at his disposal and which he may appropriately use as a member of his speech community' (1975, p. 35). While the ideas of speech community, membership and appropriacy have all been subject to critical scrutiny, the notion of having linguistic resources externally 'at one's disposal' rather than internally as part of one's competence is potentially useful. By understanding repertoire as available resources, and including within our purview songs, snippets of diverse languages and the wider semiotic surrounds, we can start to envisage an interaction between the resources brought to the table by individual trajectories (with all the social, historical, political, economic, and cultural effects this may entail) and the resources at play in a particular place.

In this sense, a repertoire is not exclusively owned and controlled by a person – Nabil, for example – or the worker-customer community of *Petit Paris*, but rather is a product of the multitasking interactions, the resources such as pizza, *denpyō*, English words, French words, words hard to pin down and the dynamic movement of people, objects and activities. Thus, rather than equating repertoires with the 'social and cultural itineraries followed by people' (Blommaert & Backus, 2013, p. 28), we are interested in the relationships between the individual and spatial resources that converge and diverge in producing place. Language is emergent not only from social interaction (Harissi, Otsuji & Pennycook, 2012) but also spatial interaction. From our point of view, then, we need to understand the relations between linguistic trajectories, current activities and spatial organization in order to account more fully for the language practices described above.

Seeking a way forward here, and drawing on the insights of Blommaert and Backus (2013), Benor (2010) and Busch (2012b; 2013) on repertoires, as well as Li Wei's (2011) notion of 'translanguaging space', we have expanded the notion of repertoire in relation to the more extensive dynamics between language and urban space that metrolingualism requires; hence the notion of *spatial repertoires,* which links the repertoires formed through individual life trajectories to the particular places in which these linguistic resources are deployed. Following Thrift's (2007) *non-representational theory*, which he glosses as '*the geography of what happens*' (p. 2), we are interested here in what we might call a *geography of linguistic happenings*, the social space and place of language practices.

The notion of spatial repertoires differs from common sociolinguistic terms dealing broadly with context or situation of language use (Hymes, 1974) such as domain (Fishman, 1972) along several dimensions. Domains have generally been considered in terms of language functions and the attendant language linked to each function (one language serving certain purposes in one domain and a different language serving different purposes in another) (Mesthrie, 2014). As Haberland (2005) explains, however, it is 'difficult to apply the domain concept to those situations where extensive code-switching is part of the linguistic repertoire of the interlocutors' (p. 234). Clearly the context with which we are dealing here is not one in which one language serves a particular function but, rather, a range of resources are deployed. Diglossic or triglossic models of language use 'in which each language had its functional niche' (Kropp Dakubu, 2009, p. 22) cannot account for the dynamics of multilingual urban interaction (García, 2014).

Spatial and individual repertoires are of course deeply bound up with each other. This is not, therefore, a reformulation of the dichotomous multi/plurilingual divide (where plurilingualism is personal and multilingualism is social), or of verbal and speech repertoires. Such separations we might see, adapting Latour (1999), in terms of the *modernist linguistic settlement* that allowed for a separation between language 'out there' and language 'in here'. Spatial repertoires draw on individual as well as other available resources, while individual repertoires contribute to and draw from spatial repertoires. The repertoires of these kitchens are organizations of the totality of linguistic resources (including menus, the name of the restaurant, labels on wine bottles and so on) brought to this place through the linguistic trajectories of the people and space. It is also, as we saw in the discussion of the *Patris* kitchen, not necessarily limited to those present.

Similar in some ways, therefore, to Gumperz's 'totality of linguistic forms regularly employed in the course of socially significant interaction', this position nonetheless does not assume a linguistic community; rather it employs spatial theory to understand the linguistics of place. Like Pratt (1987), our focus is on a linguistics of contact rather than a linguistics of community. As Pratt argues, it is not only recent diversities that problematize the idea of community, since it has always been a problematically normative and utopian ideal. Linguistic analysis, she suggests, might be better served not by studying a community assumed to share a language but rather perhaps by studying 'a room full of people each of whom spoke two languages and understood a third, and held only one language in common with any of the others' (1987, p. 50). Or, she might have said, linguistic analysis might be better served by studying urban kitchens.

Location and locution

Scepticism about the utility of the idea of community, therefore, may lead to a focus on the spatial dynamics of these contact zones rather than on individual repertoires. Cultural geographers such as Massey have similarly problematized the identification of place in terms of community on the basis that a sense of bounded and coherent social groups has become ever more obsolete (Massey, 1991). It may be more useful therefore to explore language in relation to spatial theory, by which we are referring to that broad body of work that has emerged from critical and cultural geography to address the idea of space as a category alongside the social and historical (Massey, 1994; Soja, 1996). Amid the buzz of the Produce Market at 5 a.m. (see Chapter 1), people walk in and out of the complex carrying out tasks. Even though Joseph has been operating in the same enclosed space for over 30 years, and Uncle Tony has been sitting in more or less the same place since the 1970s, the linguistic landscape is far from static. It changes over the years according to geopolitical factors, Australian immigration patterns, technological interventions (forklifts, computers, mobile phones), the day of the week (different usage of the space) or the time of the day or the products and their condition (yellow zucchini). All bring about different linguistic and cultural landscapes.

Thus while it is precisely the capacity that sociolinguistics has given us 'to examine the unfolding of social interaction, and the edges of indeterminacy, that makes it useful' (Heller & Duchêne, 2011, p. 14) for the study of contemporary language use, it is its general inattentiveness to space, movement and action that also constrains its use. One way forward here can be found in Scollon and Scollon's (2003, p. 12) *geosemiotics*, which presents 'an integrative view of these multiple semiotic systems which together form the meanings which we call place'. Place is defined as 'the human or lived experience or sense of presence in a space' (p. 214). This usefully takes us away from the modernist social scientific assumption that place is 'a location on a surface where things "just happen" rather than the more holistic view of places as the geographical context for the mediation of physical, social and economic processes' (Agnew, 2011, p. 317). This is akin to Sassen's (2005) sense of 'recovering place', which she explains as 'recovering the multiplicity of presences in this landscape' (p. 40).

While Scollon and Scollon reinvigorate place as a social category, they do so at the expense of space as 'the objective, physical dimensions and characteristics of a portion of the earth or built environment' (p. 216). To avoid the two pitfalls here of a phenomenological approach to place (our sense of place) in relation to an objectively given space – space is given, place is interpreted – we argue on the one hand for a dynamic and social understanding of place as 'articulated moments in networks of social relations and understandings' (Massey, 1991, p. 28) that are constructed 'out of a particular constellation of social relations, meeting and weaving together at a particular locus' (p. 28); and on the other hand for an understanding of spaces as 'social productions', as 'constituted by social life in such a way that "mental space" and "material space" are brought together' (Livingstone, 2007, p. 72). Practices do not just happen in spatial and temporal contexts but are rather bound up with space and time: 'interwoven activity timespaces are essential to social phenomena' (Schatzki, 2010, p. 165).

Following Lefebvre (1991) and others, Livingstone's interest in 'spaces of speech' (2007, p. 75) is itself located within a framework that sees both space and place as social categories. Places are not therefore mere instantiations of space but rather relational sites of action and interaction, sites of 'location and locution' (Livingstone, 2007, p. 75). Social spaces, Livingstone goes on, 'are shaped by speech – by what can and cannot be said in particular venues, by how things are said, and by the way they are heard' (p. 75). Place, by contrast, has to do with the specificities of space. Places are where local practices constitute and are constituted by the social and spatial (Pennycook, 2010). For cultural geographers, we aim to flesh out an understanding of the locutions that happen in particular locations; for sociolinguists, we aim to develop an understanding of these locations in relation to the locutions that occur there.

Spatial repertoires, therefore, refer to the 'throwntogetherness' (Massey, 2005, p. 140) of linguistic and other semiotic resources in particular places. Social interaction is not merely a collision of individual trajectories but the spatial organization of semiotic resources and the semiotic organization of space. This conceptualization of *spatial repertoires*, then, adds a further significant dimension to the idea of *metrolingualism* that we have been developing here. Using some of the insights of actor-network theory (Latour, 2005) – the role of 'objects' in human activity and the related sense of distributed and provisional personhood (while also pointing to some of its limitations, such as a tendency to focus on networks rather than the immediacy of an event, and to obscure the specifically human in networks of relations) – we add a linguistic dimension to Thrift's (2007) view of space as *associational*. This draws attention to the interrelated roles of space, language practices and objects in motion. Drawing on a *linguistics of communicative activity*, which insists that everyday life 'is mediated by, and constrained by, symbolic and material artefacts that carry with them historically sedimented patterns of usage' (Thorne & Lantolf, 2007, p. 188), we are attempting to grasp the ways in which individual and spatial repertoires, as well as artefacts and objects, form part of the communicative activity of particular places. We are seeking to incorporate into this view of language an appreciation of the roles of both the materiality of language and the significance of material objects.

Researching language, mobility and practices in place

The long and distinguished history of urban sociolinguistics, going back at least as far as Labov's (1972) classic work on 'black English vernacular', has taken the city as the key location of particular language forms, but has at the same time struggled to develop an ethnographic understanding of city spaces and mobility (see Chapter 2). Thrift (2007) sees space as *associational*, drawing attention to the interrelated roles of space, social practices and objects in motion. An understanding of mobility therefore needs to be central to any such approach to space. Heller and Duchêne (2011, p. 14) note that in recent years 'sociolinguistics has recognized that its traditional attention to fixed places and moments' can no longer provide the tools to address questions of language and mobility. Blommaert similarly calls for an understanding of 'the dislocation of language and language events from the fixed position in time and space attributed to them by a more traditional linguistics and sociolinguistics' (Blommaert, 2010, p. 21). This applies both to the linguistic resources that move in and out of places and to the movement of resources within such places.

As place is 'a particular constellation of social relations, meeting and weaving together at a particular locus' (Massey, 1991, p. 28), our research has been concerned with understanding the ways in which individual repertoires and spatial repertoires converge and diverge in everyday metrolingual practices. A primary focus of much research in sociolinguistics and pragmatics, Li Wei (2011, p. 1224) argues, has been 'describing structured patterns of variation and change or general maxims guiding linguistic actions'. Such apparent patterns, however, are 'long-term outcomes of original, momentary actions' that 'become patterns by being recognised, adopted and repeated by the other individuals'. Following Li Wei's (2011, p. 1224) 'Moment Analysis', which shifts the focus 'away from frequency and regularity oriented, pattern-seeking approaches to a focus on spontaneous, impromptu, and momentary actions and performances of the individual', our focus is not so much on establishing patterns of linguistic use (nor, as suggested previously, so much on the individual) but on understanding *practices in place*, those sedimented or momentary language practices in particular places at particular times. This by no means suggests that such practices are random or indiscriminate, but rather that to focus on systematicity may equally obscure the dynamics of interaction.

As well as detailed ethnographic accounts of people, space, objects and motions, we therefore need particular ways of recording language in space, as people move in and out of particular places. In order to capture these dynamics, we drew in part on Lamarre and Lamarre's (2009; our translation) 'non-static approach' (*approche non-statique*) following participant trajectories across different sites, though more particularly for our work, within different sites. We developed two principal spatial research orientations: On the one hand, we can follow an individual (often by attaching recording devices) through such spaces. This is the option we took with Nabil as he moved through *Petit Paris*. In the *Patris* kitchen, on the other hand, we focused on a fixed place (leaving an audio recorder on a kitchen shelf) in order to capture (amid the noise of cooking, washing, singing) the comings and goings of people, food and languages in and out of that particular location. Here we try to capture this sense of flow, movement and multitasking that are part of this spatial repertoire. Placing the recorder at the door of the kitchen enabled us to capture the traffic of people, food and language in and out of the kitchen as well as the ways in which multimodal semiotic repertoires form the space around the kitchen.

By highlighting two different ways in which we can look at the 'throwntogetherness' of linguistic resources – on the one hand following Nabil across space and through his different interactions, on the other observing how resources come and go in one place – we sought to relate the physical activities of work (cooking, ordering food, serving customers), the social and historical trajectories of participants (girlfriends, songs, telephone calls, and linguistic resources picked up along the way), the organization of space (the proximity of tables, the swinging kitchen door) and the language resources at play in particular places (Spanish, French, Japanese, Polish, Hindi, Nepalese, English and so on) that are part of these restaurant repertoires. Following an individual through space or following a space as people come and go does not, it should be noted, imply a focus on individual repertoires (in the first case) and spatial repertoires (in the second). Both are concerned in different ways with the relations between space and resources.

This distinction between recording from a static point and recording through space, however, becomes blurred in other contexts. Our recordings at the Produce Market, for example, sat somewhere in between these two approaches: While Talib and Muhibb were, like Nabil, wired up in order to capture their movement through this fruit and vegetable space, the recordings nevertheless captured much of what occurred at their (mobile) desk as customers came and went, and orders were called out to workers, thus also partly resembling the fixed location recordings in the *Patris* kitchen recordings. Likewise, although the *Maison Bretonne* recordings were made at the counter between the kitchen and the restaurant, the close proximity between the (open) kitchen and customers' tables, as well as the size of the restaurant, meant that a wider range of interactions were recorded than just those of people entering that particular space. The conversation between the chef and floor staff, between staff and customers as well as between customers were interwoven. The distinction between a static and non-static approach to recording, therefore, is also dependent on the spatial arrangements, work practices and interactions in any particular workplace.

While fixed audio-recording approaches may have certain drawbacks in their potential to capture the dynamics of place, action and movement, they also enabled us to capture the to-and-fro traffic of people and linguistic resources at a particular location, thus gathering together different facets of linguistic mobility and dissociating repertoires from individuals. On the other hand, tracking individuals through space also presented both limits and possibilities. While Nabil's trajectory through the bistro showed how significant his metrolingual multitasking was in producing this metrolinguistic place, this also potentially undermined the importance of other parallel and contributing activities. As our recordings in the *Patris* kitchen showed, and as Arnold Wesker's 1960 play *The Kitchen* makes clear in other ways, any such site is made up of constant overlapping language and activities that intersect and diverge. It is not so much what was going on 'around' Nabil that mattered as the ways in which activities were orchestrated. This is why ethnographic field notes were also of great significance, particularly the participatory practices discussed further in Chapter 6: Getting one's eyebrows done at the beauty salon not only helped situate the interviewee in her everydayness, but also gave the researchers a better sense of space and practices. Similarly, by being a customer, sitting at the counter of *Petit Paris* alone or with friends at a table being served by Nabil and others, or at different tables at *Patris* (sometimes near the kitchen door, sometimes elsewhere) enabled us to get a better sense of interlocking language and activities in the space.

Note

1   *Patris*, like the names of the workers there, is a pseudonym. We nonetheless tried to capture the original flavour of the Greek name of the restaurant.

5 Convivial and contested cities

'It's too many languages': suburban diversities

Common in our conversations with workers in different parts of the city were comments about their co-workers, the neighbourhood, the city and its shared spaces of multicultural and multilingual interaction. Many such remarks seemed to cut both ways, to celebrate diversity yet at the same time to revel in apparently lighthearted discrimination. Muhibb, one of the brothers trading fruit and vegetables at the Produce Market (Chapter 1) explains the diverse workforce around him.

> We've got them all. Deaf, dumb, blind, stupid … Different races … You'll find everything here. It's probably the most perfect place to be in the world. If you can work in this place you can work anywhere in the world. You won't find anywhere better than here.

Here we see that positive view: 'It's probably the most perfect place to be in the world'; but also a more playfully pejorative view of local diversity: 'Deaf, dumb, blind, stupid … Different races.' A central focus of this chapter will be on this ambivalence, of this celebratory and convivial multiculturalism that clearly suggests that the diversity of people, languages, cultures and backgrounds renders such workplaces better than anywhere else to work, but at the same time does so on terms that are at the very least jokingly disparaging of others.

A restrictive orientation towards the instrumentality of meaning and language use, towards viewing human interaction as organized around important things such as 'propositional meanings, indexical stances, identity, or subject positions' Blommaert (2013b, p. 7) suggests, has led us to overlook the fact that much of what we do is for happiness, for getting along, for making others feel OK: 'The general ambiance of communication—and its important effects on how we organize it functionally—has often been overlooked or treated as just the "key", the "general background" against which certain interactions take place' (p. 8). This then is the site of conviviality, of people enjoying and engaging in casual diversities. Although we have at times stressed the functionality of metrolinguistic practices as participants go about their daily business, getting things done with whatever resources are available, there is also a strong current in our data of conviviality, of people celebrating the diverse environments in which they work.

The double-edged nature of such interactions is paradoxically illustrated in a comment by Wafiq, who runs a store in Marrickville: 'I find it very interesting in Marrickville. It's too many languages.' Marrickville is a culturally and linguistically diverse inner Sydney suburb whose population has shifted from Italian and Portuguese to Greek, Vietnamese, Arabic Chinese and Pacific Islander (Mohr & Hosen, 2014). As discussed in Chapter 2, complex patterns of migration, labour networks and available housing lead to particular configurations of ethnic concentration in certain parts of the city. These change over time so that any such areas are constantly in a process of negotiation between old and new. In 2011, after English, the main home languages listed in Marrickville were Greek, Vietnamese, Arabic, Portuguese and Cantonese. Such statistically-based overviews of the suburb, however, as we have argued several times already, fail to capture the dynamic landscape of the place, the convergence and divergence and everyday mobility of people and objects.

The main activities of Marrickville are clustered along two main streets, with shops (such as Song's discount shop; see Chapter 1), bakeries (including *Paris Bakery*; see Chapter 6), a Turkish coffee shop and Vietnamese beauty salon (Chapter 2), banks (Cyprus Bank), dentists, lawyers and restaurants jostling alongside each other with their different languages on display (see Chapter 7). Sabiha, who works at the Turkish coffee shop, and whose grandparents first moved to Marrickville from Turkey, explains:

> Customers that come in here, we have a lot of Turkish people 'cause it's a Turkish restaurant. But there's a lot of Greek people, 'cause we have similar cultures. And Arabic as well. And a lot of, like, Vietnamese and yeah, Chinese around as well.
>
> (Interview, November 20, 2012)

Near the intersection of the two main streets Wafiq runs a store that roasts and sells coffee beans, nuts, spices and a large range of groceries, mostly from the Middle East and eastern and southern Europe. He also sells a lot of Greek, Danish, Bulgarian and Turkish cheeses and yoghurts. The signage outside has a small amount of Arabic on it but as soon as you walk into the shop, a large number of other languages become visible too: Greek on the tins of olives and olive oil; Turkish on the fresh bread and semolina; Chinese and Vietnamese on the rice bags and spice boxes. There are also sauerkraut and gherkins, Indian spices and Ethiopian coffee. The mixture of smells of coffee and spices that fill the shop come from many parts of the world, there because of the diversity of people he serves and the changing patterns of settlement in the suburb.

Of Lebanese background, like his staff, he has been running the shop for four years, and enjoys the diversity of the suburb.

Excerpt 5.1 (W: Wafiq, R: Researcher)
1. W: I find it very interesting in Marrickville. It's too many languages.
2. R: Too many?
3. W: Too many languages. You got the Greek, Macedonian, Croatian, Vietnamese, Chinese, Lebanese, Turkish … So that's seven now. Yeah, it's too many!
4. R: Why is it too many? To keep up with everyone?
5. W: No, no, actually, you know, you go to different shops and everyone speak different language. And I find it very interesting, it's multicultural. And you've got different food, different variety, different stuff. And it's really nice. The Australian people when they come here to the shop and they find all this products coming from overseas they get amazed. And it's really nice. I like it.

Here, after the initial confusion over the phrase 'too many', it became clear he was using it to mean 'very' (the distinction in English does not map onto an equivalent in a number of other languages, and Arabic speakers, like a number of others, may use one for the other). Here, then, beneath what appeared to be an ambivalence or even a negative view of this multicultural and multilingual suburb (too many languages), we find a celebration of its diversity (I find it very interesting, it's multicultural); and yet, this ambivalence never seems so far away. We shall return later in this chapter to the implications of the term 'Australian people' or the more common term 'Aussies' to refer to the Anglo-Australian community.

Despite his positive views on the multicultural suburb, Wafiq explains that it's not always easy. One problem for him is that the older Greek population, which used to form a much larger percentage of the suburb, often assumes he speaks Greek.

Excerpt 5.2 (W: Wafiq, R: Researcher)
1. W: Because sometimes you know, the Greek comes here and he doesn't understand, ah:: what they want, about the stuff you know, the products. And I don't speak Greek! I speak two languages and I don't understand what they're talking about!
2. R: And they're speaking to you in Greek?
3. W: In Greek! And I should you know, as a shop owner, understand them. And some people get upset you know, but it's not my problem you know, I don't know. They're old people … and they've been here for 40 years.

Here Wafiq's pragmatic orientation to the needs of business – as a shop owner, he should be able to understand the languages of his customers – as well as his acknowledgement that old people who've lived in the suburb a long time may have legitimate expectations about that languages they can use, meets a level of frustration that these customers don't realize the shop has changed hands and languages. Nonetheless, as he later explains, he's been learning some Greek and this pays off as he meets older Greek residents in the street.

When I go onto the street to pay bills or to get something from other shops, elderly people 'hello!' 'hi!' 'how are you?' they want open conversation. Old and young. Which is nice. Some other people you know, in different areas, they wouldn't say hello to you. This is kind of social life, it's nice to get in contact with other people and find out how they think, how their languages … I been picking up a few words and it's alright! [People say] 'Ah, you speak Greek!' I say, 'Yeah, yeah, I'm just learning, I'm just learning.' Yeah, it's nice to get some sort of different language.

The owner of a neighbourhood discount shop a block away from Wafiq's shop has a slightly different take on this. Among small statues of Hindu gods next to Christian iconography, Australiana next to plug-in, light-up framed holograms of Mecca, plastic flowers and a wooden tablet in Thai wishing health and prosperity for someone's home, and all the bric-à-brac of a globalization-from-below discount store in a multiethnic suburb, the co-owner of the shop, Song, and one of her regular Greek customers are having a light exchange at the cash register, talking, laughing, hugging: 'See you tomorrow' says the Greek woman, who works in a nursing home and visits Song to buy something almost every day.

Excerpt 5.3 (G: Greek regular customer, S: Song, R: Researcher)
Greek: **bold**, English: plain (translation in brackets)
1. G: She know Greco. Greco forget.
2. S: Yeah, **yashou yashou**. [jaʃu] (hello hello.)
3. R: You can speak Greek!
4. G: **Yassou, kala, afharistro**. (hello, good, thank you.)
5. S: **Yassou**. (hello.)
[laughter]
6. G: See you tomorrow!
7. S: Yeah, see you!

Song's discount store is filled not only with a range of products jumbled together but also with such linguistic items. From her regular interactions with her Greek customer, she has learned a few Greek ('Greco') resources, such as **yassou** (hello) (pronounced [jaʃu] by Song). Her friend lists a few other daily terms she has apparently taught Song over the years: **kala** (good), **afharistro** (thank you). This type of exchange apparently had been going on for a long time. When asked how long they had known each other, they replied, laughing and joking.

Excerpt 5.4 (G: Greek regular customer, S: Song)
[both women shouting]
1. S: 20 year. [laughs]
2. G: More! More! More!
3. S: More than 20!

Song and her husband are of Chinese Lao and Thai backgrounds. She speaks Thai, Lao, Teochow (a brief exchange occurs in Teochow with a long-term customer while we are there), Mandarin and English, and has picked up, by her account, bits and pieces of Cantonese, Vietnamese, Greek and Fijian in the 22 years she's worked in the shop. Song seems to take particular interest and pride in learning different languages, and she perceives it a necessity for running her shop and satisfying the needs and desires and language abilities of her regular customers:

> they speak a little bit of English, but when they come in here to buy they speak Vietnamese. That's why I have to try to learn … some words I can learn. Sometimes I say to people, 'you look yourself' […] if I not understand some Vietnam, I have to say, 'Oh, OK, you have to look yourself'.

So while this is clearly a light knowledge of various languages, she also takes pride in her abilities.

Excerpt 5.5 (S: Song, R: Researcher)
1. S: Some from … I don't know … I think Fiji. They come and they just speak 'how are you'. And I can answer a little bit, [and they say] 'Ahh! How do you speak'! [laughs] Just a little bit …
2. R: So you understand a little bit of Fijian?
3. S: No no no but just a little bit!

Here we see that mix of sociality, compromise and negotiation that are part of everyday metrolingualism, as well as the spatial repertoires of such stores and the wider suburb. This aspect of everyday multilingualism, as people expressed their pleasure at the sharing and mixing that goes on in everyday multicultural encounters, was something we repeatedly encountered. It is the tensions between the conviviality of such encounters and the labeling and naming of difference that we focus on in this chapter as part of the wider struggle over ownership of space, language and identity.

Conviviality and the city

Cities are places where different people are constantly encountering others in close proximity; cities are built on the propinquity of difference. Because trade and transport have always been integral to the development of any city, they are inevitably on trade routes. Traditionally, this often meant proximity to water (rivers, oceans and later canals), though not always. Cities such as Samarkand grew up in the arid regions of what is now Uzbekistan on the busy trade route known as the Silk Road. Cities are always marked by internal differences, both cultural/linguistic and economic. Cities attract, often through trade and then through more settled patterns of migration, people of different backgrounds, and these people must then get on with each other. The density of settlement and the diversity of people mean that the proximity of difference is always part of life.

Cities grew as people moved from the countryside to the city (a result of land reforms, the industrialization of farming, as well as the work and educational opportunities afforded by cities). Now, in the twenty-first century, people may still move from the countryside to the city, but this may be from rural Guatemala to New York, from the hills of Laos to Los Angeles, from the coastal villages of Sri Lanka or the cyprus groves of Lebanon to Sydney, from the reefs of Tonga and Samoa to Auckland, from the barley fields of Anatolia to Berlin, from the millet crops of Mali to the suburbs of Paris, from the cotton fields of Bangladesh and Pakistan to the industrial cities in the north of England, from the cane fields of Paraguay to the *favelas* of Saõ Paulo. Movement is of course also from city to city, from the nightclubs of Bamako, Libreville and Dakar to the recording studios of Marseille, Lyon and Paris, from the rubbled outskirts of Port-au-Prince to the taxi ranks of Montreal.

Not surprisingly, many of the people we worked with in this project had similar trajectories: from a small village in Bosnia to Sydney (Vukasin from Renewal construction company), from Ostrowiec Świętokrzyski, a small village in Poland, to Sydney (the Polish brothers in *Patris*), from Tipaza to Paris to Tokyo (Nabil from *Petit Paris*), from central Brittany to Tokyo via Paris (Denis from *Maison Bretonne*), from Nīgata to Sydney (Yama-san from the ramen shop in the Japanese alley), from Réunion to Tokyo (Pierre from *Petit Paris*), and a small town in Aomori prefecture to Tokyo via Paris (chef from *Carthago*). The movement is almost always towards the city, yet that city space may also be differently interpreted. As Nabil explains, echoing in some ways Wafiq's account of the convivial relations on the streets of Marrickville:

> I loved the first time Kagurazaka. Because Kagurazaka for me it's not Tokyo … It's a small village. Kagurazaka is really really France small village, everybody know, hi hello, good morning, good morning, good morning (…) For me, it's a small village … For me, we are completely not in Tokyo.

Meanwhile Mariko-san, who runs one of the corner Japanese grocery shops in the Japanese alley in Sydney, describes this *Shoten-gai* (shopping alley) as having a 'downtown' feel, referring to an area of Tokyo (*Shita-machi*) that dates back to the Edo period, a hub for merchants and artisans, and with a reputation for being friendly and casual.

Excerpt 5.6: (M: Mariko-san, R: Researcher)
Japanese: Japanese fonts (translation in brackets)
1. M: 日本で言う何ですか… 商店街っていうか下町っぽい … 下町って何て言うんですか? … 下町っぽい感じがあるから,
   (what is it called in Japan… a shopping alley or Shita-machi ambience … how do you say Shita machi? … It's got a Shita-machi ambience,)
2. R: Downtown … yeah different
3. M: ダウンタウンぽいのが, この場所にはあるのでそれをちょっと崩したくないな.
   (Downtown ambience, this space has this. I don't want to ruin it.)

We do not therefore assume the centrality of the urban over the rural but rather see these as interrelated and perspectival spaces. Rural and urban are interpretive as well as spatial categories, and the diversity of places such as *Petit Paris* (as well as other spaces such as construction sites and markets) also represent a convergence or levels of rural-ness rubbing together: The chef from a small village in Réunion sings Japanese songs in the kitchen, while the owner from Tipaza in Algeria is busy on the restaurant floor, putting in an order for 'two Bordeaux onegaishimasu' (two glasses of Bordeaux please) to a Japanese staff member who is from a rural city in Japan. Meanwhile workers from country towns in Fiji, Serbia and China sit next to each other and share food in a small basement room of a building site in central Sydney, where rapid urbanization is changing a suburb with a long Indigenous history. The urban is the space that takes in all these people and practices and artefacts and requires that they figure out how to get along.

Sydney's mayor has been pushing the idea of Sydney as a city of villages. Nabil, the owner of a French bistro in Tokyo, likens an inner city suburb of Tokyo to a small French village. The collection of small Japanese businesses on the lane in Sydney leading from the station has a communal, 'shitamachi' village-like feel, enhanced now by a pepper tree planted by the local council. When the new coffee shop opened (run by three young men classified as 'completely Aussie' – see later) Ishikawa-san brought a welcome cake with 'congratulations for opening' in icing on top. The coffee shop owners responded on Facebook: 'Bit of courtyard love from Ishikawa-san' with a picture of the cake. The gym owner across the street sent a welcome case of beer to the coffee shop. Yama-san, the owner of the ramen shop opposite is a friend of the father of one of the owners of the coffee shop and is a fatherly figure in the alley. The kitchen staff from the sushi restaurant rush to the corner grocery shop when they are running out of *mirin* (sweet rice wine), and customers can get a cup of coffee delivered from across the way; Mariko-san looks after Ishikawa-san's shop while she goes to deposit money at a bank on the other side of the station.

This village and community feel is extended outside the alley: Mariko-san provides lunch boxes for local schools and companies, promotes local events and activities on large notice boards inside and outside the shop, helps cat owners relocate and supports the local Japanese Buddhist temple. Establishing ongoing social relationships, she suggests, is more important than transactional encounters. Such relations should not be like one-off transactions after purchasing ('お店行って買ったら終わり、はいぽん、じゃなくて'). Likewise the Polish cooks from *Patris* pizzeria nip across the intersection to the pub after work on Tuesdays (when the beer lines are being cleaned), exchanging pizzas for a few glasses of beer. Less often, and with different motives, they also take pizzas to the young Japanese women working at a nearby Japanese restaurant. People, objects activities and desires intersect across this village-like yet cosmopolitan intersection, maintaining and developing a sense of conviviality.

The inner city, suggests Millington (2011, p. 205), has been 'an iconic site of immigrant settlement, racial and identity politics, and conviviality'. The idea of conviviality opens up ways of seeing the lives and cultural and linguistic productions of the city as not only forged in terms of industrialization, the built environment and the search for work, but also in the process of trying to get along, in the ordinary, everyday interactions of people in the city. To the extent that this everydayness of getting along has been central to this book, so too has the idea of conviviality.[1] The basic notion contained in the idea of conviviality –living together – implies a happier state of cohabitation than more neutral terms such as propinquity. This will also connect to the discussion of commensality – eating and drinking together (see also *symposium*) – in the next chapter where people eat lunch together at construction sites and *makanai* (restaurant-provided lunch) at *Petit Paris*, and the young staff at *Patris* drink together after work.

Gilroy (2004) takes up the notion of conviviality in his depiction of everyday multicultural life, the lively, everyday interactions between people of diverse backgrounds in inner cities. This is akin to what we have been calling in this book multiculturalism from below, or what Noble (2009) refers to as corner-shop cosmopolitanism, banal cosmopolitanism, pragmatic-being-together or unpanicked multiculturalism. For Gilroy conviviality can be explained as 'the processes of cohabitation and interaction that have made multiculture an ordinary feature in Britain's urban areas and in postcolonial cities elsewhere' (2004, p. xv). This then is the everyday necessity of getting along in urban contexts. It also, as Gilroy notes, helps us get away from the notion of identity with all the limitations this focus has brought for understanding class, race and gender relations.

Hinchcliffe and Whatmore's (2006) notion of a *politics of conviviality* likewise focuses on the idea of *living cities* in which 'the life patterns and rhythms of people and other city dwellers are entangled with and against the grain of expert designs and blueprints' (p. 134). Echoing Latour's (1993; 1999) rejection of the *modernist settlement*, they argue for the need to refuse the old settlements between society and nature, humans and non-humans, in favour of 'a politics of conviviality that is serious about the heterogeneous company and messy business of living together' (p. 134). Our interest is particularly in the linguistics of conviviality, the entanglement and 'messy business' of talking to each other; but it is also about the ways in which such conviviality is often double-edged, leading back to forms of exclusion and discrimination.

'I'll fix you up, ya Lebs!': everyday contestation

While convivial multilingualism, a fairly harmonious getting along together, seemed to be a common feature of many of the workplaces we explored, it also often had its down side. There are many examples of more conflictual relations. As Loosemore and Chau (2002) and Loosemore and Lee (2002) note, for example, alongside the picture described in Chapter 2 of the more or less smooth running of the multicultural construction site, there are quite extensive reports of workplace discrimination and communication difficulties. In our data we found numerous examples of 'positive multiculturalism' that was at the same time reductively discriminatory. As Phillip explains one case at his worksite:

I had a guy here from Sierra Leone working for me. And he had ... he told us about his two wives that he had and that was a great discussion point 'cause we had a lot of fun with that, without being racist, we had a lot of fun.

(Interview, 31st October, 2012)

Our discussion of the everyday by no means therefore assumes that everydayness is free of discrimination, contestation or rubbing together that causes friction. As Hill (2008) makes clear in her examination of 'the everyday language of White racism' in the USA, it is precisely its ordinariness, its pervasive mundanity, the ways in which it seeps into daily talk, that makes it so pernicious. When folk theories of race (that races are a biological rather than a human construct, that people can be assigned to different races according to certain characteristics, for example) are part of everyday articulations of difference, racism is constantly being remade. As Alim and Smitherman show (2012), such everyday racism may emerge in comments that, for example, Barack Obama is 'articulate'. This patronizing acknowledgement that he speaks in a way White people can be comfortable with (this is not the articulation of a Black rapper), that he can sound quite White, not only hides its racist implications beneath a seeming compliment but also of course conceals the realities of underlying racial attitudes: 'The somber reality for many African Americans is that, still, no matter how "articulate" yo ass is, upon visiting in person, can't nuthin fool the landlord now, baby – you Black, Jack!' (Alim & Smitherman, 2012, p. 55).

Australia too has a long history of White racism. While the Chinese market gardeners interviewed in Chapter 2 still struggle to make ends meet because of their age, limited language abilities and the competitive vegetable pricing, they nonetheless are working in an age of newly affluent and growing Chinese populations who are finally escaping some of that long history of anti-Chinese racism that has marked Australian history. Already by the 1860s, following violent conflicts between Chinese and non-Chinese workers in the goldfields, legislation was put in place to restrict Chinese labour. As Williams (1999) notes, apart form Indigenous Australians, people of Chinese origin in NSW had more legal restrictions placed on them than any other people. These laid the grounds for the White Australia Policy (Fitzgerald, 2007; Markus, 1979), which is still a clear memory for Uncle Tony: 'Hong Kong. China ... from China. Not easy to come, you know, before ... the White Australian Policies. See it's very hard to come, yeah.'

Chinese market gardeners suffered a variety of discriminations. One newspaper account from the end of the nineteenth century (Our Market Supply, 1897, p. 5), while reporting the news that three men were standing trial for stealing vegetables from Chinese market gardens ('having, under cover of night, taken a horse and cart and raided the Chinaman's garden of about £7 worth of vegetables, which were, according to the police, driven into the market and sold'), nonetheless does so with a representation of the English of the Chinese workers in court that is surely discriminatory. One witness, Mr. Ah Cooey, is reported as explaining that 'the goods were "Allee light" the night before, but when next morning he "go'em look, an' cabbage em all all gone"'. Throughout the article the reporter dwells on the pronunciation of Barrack ('Ballack') Street and other such names: 'At great length, Ah Ling told of how he went to the "Lailway" station, where the "tlane" was, and he "ask 'em the guard who blought them".' The witness caused some little amusement in court by the way in which, when Sergeant Duncan was questioning him, he interrupted with 'Allee light'. It is against this backdrop of discrimination, peripheralization and immigration that the current networks of Chinese vegetable growing and selling needs to be understood.

It is also against this backdrop that the more general relations between White Australians and others need to be understood. This is always the tension in the reductive multiculturalism of popular discourse, where the seemingly celebratory nature of multiculturalism or the accommodation of others' practices and beliefs slides from a fluid negotiation of everyday disparity into a fixity of difference. Leading the 'Toolbox meeting' (a meeting to ensure the safety of the site – held in an air-conditioned room with about ten workers including Bosnian, Afghani, Lebanese and one of white Australian background), for example, Phillip is addressing an incident of sexual harassment outside the building when a track worker had whistled at a female passerby.

Excerpt 5.7 (P: Phillip, W: Worker)

1. P: OK, so, please, out the front … you're my eyes, you're my eyes … I don't want to see that happen again. And you're my eyes, OK. We work well out the front, we're all working well together but just something silly happened today and I can't let that happen. OK? I've been to court over sexual harassment of women, and I've also had the unions involved with two men with sexual harassment. So I don't want to go down that track. [gesturing to one of the young Lebanese men] And given your culture, I'm sure that you would respect women. Is that right? Yeah? Is that right?
2. W: Yes.
3. P: Yeah, of course it is. OK … is there anything else? Is there anything there that I've said that everybody doesn't understand? Does everybody understand what I've just said?
4. W: Yeah. Everybody.

As he asks his workforce to collaborate in avoiding instances of sexual harassment (not, we might note, on the grounds of not harassing women, but more in terms of avoiding legal action), he very clearly picks on one worker of Lebanese background to gain agreement with his point. In our exploration of Sydney worksites, however, we did not in fact talk to many such 'Aussies' (as White Australians were almost always called). So here we want to turn our attention more closely to the complexities of interaction among the non-White population. As we saw in the opening comments by Muhibb, 'the most perfect place to be in the world' may be characterized in playfully pejorative terms: 'Deaf, dumb, blind, stupid … Different races'; or here, as Talib and Muhibb deal with a customer, we see a more edgy naming and threatening, as the customer engages in that common mixture of banter with racial overtones.

Excerpt 5.8 (T: Talib, C: Customer)
Arabic: *italics*, English: plain (translation in brackets)
1. T: I don't think so. *Shibak* Johnny? (What's wrong Johnny?)
[yelling in the background]
   Huh? *Wallah ma ba'ref.* (I swear I don't know.)
2. C: I'll fucken fix you up don't worry! Wait to see. Yeah I'll fix you up,
   ya Lebs! [laughs] [shouting back to someone else]
3. T: Muhibb, *wan el koosa elrakhis?* (where is the cheap zucchini?)
   Arkhas eshi. (the cheapest ones.)

Here as Talib and Muhibb maintain their constant busy activity, moving back and forth with Arabic and English, their frustrated customer uses the common phrase 'Lebs' as he threatens, jokingly, 'I'll fucken fix you up don't worry!' In such moments, the everyday multilingualism that allows such interactions to happen also crosses into that uneasy territory of discrimination, exclusion and racism.

It has been widely noted, of course, that it matters fundamentally who utters what terms to whom. It was possible for the great Yiddish actor Joseph Adler to perform Shylock in the Merchant of Venice to a Yiddish-speaking audience in New York in 1901 (Simon, 1992), for example, or for terms of abuse such as *nigger* or *queer* to be used within and to be appropriated by those very groups at which they are aimed. Nigga: '1. Close friend, someone who got yo back, yo "main nigga"' (Smitherman's *Black Talk* cited in Alim & Smitherman, 2012, p. 112). It is nonetheless arguable that the circulation of such terms in and across communities, while not always simply classifiable as 'racist', is always potentially prejudicial. This is where those elements of fixity that make fluidity possible take on not merely an essentialist but also an injurious edge. There is often, then, at the very least an ambivalence, two sides of the coin, in the give and take of multilingual and multicultural relations. In looking at the fluid metrolingual practices that often characterize urban encounters, therefore, we are equally attentive to the play of what we have elsewhere (Otsuji & Pennycook 2010; 2014) called *fixity* and *fluidity*. We cannot ignore the continued deployment of fixed categories of linguistic and cultural identity. These are still very real as part of the discursive world in which we operate, and such categories may equally and simultaneously be deployed by those who also revel in the fluidity and conviviality of everyday multilingualism. There are several layers of complexity here, therefore, that we need to briefly unpack.

Language practices and identity are formed in a constant push and pull between fixity and fluidity. Like Rampton (2009), we see the dangers of an overemphasis on fluidity, since it may highlight only the possibility and the desire to operate in a world of constant flexibility. We may, as Appadurai (1996) noted, live in a world of flows, but we also live in a world of fixities. Not only are there political and economic limits to the degrees to which language and cultures can ebb and flow, but there are also strong attachments to fixed identifications. Work that has focused on identity or hybridity, while making multiplicity or instability a central aspect of its discursive framework, has often been equally complicit with the reification of categories: 'We tease out a so-called "identity" from the polyphonic discourse, and, ultimately, we guarantee the categories which permit the politics of classifying, creating hierarchies, and monitoring the population' (Canut, 2009, p. 99). As we seek to identify identities, we all too often reinscribe particular modes of categorization. Likewise, as we argued in Chapter 3, the notion of hybridity is frequently 'predicated on an assumption that there exist two distinct codes or separate entities which are combined' (Makoni, 2011, p. 683). To invoke forms of diversity and hybridity, then, may be equally to invoke forms of stability on which such difference depends.

This is a basic theoretical and practical predicament posed by notions such as hybridity. The notion of transgression raises similar concerns. Although, as Jervis (1999) argues, 'transgressive sexuality is an offence against the "real", the modern structure of reality and illusion; it is an ontological "crime", before it is a moral one' (p. 177), such transgression depends on predefined gender roles in order to be transgressive. Limit and transgression, as Foucault (1977) points out, depend on each other, for 'a limit could not exist if it were absolutely uncrossable and, reciprocally, transgression would be pointless if it merely crossed a limit composed of illusions and shadows' (p. 34). This, then, is one of the dilemmas we are trying to deal with in this book: While we are very aware of the fixed identity categories often invoked by our participants and that also circulate in both popular and academic discourses, we do not see metrolingualism as a hybrid mixture of such fixities.

Nor do we wish to suggest that metrolingualism is unbridled fluid language. Rather, it involves the interplay between a given diversity and its static institutional and discursive nemesis. Foucault suggests that transgression

> is not related to the limit as black to white, the prohibited to the unlawful, the outside to the inside, or as the open area of a building to its enclosed spaces. Rather, their relationship takes the form of a spiral which no simple infraction can exhaust.
>
> (p. 35)

Similarly, when considering metrolingualism, therefore, we are by no means blind to the fact that people also incorporate fixed modes of identities. Metrolingualism is not so much convergent diversity (the blending of fixed elements) but dynamic emergence in the form of a spiral as people move between fixed and fluid understandings and uses of language and identity.

The contested city

The city is always a site of struggle. Raymond Williams' (1980, p. 9) injunction that 'it will always be necessary to go again to Hyde Park' harks back to the 1866 demonstrations in favour of the vote in London, as well as the response by writers such as Matthew Arnold who saw anarchy in such demonstrations for voting rights and called instead for greater law and order. Public spaces have long been the site for public demonstrations, viewed by some as riots, anarchy and a decline in law and order, but by others as part of a democratic right to public space. The wave of *occupy* movements across the world – from the *Indignados* in Spain and the *Aganaktismenoi* in Greece to occupations in Cairo, London or Washington – were both spatial and linguistic (Rojo, 2014; Chun, 2014; 2015). Cronulla beach in Sydney, normally a peaceful place to swim, relax or have a BBQ, became in 2005 the site of racial and ethnic conflict against people of Middle Eastern background, with chants and slogans claiming, 'We grew here, you flew here', or more simply, 'Fuck off Lebs!', 'Aussie Pride', 'Fuck off wogs!' (Collins, 2009). This physical and verbal contestation was a claim to space, the city and Australian identity.

These arguments take us back to Lefebvre's key 1968 text (another important year for people and the streets) *Le Droit à la ville* (The right to the city). Central to Lefebvre's argument, later expanded in his writing on *the production of space*, was his contention that space and cities were in effect works in progress produced by inhabitants. Lefebvre's (1968; 1973) arguments have been influential on the development of many of the themes in this book: the *public* nature of city life, the need to engage with *difference* and thus, importantly for this chapter, the ways in which city life involves struggle. For Lefebvre it was crucial to emphasize the rights of different people to participate in this production of the city space. 'The production of public space', argues Mitchell (2003, pp. 35–36), the means through which 'the right to the city is made possible' is always a struggle over the idea of the public sphere, with particular social and spatial implications (Purcell, 2002).

Graffiti writing is one such domain of contestation (Pennycook, 2009; 2010), including overt challenges to ownership and property, as in this challenge to property owners in Berlin (Image 5.1), which reads (bilingually) 'Wohnungen zu verkaufen' (accommodation for sale) and 'Buy Yuppie Scum'. While city authorities may see graffiti as vandalism, or as 'incomprehensible hieroglyphic signatures that aggressively pollute the visual space of the inhabitant' (Milon, 2002, p. 87), for the artists themselves, they are often part of the struggle over the meaning, look and space of the city (Millington, 2011; Modan, 2007). The question, in part, is who has the right to author the city? When a bank's cash machines (ATMs) are dressed up in new sparkly outfits (Image 5.2) for Sydney's Mardi Gras festival, it matters who has authorized this public display.

City spaces – from piazzas to shopping malls – may be shared and inclusionary or secured and exclusionary spaces. Guards at the doors of expensive shopping malls in many cities overtly police who should be let in, and sometimes, whether someone should be let out again. The Japanese pedestrian alley was far from convivial when Yama-san opened his ramen shop in the early 1990s: it was known as a dark and dangerous place on the wrong side of the tracks. According to Adam from the local historical association, 'Businesses have never succeeded there. It's the poor side of town. The other side of the railway line is where the activity's always been, it's where there's been success'. Carolyn, his colleague, concurs: 'And I guess if that attitude has always been there, though ... you don't come to this side of the railway line, everything's on the other side ... these guys are doing a great job'.

Image 5.1 Berlin graffiti.

Image 5.2 GAYTM.

The low rent and convenience (next to the station and ample parking space around) were the deciding factors for Yama-san to choose the venue, but this came with a price: the alley was also a place where theft and drug deals were common. As he says: '開店した時は、もうバットとか常にもっていました' (When I opened the shop, I used to keep a baseball bat handy). Eventually, however, as other shops opened (at Yama-san's suggestion) – such as Ishikawa-san's grocery store and *Furuhonya* (second-hand bookshop) – the joint efforts of the shop owners and the local council paid off and the pedestrian alley gradually turned into a family-friendly space. This claiming of the alley by Yama-san and the other owners has now changed the meaning of the space even if at times they still stand guard at the entrance of the alley (Yama-san and Makoto-san from the sushi restaurant, according to Mariko-san, guarded the alley when two 'junkies' were hanging out there). Mariko-san also explains how she and Ishikawa-san (whose shop is opposite) warn each other with a shared secret sign language when they witness shoplifters.

Now it is shoplifters and junkies who are excluded from the area. This understanding of the lived space of the city enables us to conceive of the city not only as an urban environment but also as a space that is made and remade by people and to which we claim rights. As Harvey (2008, p. 23) explains: 'The question of what kind of city we want cannot be divorced from that of what kind of social ties, relationship to nature, lifestyles, technologies and aesthetic values we desire.' The right to the city is therefore 'far more than the individual liberty to access urban resources: it is a right to change ourselves by changing the city'. This is, as we see in the examples given earlier, a collective rather than an individual right since 'transformation inevitably depends upon the exercise of a collective power to reshape the processes of urbanization'. The freedom to make and remake our cities ourselves, Harvey argues, is 'one of the most precious yet most neglected of our human rights' (2008, p. 23).

In Watson's (2006) view, we have on the one hand the 'contemporary phantasmagoric "multicultural" city' in which people of diverse backgrounds – different class locations, races, ethnicities, sexualities, ages – live side by side. From this point of view *living with difference* is 'quintessentially what city life is about' (p. 1). And yet the social, economic, political, cultural and physical forces that bring about this close engagement with difference also divide the city. Alongside this inclusionary, celebratory narrative, therefore, is also the city as a divided space, 'a space of segregation, division, exclusion, threat and boundaries' where the positive account of people mingling and exchanging intercultural moments is replaced by antagonism, fear and exclusion (p. 1). In the case of the Japanese alley, it was the railway line that used to divide the two areas. As Carolyn and Adam said, everything was on the other side of the tracks and people rarely came to this side.

The area of Sydney where the construction workers were eating their lunch (see Chapters 3 and 6) is an inner-city suburb with a rough reputation, extensive public housing and a large (about 50 per cent) overseas-born and Indigenous population. But the presence of these construction workers is also part of its redevelopment, with house prices going up, new people moving in and these older residents being pushed out. This process of struggle and change is echoed in cities around the world. Sanya (山谷) in Tokyo used to be an 'untouchable' area during the Edo period; cheap 1960s accommodation was turned into temporary residences for day-labours, which in turn have now become cheap places for foreign backpackers, with English and Japanese signs on hostels and internet cafés. Cities are always going through these periods of shared settlement. They are restive places, marked by marginalization, resistance, order and disorder.

For Zukin (1991; 1995), there is a basic tension and struggle between what she calls the *landscape of power* and the *vernacular*, the first typically expressed in the gleaming vertical buildings of the financial sector, the latter in the low-lying, horizontal residential areas. From a different framework, this division has also been discussed in terms of the *citadel* and the *ghetto*, again pointing to the sociospatial inequalities between the two worlds of office towers and poor suburbs (Friedmann & Wolff, 1982).

> If we consider that global cities concentrate both the leading sectors of global capital and a growing share of disadvantaged populations (immigrants, many of the disadvantaged women, people of color generally, and, in the megacities of developing countries, masses of shanty dwellers), then we can see that cities have become a strategic terrain for a whole series of conflicts and contradictions
> (Sassen, 2005, p. 39)

Class and ethnic divisions are built into the city. To live in the urban periphery of Paris, for example, where the 'peripheralisation of poverty' started with Haussmann's renovations in the nineteenth century and 'came to a head with the construction of mass housing (the *grands ensembles*) on the northern and eastern peripheries of the city in the 1960s' (Millington, 2011, p. 159), or the differently racialized ghettoes of cities such as Chicago, is to be subject to advanced forms of marginalization, to be an urban outcast, as Wacquant (2008) argues, to feel not only the stigmatization of class, racial and ethnic prejudice but also the spatial exclusion of being from the *banlieues*[2].

Akin to Nandy's (2006) argument that the relative harmony among the many communities in Kochi (Cochin) has been achieved by a stable but mutual dislike of each other (an understanding that while you may dislike the others, they are nevertheless part of you and part of the city), Simon (1997) suggests the highly diverse Parisian neighbourhood of Belleville (straddling the nineteenth and twentieth arrondissements) (Images 5.3 5.4, 5.5) survives through a series of compromises, the *compromis bellevillois*. As Belleville has passed through typical stages of a changing inner-city area – from Armenians, Greeks and Ashkenazi Jews, to Chinese (it is home to one of the Paris China Towns) and North and Subsaharan Africans – it has become in popular imagination not only a working class and artistic area (Edith Piaf is said to have been born under a lamppost there) but also 'the archetype of the cosmopolitan district … this magical place where extremes live together without apparent strife' (Simon, 1997, p. 34, our translation).

Image 5.3 Belleville Chez Yu.

Image 5.4 Belleville Boucherie Caïdi.

Image 5.5 Belleville Cheary Horlogerie.

This is achieved, however, by a scrupulous respect for each other's space, particularly in public places. In Belleville everyone waits in line and avoids encroaching on their neighbour. A certain closing of borders (*étanchéité des frontières*) preserves group autonomy but at the same time limits mixing (*limite les brassages*) (p .35).

It is these tensions that new arrivals in a city have to work out. Immigrants from Central America to the huge US conurbations have to negotiate a complex linguistic world: '*Cuando quiero hablar con ellos, mezcho los cuatro idiomas*' (When I want to speak with them, I mix the four languages) remarks a Guatemalan immigrant working in a Korean workplace in New York (Velasquez, 2013, p. 10), the four languages (*cuatro idiomas*) he refers to being Spanish, English, Korean and Kaqchiqel. Such multilingual negotiations are on a very uneven territory. As Han (2009) makes clear, in a context where 'Korean workers take the orders and collect the money while Latino workers replenish the shelves, clear the tables and wash the dishes' (p. 237) and where Latino workers can be hired cheaply and are often compliant because of their (il)legal status within the country, resentments, prejudices and differences also run deep.

Spaces and work in the city are also deeply gendered, a division that is intertwined with the nature of different kinds of work and the background of people who do it. As we saw in the discussion in Chapter 2 of the different linguistic and cultural affiliations that lead to people of related backgrounds – Chinese gardeners and fruit sellers, Serbian painters and plasterers, Vietnamese manicurists – linking up, these affiliations often work along gendered lines. From female garment workers, and Irish construction site traffic directors (many of the women holding the *stop* and *slow* signs around construction sites in Sydney turn out often to be of Irish background) and the women working in beauty salons, to the taxi drivers, construction workers and cooks, we find language, ethnicity and gender line up in particular formations. Joseph explains one reason he enjoys the work in the Produce Market.

> Look. Why do I like it? Why do I like it? I like the market. It's a male ... it's a large male club. When I'm talking club ... you talk to everybody, have a chat with everybody, you pack up and go home, you don't have to go anywhere. Don't have to go to your local pub or local club. You've already had your chat. It's a very good social place. And I've found over the years a lot of elderly people who have retired from this place who still live close by ... they still coming down and grab a coffee and have a chat and tell everyone about ... They work 40 years, 45 years in the market and they handle the produce on their shoulders, unloading.

When we look at language affiliations, work and social relations, we also need to see the ways in which these are bound up with the class and gendered lines along which social organization also occurs.

The sense of ownership, of the right to the city, of how the city looks from working class and ethnic minority perspectives and how this may be deeply gendered is nicely captured in Monica Ali's (2003) novel *Brick Lane*. For an outsider, a tourist, a visitor, a city such as London presents itself through its famous buildings, bridges, streets, river and shops. For an inhabitant, these are part of the cityscape, buildings one may view in passing from a bus or stroll past on the way to somewhere else. Monica Ali (2003), however, gives us a glimpse of the city as viewed by Nazneen, whose closed and claustrophobic life is spent largely at home, near Brick Lane in East London (and see also Chapter 7 for further discussion of this area of London). Thirty years after he came to London, her husband, Chanu, decides to take the family on a trip into the city: "'I've spent more than half my life here," said Chanu, "but I hardly left these few streets'" (p. 238). Nazneen takes a picture of her husband and daughters in front of Buckingham Palace, a photograph 'that would live in the kitchen, propped up against the tiles at the back of the work surface, accumulating a fine spray of turmeric-stained grease from her cooking pot' (p. 243). This is, in a way, an attempt to claim one's right to the city, to make the city one's own, even if its end result is not so much a sense of city ownership but a memory of a trip captured in a fading photograph next to the stove where she is destined to spend much of her time.

The participants in our study struggled with the city in many different ways. From Nabil (*Petit Paris*) and the chef at *Carthago*, carving our their little city spaces within the wider metropolis, to Yama-san guarding the alleyway with a baseball bat, or the market workers with their linguistic territories, all are busy claiming rights to some part of the city, and changing what the city means as they do so. By contrast, while the vegetables the Chinese market gardeners (Chapter 2) grow (including the *gwai lou coi* – foreign vegetables) may travel across the city to a Bangladeshi-owned shop, a Lebanese-run fruit and vegetable kiosk in the northern suburbs, or a Chinese restaurant in Hurstville to the south, their lack of transport, run-down hut beside the gardens under the flight path into the airport, their limited linguistic repertoires and their long hours of labour with tired bodies, restrict their claims to the city.

Aussies and 'the worst general Asian ever'

The idea of foreign vegetables takes us back to the questions of naming the Other, which, for many of our participants meant the 'Aussies' or 'オージー' (Ōjī). As noted at the beginning of this chapter, Wafiq, the Lebanese store owner, along with his quirky use of 'too many' also noted the excitement 'Australians' felt when they came to the shop. This terminology is used by both insiders and outsiders to this community: In the following excerpt, an Anglo-Australian also maintains this distinction in his description of working some years before at a construction site in Smithfield.

> Smithfield is a very much a multicultural society, back then it was very much the Italians and the Greeks that lived in there. But I worked with a lot of Turks and a lot of Maltese and a lot of Italians and a lot of Greeks and a lot of Germans and a lot of, ah, Yugoslavs, and I also, there was also a mix, a lot of English people in there, Pommies, and there was also the Aussies in there as well.
>
> (Phillip, interview, October 31, 2012)

Meanwhile, Mariko-san describes the clientele at her shop as: 'そうですね, 最近は半分 … え::50, 30, 20 で 50がジャパニーズ, で 30 がオージー, 20 がチャイニーズ, ベトナミーズぐらいでしょうか' (Well, recently, half … we::ll 50, 30, and 20. That is, about 50 Japanese [ジャパニーズ], 30 Aussies [オージー], 20 Chinese [チャイニーズ] and Vietnamese [ベトナミーズ]). Instead of listing the ethnicities in Japanese (日本人: nihonjin – Japanese; 中国人: chūgokujin – Chinese), Mariko-san's terms 'ジャパニーズ' (Japanīzu), 'チャイニーズ' (Chainīzu), and 'ベトナミーズ' (Betonamīzu) orient towards an 'Australian way' of identifying ethnicities, including her own Japaneseness. But she also speaks of 'オージー' (Ōjī), a Japanese version of saying 'Aussie'. This use of 'Aussies' occurred frequently: A Nepalese worker in a restaurant talked of 'mostly Aussie customers'. When asked whether there were many Vietnamese customers at the manicurist shop where she works, Lim replied 'Not much Vietnamese … um … come here. No. Aussie. Aussie and other … other. Local. Mmm' (Interview, November 20, 2012).

'Aussie' can refer to anything from language to vegetables: As the owner of a Lebanese Grocery shop put it, 'I speak to Lebanese in Lebanese, I speak to Italian … No! Mostly the language is Aussie, English … ' When asked about cucumbers, he explained, 'Before you used to use Aussie cucumbers … nobody buys them anymore'. A Japanese store owner, Ueki-san, in the same shopping mall explained:

Excerpt 5.9 (U: Ueki-san, R: Researcher)
Japanese: Japanese scripts (translation in brackets)
1. U: ローカルの人…はあんまり…使わない.
    (Local people … don't … spend very much.)
2. R:ほんとに?(Really?)
3. U:うん. (Yeah.)
4. R:お金を?(Money?)
5. U:まだ. (Not yet.)
6. R:やっぱ高い? 日本の食べ物高いから?
    (Expensive? Because Japanese food is expensive?)
7. U:う::ん, いや, もうそれは…そういうことじゃないと思う. たぶん…あの::そういう文化. (M::mm, no, it's … not something like that I think. Probably … we::ll it's culture.)
8. R:日本食, (Japanese food,)
9. U:オージーはそんなにお金は使わない. 食には.
    (Aussies don't spend much money on food.)
10. R:ああ, そっか そっか. (Ahh, I see I see.)
11. U:普通の人間, 普通のオージーは使わない.
    (Normal people, normal Aussies don't spend much.)

Not only does this store owner lament the fact that 'Aussies' do not spend much on food (the majority of this shop owners' customers were Japanese, along with some Korean and Chinese), he also categorizes this mainstream majority as '普通の人間' (normal people). Unlike his more hesitant responses in lines 1 and 7, his utterances in lines 9 and 11 are more definitive (falling tones) when he claims that 'オージー' (Ōjī) don't spend much. A Japanese sushi restaurant owner in a different suburb, however, had a different experience. When asked about the clientele of his restaurant, for example, he replied: 'ええっとですね…変なんですけど, オージーのお客さんが多いんですよ' (Let me see … it might sound strange to you, but we have many Aussie customers). He goes on to suggest that some 70 per cent of his customers are Australians: 'でコリアンかチャイニーズか…ジャパ, あの:: オーストラリアンですね. オーストラリアンが大体…70% 来るかなって言うぐらいですね' (And Korean or Chinese or Japa, errm, Australian. Seventy per cent of the customers are Australian, I would say). This he puts down to the balcony and outdoor deck. While these two small business owners may have different experience of 'Ōjī' consumer practices, it generally seems that they are either a broad category of White Australians or more generally non-Asian Australians.

His classification of 'Aussies' or 'オージー' (Ōjī), however, is not simply along lines of colour, since he also goes on to refer to people of mixed background, particularly the guys that run the coffee shop opposite, as 'completely Aussie': 'まあでも, もう完全にオージーですけどね' (Well but, they are already completely Aussie). Indeed, he even goes on to suggest that his own son, born to Japanese parents but having grown up in Australia, and with whom he speaks English, might be similarly classified. The young men who run the newly opened coffee shop are thus also classified as 'オージー' (Ōjī) even though one is of mixed Japanese and Anglo-Australian parentage (it is through his father's connection to the owner of the ramen shop that they came to take over the coffee shop opposite) and the other of Chinese background. For the sushi shop owner 'Ōjī' is a cultural and linguistic label as much as a racial one. Ben from the coffee shop, however, acknowledges these conflicting identity pulls. When asked about his Chinese background, he explained, 'I don't even know! I am the worst, like, general Asian ever! [laughter] It's terrible! I can't even speak Chinese'.

Here in the convivial and contested space of the multicultural city, Ben feels that occasional pressure to be Chinese rather than 'general Asian' or 'Aussie'. With his fluid and mobile history of a Chinese family in Papua New Guinea migrating to Australia and marrying into another Chinese-Australian family (and his grandmother on this side sounding as if she might have 'blonde hair and blue eyes' on the phone), there is also the occasional pull towards the fixity of Chineseness, of speaking Chinese. 'So I'm half Chinese. Actually, officially, I'm seven-eighths Chinese and one-eighth Irish! So … I'm half, though. Like, I'm Chinese on the outside, but I can't even speak Chinese. I can understand a little bit, but … I'm pretty useless.' He is caught in Ang's (2001) dilemma of 'not speaking Chinese'. While he may be classified as 'Aussie' by the Japanese sushi shop owner opposite, he also feels that pull of ethnic identification that perhaps he ought to speak Chinese, and by not doing so he becomes nothing but a generic Asian. In the convivial space of the Japanese alley, a space to which the various small business holders progressively staked their rights, the fixities and fluidities of identity claims are always under contestation as 'the worst, like, general Asian ever', the 'seven-eighths Chinese' who 'can't even speak Chinese', the 'オージー' (Ōjī) who is running the coffee shop, works out his possible ways of being.

Research and stories: the chicken mime

As we talked to many people across workplaces in the city, much of what we heard came in the form of stories. As many discussions of narrative inquiry (e.g. Bruner, 1991) have told us, this is the way people make sense of their lives, turning their lives, or particular episodes and encounters, into recountable stories. Our interest in such stories therefore was not in the Labovian tradition of sociolinguistic research where stories are encouraged in order to elicit a less formal style in interviews to enable analysis of sociolinguistic variables (Mesthrie, 2014), but rather to help us understand how participants in the research understood themselves, how they located themselves discursively, culturally, spatially. These are 'small stories' that give sense to people's understanding of their lives in the city (Bamberg & Georgakopoulou, 2008).

Some were personal stories, such as Ben's from the coffee shop. The background to his statement that he was 'the worst, like, general Asian ever' needs to be heard through his own family story: 'Yeah, so, my mother and her grandmother … and mother … yeah, there was about eleven of them, and they moved here from Papua New Guinea when she was a kid. 'Cause, you know, there's a big Asian community, Chinese community [in PNG]'. His grandfather, he explains, worked as a barber in PNG before moving to Australia after WWII:

> When he was a kid in Papua New Guinea, I think some Japanese fire – uh, Japanese fighter planes went over and I think they shot his leg off. I've never actually seen his leg. Like, he won't show us. But uh … yeah, it's one of those things. I don't even think my mother's seen it. So … I think it's just a sore point for him. I mean, even still, he's got Japanese friends.

His mother met his father in Australia: 'Even my dad's half-Chinese as well, but if you spoke to his mother, you'd think she had blonde hair and blue eyes on the phone even though she's Chinese. But she grew up in the inner-west.' Such stories are, of course, always mediated by the sedimented history of retellings, by the type of story members of this family wish to tell, by the discourses that construct them, by the people to whom they are being told. They are stories that need to be read as part of the metrolingual history of the city.

Other stories are not so much personal stories as accounts of a more general community nature, of increasing fixity, akin in many ways to urban myths, that seemed to narrate a particular way of representing aspects of the multilingual migrant experience. Wafiq, for example, gives us one account of a recently-arrived immigrant in the 1960s who had just moved to Sydney and knew little English. Hoping to buy some eggs in a local store, he looked around but couldn't find any. With his English not up to finding a way to ask, he tried another option and started miming a chicken laying an egg. Up and down he walked in the shop, clucking and flapping his wings, but taking care to show that his interest was not in the chicken itself, but the carefully mimed egg that he was laying. Eventually he got his message across, and managed to negotiate the buying of the eggs. It was not until some time later that he learned that in fact this grocer also spoke Arabic and indeed was a Lebanese immigrant too.

The stories we heard could be amusing like Wafiq's, romantic like Zlatan's – 'I met her in Montenegro. She went to:: she was on holiday and I met her and … after half year I come to Australia and married here' (Zlatan, interview, February 14, 2012) – or profoundly sad. Migration is often a result of major disruption to lives, including wars (the Lebanese civil war, Bosnian wars, World War II, the Algerian War). At the dining table of Emi's apartment, Igor, the construction worker who insisted that he spoke 'Yugoslav' not Serbian (see Chapter 1) disclosed a heartbreaking tale about the Bosnian war. He moved to Australia because to going too far of my country, to can't back. Because I no like anymore to going back. Because my father is died there, my mother is die, my sister is die. My sister is now being thirty-one, but everybody die in the war. Yeah, I no want to going back.

(Igor, interview, December 3, 2011)

Despite the gravity and sadness of his story, he smiled and continued: 'It's very hard to leave your country. But when you thinking what's happened, what bullshit is happened there, only for religion, because you Croatian, I am Serbian, this bullshit' [laughs]. Such stories, of course, rarely emerge in early encounters. It was only after a few months of casual chat and daily greetings, and during a break from work sitting in Emi's apartment, that he told this story.

The story by Yama-san, the ramen shop owner has, again, a slightly different flavour. For him it was neither romance nor war that brought him to Australia, but a passion for *ramen*. When we praised the soup, Yama-san started talking passionately about his philosophy and art of cooking the ramen stock; simmering Japanese kelp (*kombu*) for hours early in the morning when, according to Yama-san, it is the best time to make the most of the Earth's energy. Of an interview lasting an hour and a half, one hour was spent on the philosophy and virtue of making ramen. Yama-san was the first to open a Japanese-related business on the 'wrong' side of the railway tracks, an area that has now turned into a Japanese precinct. While looking for a suitable venue, he stood at the exit from the station and observed the behaviour of the commuters: '2, 3 ヶ月僕ずっとこの駅のこちら側に立って，ずっと何人通るか計算したんですよ' (For two or three months I stood at this side of the station and counted the number of people passing). According to his estimate, approximately 3,000 people passed through the 'dangerous' alley every evening. His observation led to another finding; although most people seemed to be eager to rush through the alley, there was one particular spot that seemed to always come to their attention as soon as they left the station, and this is where his ramen shop stands today.

Listening to these stories was also closely tied to our participatory research practices (see also Chapter 6) as we slurped noodles, had our eyebrows done, drank vodka, bought fruit and vegetables. This is about building rapport and relationships that also allow us to be a part of the participants' worlds. The stories recounted by our participants gave us insights into their life trajectories, their histories, their deeply-held views and passions. Such stories, however apocryphal and changed, however much in need of being spoken and enacted, are also the stories of the double-edged world of multilingual Sydney. As researchers, we have to learn how to put our participants at ease so they will tell us these stories, how to listen to their stories (and not interrupt with 'research questions') and how to interpret and appreciate these stories for all they tell us about language, lives and the city.

Notes

1   Noting the problem with the term conviviality in English (which differs in various respects from its French and Spanish cognates) where it tends towards a lighthearted jolliness, Illich (1973) suggests a meaning closer to *eutrapelia* or *graceful playfulness*. Conviviality, then, for Illich designates the 'opposite of industrial productivity. I intend it to mean autonomous and creative intercourse among persons, and the intercourse of persons with their environment' (p. 6).
2   The meaning of *suburbs*, as Kramsch and Thorne (2002) show, can be very different between France and the USA, for example, the former being peripheral, immigrant and working class, and the latter green, spacious and bourgeois. Likewise the meaning of 'downtown' discussed above in Japanese contexts can have very different meanings historically and geographically.

6 Talking food

Commensality and the city

The *Fanta* is always greener back home

One thing that became very clear to us throughout this work was the close connection between food and language. We have already pointed to this in our discussion of markets, vegetables, kitchens and restaurants (see for example Chapters 2 and 4), but here we want to look more closely at metrolingualism and talk about and around food. This is the everyday stuff of commensality (eating together), conviviality (living together – see Chapter 5) and language. On the construction sites, for example, different trade groups take their coffee and lunch breaks at distinct times. As noted in Chapter 2, the linguistic and ethnic affiliations that bring people together in particular areas of the construction industry therefore have concomitant linguistic implications. Here Drago (of Serbian background, moved to Australia a year and a half ago) and Marko (also of Serbian background but moved to Australia at the age of ten) are having a conversation while they eat chips and chicken kebabs bought by Drago from the corner chicken shop (across the street from Lynda's Hungry Café – see Chapter 3), while Nemia (Fijian background) sits next to them eating his own lunch brought from home.

Excerpt 6.1 (M: Marko, D: Drago)
Serbian: *italics*; English: plain; Fijian derived word: **bold** (translations in brackets)
1. M: *Pa jebi ga sad su krenuli.* (Well, fuck it, they've started now.)
2. D: *Pa sto ti … to radi?* (But why … everything he does?)
3. M: *Ne adresu gde je radio svaki dan i datum.* [To Nemia] **Ula** have some chips mate, [to Drago] *uzmi jos* chips.
    (No, the address where he worked every day and the date. **Ula** [address term] have some chips mate, take some more chips.)
    [someone passes something to Marko]
4. M: Thank you.
5. D: *Ovo Fanta, tako*? (This is Fanta, yeah?)
6. M: Yep.
7. D: *Nema kao kod nas jebi ga*! (Not like ours fuck it!)
8. M: Yeah.

9. D: *Hoces jos koka kolu*? (You want some more Coke?)
10. M: *Ne hvala. Kod nas Fanta zelena jebote. Zuta, zuta. Pa uzmi.* (No thank you. Back home Fanta is green fuck it. Yellow, yellow. Take it.)

Here Serbian dominates, though also, given these workers' varied trajectories, these are different varieties of Serbian mixed with some English. Marko, who has lived a substantial time in Australia, often uses English. When Drago returned with the chips just before this exchange, he thanked him in English: 'Thank you very much. Is this for me? Thank you. I think this is too much ... Oh yeah'. Drago's response was in Serbian: '*Uzeo sam ove*' (I got these), to which Marko again replied in English, 'Ahh. Thanks Drago'. Marko's use of English seems to be both out of habit and to be inclusive to Nemia who is sharing the space. Marko's '*Ne hvala*' in line 10, furthermore, seems slightly out of place in Serbian: such terms for please and thank you are less commonly used in Serbia, and this phrase has the feel of the English 'no thank you' transferred into Serbian. So even though they are speaking ostensibly in Serbian, this may also involve other cultural and linguistic practices. As the eating, sharing and offering of food is deeply bound up with such cultural and linguistic practices, this is a common space for this drift to occur.

In line 3, in the middle of the conversation in Serbian, Marko offers chips to Nemia in English, '**Ula**, have some chips mate' and then in Serbian to Drago, '*uzmi jos* chips'. According to Marko, **Ula** (he later spelled this out to us as U-L-A) is an affectionate Fijian term of address, a term he picked up from other Fijian workers at other construction sites. '**Ula**' in fact appears to be derived from the common Fijian address term *bula* (literal meaning 'life'), which has a number of meanings (akin in some ways to Hawaiian *aloha*): hello, wishing good health, greeting and so on. Here, picked up in the contact between Balkan and Fijian construction workers, and changed from *bula* to '**Ula**', it operates as one of those small items of accumulated language resources that become part of the commensal spatial repertoire in the basement of a construction site.

There is sharing of food and drink, here of some chips – construction workers are frequent visitors to local cafés and fast-food places – and drink. Here too we see how the food becomes a referent for 'things back home' though not in this case around traditional food but around a discussion of *Fanta* being green or yellow.[1] Here the discussion is not so much about an obviously ethnically oriented food (we turn to a discussion of *moussaka*, for example, later in this chapter) but about an apparent difference in a common soft drink. In this all-male Serbian-dominant construction-site lunchtime, this is not, of course, a place of polite chat, though this friendly, male banter, this sharing and talking about food, nonetheless can still be seen as convivial, as everyday commensality, eating together, with food and language mixed together in one busy hotpot.

Talking food

It is perhaps not surprising that food has emerged as a significant theme in our research. In looking for the urban life of language outside both the private (at home or in family gatherings) and institutional (school or other public institutions) domains, we have perhaps inevitably ended up in restaurants, markets and shops where food is a focus of doing and talking. Food is central to human life, both on a basic physical level, as well as in cultural and economic terms. 'Food lies at the very heart of human existence. Just as the individual person must eat, so too does any form of social order have to organize the production, distribution and consumption of foodstuffs' (Inglis & Gimlin, 2010, p. 3). As Duruz, Luckman and Bishop (2011, p. 600) note, the sharing of food or exchanges over food 'is one of the core ways in which cultural exchanges across ethnic boundaries take place'. According to Wise (2009, p. 23), therefore, 'cultural difference can be the basis for commensality and exchange; where identities are not left behind, but can be shifted and opened up in moments of non-hierarchical reciprocity, and are sometimes mutually reconfigured in the process'.

Food has therefore long been a focus of intellectual interest: from health to the economics of global food distribution and sustainability, to the development of McDonald's as an index of neoimperialism, to the politics of movements towards local production, food becomes a major focus for understanding access, inequality, globalization, big business, technologization of production and much more. There are studies of ethics and food choice (Singer & Mason, 2006) and foodies and foodscapes (Johnston & Baumann, 2010; Mikkelsen, 2011; Yasmeen, 2006). As Mohr and Hosen put it, 'food is an element of social identity and cultural capital' (2014, p. 101). According to Belasco (2008), however, much of this focus has been on topics such as nutrition and malnutrition, agriculture, marketing, the gendered nature of food labour and so forth, rather than on the cultural meanings of food. As he suggests, there are a number of reasons for this focus, including a gendered hierarchy of (male) public production over (female) private consumption, a sense that cooking and eating are trivial matters and that, like language, food is so mundane and pervasive, its meanings are taken for granted.

The cultural turn towards the body, materiality, situatedness and discourse, however, has opened up a range of other concerns to do with food. When we eat, suggests Probyn (2000),

> we grapple with concerns about the animate and the inanimate, about authenticity and sincerity, about changing familial patterns, about the local and the global, about whether sexual and alimentary predilections tell us anything about ourselves, about colonial legacies of the past for those of us who live in stolen lands, about whether we are eating or being eaten.
>
> (p. 3)

Food, suggests Probyn, is also an encounter with gender, sexuality and identity since the 'hands-on encounter with food' in its preparation and consumption 'connects us with surfaces, textures, tastes, smells, insides and outsides' (2000, p. 60). More importantly for this book, it is the connection between food and ethnicity, of the particular eating practices of different communities and of the availability in urban spaces of a multiplicity of *ethnic* restaurants and the practices of 'eating the other' that are of interest to us.

'Eating the other' is a phrase Hage (1997) uses to differentiate 'culinary cosmo-multiculturalism'– those inner-city experiences of cosmopolitan consumption where people dine out on 'ethnic food' – from the multiculturalism of the home – where 'home-building' may be constructed around the preparation of particular dishes representative of certain migrant community cultures. *Eating out* can be located in the context of hospitality (see Derrida & Dufourmantelle, 2000) or more broadly in how we understand social relations as played out in the social spaces of bars, restaurants and cafés in the city. The 'hospitable city' as Bell (2007, p. 8) puts it, welcomes guests through its 'diurnal flow of visitors who come into the city' to partake of the commercial hospitality on offer in its bars, restaurants, cafés and clubs. While we might prefer to interpret such interaction more in terms of economic transaction than as a form of hospitality, Bell argues that

> the ways of relating that are practiced in bars, cafés, restaurants, clubs and pubs should be seen as potentially productive of an ethics of conviviality that revitalizes urban living. The encounters in those spaces should, therefore, be reinstalled in discussions of the ethics and politics of hospitality.
>
> (p. 12)

As the discussion in Chapter 5 highlighted, however, conviviality needs always to be set against the questions of rights and contestation – of who gets to eat out, who can afford to do so, who is allowed into the pub or kicked out of the club, as well as the questions around the workforce providing such hospitality: gendered, poorly paid, insecure, working difficult schedules. When *eating out* is also a practice of *eating the other*, we need to understand such culinary practices in the context of the politics of multiculturalism. Like Noble's (2009, pp. 49–50) shift of attention to the significance of 'being together', of the 'local but not enclosed relations of intercommunal practice', the examples we are focusing on in this chapter fall into that space where eating out and eating at home intersect, focusing particularly on talking about and around food in the workplace. These are the decisive moments in which metrolingual practices are produced through talking and sharing food as people of varied backgrounds rub up against each other in the everyday.

If food is central to human life, so is language, and the two intersect at several crucial junctures: We come together to eat and talk; those occasions when silence accompanies food are the remarkable exceptions. When talk is banned at mealtimes, it is often either for religious reasons – religious orders that have taken a vow of silence (some Belgian beers are brewed in silence by Trappist monks) – or as part of familial or patriarchal rule (Stravinsky forbad his family from speaking over lunch lest his composing mind were disturbed; Modjeska, 1999). We talk about food. We watch cooking shows on TV – indeed there is now a Cooking Channel devoted to food preparation – and *Master Chef, The Naked Chef, Iron Chef, Yan Can Cook* and the many celebrity chefs (Jamie Oliver, Gordon Ramsay, Nigella Lawson, Julia Child, Martian and Stephen Yan) combine food and talk in intriguing mixtures (even if, in Gordon 'It's enough to make anyone turn fucking vegetarian' Ramsay's case, this seems mainly to constitute swearing at staff[2]). As a study of Jamie Oliver and Nigella Lawson's food shows suggests, what matters in these shows may not be so much the food and the possibility of cooking it as the performance and the talk, which may vary from the 'self-assured, chipper, working-class Jamie' to the 'sensual and classy Nigella' (Chiaro, 2013, p. 101).

Since much of group belonging is constructed discursively, and since the sharing of food – commensality – is also a crucial part of social and cultural solidarity, 'discourse about food is actually doubly constructive of belonging' (Karrebæk, 2012, p. 2). Observing two school children of different cultural and culinary backgrounds swapping lunch between beef sausages and curry puffs, Noble argues '(i)t is the exchange itself that is significant' (2009, p. 58): the act of sharing has 'a broader recognition of the social and cultural importance of food in creating cultural meaning, social bonds and senses of personal identity'. Of course, as the previous chapter indicated, conversations over different lunchboxes may equally be a site of contestation. The Australian comedy *Legally Brown* (2013) captures this nicely in a skit reversing the common trend to mock the 'smelly' food some people bring from home: Here two 'Asian' men on a construction site ask a White guy to open his lunch box and mock his stinky white-bread sandwiches: 'What're you having for lunch?' [reaches over and opens White guy's lunch box] 'Paw,' [waves hand in front of nose] 'bread. Aw, stinks.' As Mohr and Hosen (2014, p. 102) put it, 'Food choices can therefore be divisive, when different dietary regimes are taken to represent essential elements of social identity, for instance when obesity and bad diet are related to moral failings, or when halal food is related to terrorism'.

Talk about food, and especially the processes of mealtime socialization (Ochs & Shohet, 2006; Paugh & Izquierdo, 2009) can also strongly influence how we understand the food we eat. From moral discourses about healthy eating ('eat your greens') or eating what you are given ('eat what's on your plate'), or more sensual discourses about the pleasure of tastes and smells, we are thus socialized into ways of eating and drinking, and into ways of thinking about what we eat and drink through table and kitchen talk. As Karrebæk's (2012) research shows, since 'food practices are used to construct, demonstrate and interpret individuals' affiliation to social communities' (p. 3), discourses about what counts as healthy food, particularly in the context of immigration and school lunchboxes, become a site of not only food, but also health and moral regulation.

Despite the obvious and deep connections between talk and food, little research has been done on talk about food in the workplace (Holmes, Marra & King, 2013); and yet, in their own analysis of workplace discourse, Holmes *et al.* note that 'food makes a contribution similar to that of other aspects of relational workplace interaction, such as humor, small talk and narrative' (p. 205). Likewise, we have elsewhere noted the importance of talk about food, or more particularly drink, in

Australian workplace settings (Otsuji & Pennycook, 2010; 2014). Holmes *et al.* found that food talk tended to occur at the boundaries of interactions (at the beginning and end of meetings, for example), and may be deliberately deployed to mark boundaries, build rapport or lessen formality, though it also seemed to generate problems and discomfort if it became a formal topic of meetings. Our research differs from that of Holmes *et al.* in several ways: Their focus is on mainstream *Pakeha* (White New Zealander) interactions around meetings in the workplace, whereas our focus is on the relations between food and metrolingualism in informal workplace contexts. By focusing on those informal spaces such as construction site lunches, restaurant lunches or serving and selling food, furthermore, we have drawn into our ambit the commensal space of eating together that is neither commercialized (restaurants, cafés etc.) nor domesticated (having people over) nor family or community based (a family BBQ in the park), but rather is a space of work commensality.

Our interest in talk and food in the workplace, furthermore, looks at such commensality as a critical site of metrolingual interaction: This is about the city, the foods that come together in the city and the language that occurs over, about and alongside shared meals. As we saw in the previous example, while this may involve the rough language of the workplace – '*Kod nas fanta zelena jebote. Zuta, zuta. Pa uzmi*' (No thank you. Back home Fanta is green fuck it. Yellow, yellow. Take it) – this lunchtime conversation involves not only, for example, a casual blending of Serbian and English, but also sharing of food, talk about food, markers of identity (back home Fanta is green) and a sense of 'being together' by crossing culinary borders. Marko, Drago and Nemia's supervisor, Vukasin, explains this in the following excerpt.

Excerpt 6.2: (V: Vukasin, R: Researcher)
1. V: Yeah. Again, different cultures, different things. It's always, always interesting. When we have breaks, you will see all different food from different countries. So it's interesting. It's quite different.
2. R: Do you talk with them during the break?
3. V: Of course, yes, and we try each other's food.

Food is often 'assumed to bridge cultural gaps. It is a universal need and desire that can be shared between cultures, even overcoming linguistic differences' (Mohr & Hosen, 2014, p. 102).

In the following example, again at lunchtime in the construction site in the same basement as in excerpt 6.1, Drago is eating *moussaka*, which has been made by his girlfriend of Macedonian background. The question of whether it is traditional Serbian/Macedonian food triggers a quick history lesson from Marko.

Excerpt 6.3: (D: Drago, M: Marko, R: Researcher)
1. D: Yeah. I think this is something like a traditional food. I'm not sure. Marko?
2. M: What's that, sorry?

3. D: Moussaka. It's traditional food, or?
4. M: I think it's ... maybe it's Turkish?
5. D: Turkish?
6. M: Yeah! Moussaka.
7. R: Moussaka! Ah ... Moussaka is with mashed potato, no?
8. M: Yeah, my mum makes that every now and then.
9. R: Yeah?
10. M: Yeah. Moussaka. Moussaka.
11. R: It's Turkish?
12. M: Yeah, that was ... ah ... some parts of all Yugoslavia back in I don't know how many hundreds years ago were under the Turkey, for ... five hundred years. Yeah, and then, we got a lot of their words as ... not a lot ... a few words
13. D: A lot, a lot.
14. M: A lot! Yeah? A few words that they use, a lot of foods that ... coffee for example, short black.

Moussaka was one of those food items – like cucumbers (see Chapter 7) – that seemed to keep turning up in our data: *Moussaka* appears on the menu in *Carthago* (see Chapter 3) in Nakano, Tokyo, as a Turkish dish (*Patlican musakka*[3]) as well as on the menu in *Patris* pizzeria in Sydney owned by a second-generation Greek migrant. Here Marko gives a quick history of the Ottoman Empire to explain how this food and word became relocalized in parts of Yugoslavia, in response to Drago's request for confirmation in line 3 whether *moussaka* is a traditional food of the region. While this clarification of the origin of *moussaka* can be related both to establishing and complexifying ethnic identity (*moussaka* is traditional Serbian food brought by the Turks), his explanation of the introduction of coffee (line 14), meanwhile, also places this squarely back in Australia, with his use of the Australian English 'short black' instead of the more common global/Italian term *espresso*. The mobility of markers of local identification (Noble, 2009) can be observed in this brief conversation: from Macedonia, to Turkey and the Ottoman Empire and to Australia. In this commensal space in the basement of a construction site (very literally metrolingualism from below), people share not only food and space through seemingly mundane culinary practices but also rework their everyday cultural and regional affiliations.

'Makanai des pauvres'

Excerpt 6.4 (Na: Nabil, R: Researcher)
Japanese: *italics*; French: **bold** (translations in brackets)
[Setting up the table for the regular staff lunch (*makanai*) at *Petit Paris*, Nabil jokes]
1. Na: This is a poor *makanai*.
2. R: e::? Poor *makanai*?
3. Na: Yes ... *Makanai* **des pauvres** ça. (Poor people's Makanai, this.)

Playing with the Japanese word for a staff meal in Japanese, *makanai,* Nabil refers to their lunch as 'poor *makanai*' (first in English) and then in a slight variant as '*Makanai* **des pauvres ça**'. The '**ça**' (this) in sentence-final position, the tendency away from word-final stress in words such as **appétit** or bolognaise (see below), the raised vowels in such words and the use of apical (front) [r] rather than uvular [R] are all common in Maghrebi styles of French (Sayahi, 2014). These features, as well as other aspects of his French, also cross into his ways of speaking English and Japanese and, as we observed in Chapter 4, his ways of speaking Japanese, especially in the fast-paced metrolingual multi-tasking in the restaurant, also influence his use of English and French.

Makanai in Japanese is lunch prepared with the leftover ingredients available in the kitchen, and here Nabil explains this dish of spaghetti is a very ordinary affair. Makanai in *Petit Paris*, however, is often far from 'poor *makanai*' since it may be used as an occasion to try out new dishes for future menu items. On a separate occasion Nabil explains that '*makanai* is the appraisal space for a dish. We can check how the food is grilled, if it's suitable for the dish, and the quality of ingredients. It is more effective than cooking something separately for a trial' (Takano, 2012, p. 139, our translation). Thus, the staff eat, share plates and talk about the quality of the dishes. So here, unlike the basement lunch, the commensality has a more specific focus on the food.

Petit Paris offers lunch (11:30–15:00) and dinner (17:30–2:00). In between, Nabil, the chef and other staff eat *makanai,* walk around the area, smoke outside the restaurant or rest in a stock room in the next building. The two hours between is the time that they rejuvenate after the buzz during the lunch hour and get ready for the evening shift. The day excerpt 6.5 was recorded, spaghetti bolognaise (a mundane dish for Nabil, hence '*Makanai* **des pauvres ça**') is being served, and a bottle of wine has been placed on the table. The researcher has joined Nabil, Stéphane (floor staff), Chef (Patrick) and Hata-san (the Japanese manager) at the table.

Excerpt 6.5: (Na: Nabil, S: Stéphane, C: Chef, R: Researcher)
Japanese *italics;* French: **bold** (translations in brackets)
1. Na: **Bon appétit.** (enjoy your meal.)
2. S: **Bon appétit.**
3. Na: We have a pasta:: bolognaise.
4. R: hmmm *mainichi*? (everyday?)
5. Na: no no no everyday … can't … Of course *mainichi ja nai* (not everyday) Depend depend the **humeur** (mood) of chef.
6. R: ah Chef … *wa tabenaino*? [To chef] You are not … *tabenaino*? (Chef is not eating? You are not … not eating?)
7. Na: Chef eat ahm from nine until three he eat. At three we start to eat, he stop. **J'ai dis que vous mangez de neuf heures à quinze heures.** (I said you eat from nine o'clock to 3 o'clock.) [laughter]
8. C: *Go ji.* (five o'clock.)
9. R: *Go ji*? (five o'clock?)
10. Na: He prefer after.

Nabil has only one day off on Tuesdays and because of the long working hours, he does not have much time to spend with his daughter, Rami (about one year old at the time) and his Japanese wife, Narumi. *Makanai* break time is, therefore, also the time that Narumi and Rami visit *Petit Paris* to spend time together as a family. At this time of the day, the dynamics and rhythms change again as the space/floor turns into the intersection of professional, social, family and recuperative (private) space during the lunch time. Here, in the downtime at *Petit Paris*, we see the different rhythms (see Chapter 3) of the restaurant world, with lunch for staff taken between the lunch of the restaurant and the start of evening preparations. The cook, who Nabil jokingly suggests has been eating while cooking from nine in the morning till three in the afternoon, joins them at the table for their 'poor people's lunch' but doesn't eat, preferring to have something as he starts work again at 5 p.m.

This commensal space is a mixed one, combining work (discussing meals, cooking, new dishes), social and family talk, mingling French, English and Japanese, and merging both a Japanese emphasis on eating together in the workplace (*makanai*) as well as a French orientation towards lunch as a relaxed and communal space for eating and talking. Although it shares in a number of ways similar qualities of rapid language mixing described elsewhere (Chapters 1 and 4) in terms of metrolingual multitasking, here the mood is relaxed and the deployment of language resources more constrained. Yet, while the researcher uses informal Japanese to the chef ('*tabanaino*?'), Nabil nonetheless uses the more polite **vous** form (**'vous mangez'**). Without the customers and the hectic pace of cooking and serving, the space has changed, the spatial repertoire has shifted. Yet *Petit Paris* maintains a space of perpetual multiplicity culturally, linguistically, socially and professionally. This parallels a lunch time break in the basement of the construction site where Vukasin visits the site during the break, Nemia calls his friends in Fiji, Marko tells Nemia about his fight with his wife the previous night over a shower panel and Marko sings a traditional Serbian folk song while waiting for Drago to bring back chicken kebabs and chips from the corner shop.

'*Ma fi* fruit *bi nom*? (There's no fruit at all?)'

Food becomes part of metrolingual practices across multiple domains: growing, buying, cooking, eating, sharing and talking about and around food. Other spaces of food talk are more functional than the shared lunches of workers; market talk around food, for example, being generally about prices and quantities. Amid the busy early morning trading at the Produce Market (see Chapter 1), there are the usual switches from dealing with customers in English and greeting other Arabic speakers, the comments about other workers (see Chapter 5), the shouted orders to workers, the negotiated prices and the urgent instructions.

Excerpt 6.6: (T: Talib, M: a male passerby, C: a customer)

Arabic: *italics;* English: plain (translations in brackets)

1. T: Here. I dunno, ask my brother. *Assalamu alaykum.* (Peace be upon you.)
2. M: *Wa alakum assalam wa rahmat allahi wa baraku.*
    (And may the peace, mercy and blessings of God be upon you.)
3. T: *Ma indna ilal halabeh byishteghloo endna.*
    (We only have the incompetent working here.)
4. T: *Hada dollar wa noos endeef.* (That's $1.50, clean.)

[various exchanges and pause]

5. T: That bloke wanted half a box of bananas, doesn't matter, just give it to him. … *Tamana, Tamana* (eight, eight)… *Or lak tnan elhabeh kabira badok yahoon?* (Or look there's two. The fruit is big do you want them?)
6. C: *Mabaref.* (I don't know.)
7. T: *Wal sita endaf.* (And the six are clean.) … You right mate? Limes? Yeah. Thirty-six. Thirty-six bucks.
8. C: Thirty-six? That's the price? You got anything cheaper, or?
9. T: No that's it. Thirty-five doesn't matter, but … [noise/chatter] Get those two lemons from over there. No, no, two lemons. Lemons. Far. Come on Saleh man. It doesn't matter. Just behind them. Doesn't matter.

The use of Arabic and English, use of different styles of both, artefacts being bought and sold, importance of the space (with greetings intended for passing others: lines 1 and 2), directions to others to fetch produce ('Get those two lemons from over there. No, no, two lemons. Lemons': line 9) and the negotiations over fruit and price (*Or 'lak tnan elhabeh kabira badok yahoon?'* [Or look there's two. The fruit is big do you want them?: line 5] '*Mabaref*' [I don't know: line 6]) are all part of the metrolingual multitasking and spatial repertoire of this part of the market. Sometimes the style and speed change from these fast-paced, shouted exchanges. When a woman comes too late to get any strawberries, the tone is softer, more jocular.

Excerpt 6.7: (F: Female customer, T: Talib)

Arabic: *italics;* English: plain (translations in brackets)

1. F: *Ma fi* fruit *bi nom*? (There's no fruit at all?)
2. T: [laughing] *la.* (no.)
3. F: *Alwahid byistahli.* (A person craves.)

[various exchanges with others]

4. F: *Maba' andak frez?* (You don't have any more strawberries?)
5. T: *La wallah.* (No, I swear.)

Amid the frenetic shouting and bartering, this female customer makes a slightly different plea to see if there might still be some strawberries (*frez* – cf French *fraises*) after all. Talib laughs and replies with the fairly blunt '*la*'(no) in line 2. Yet when she asks again, with the more poetic '*Alwahid byistahli*' (a person craves) and then '*Maba' andak frez?'* (You don't have any more strawberries?), Talib softens his tone with the common Arabic phrase '*La wallah'* (No, I swear [by God]) by way of reply. *Wallah,* or *Wallahi* as Ayoola (2009) also notes in the context of Yoruba speakers in a Lagos market – even those speaking Nigerian pidgin with a customer: 'Wallahi, nobody go answer you for this market!' (I swear, no one will attend to you in this market!) (p. 398) – is a common term to convince customers that one is telling the truth.

Such appeals to truth are common in market discourse: In the market discussed in Chapter 8, we also find repeated claims to the voracity of the sales pitch: '真係 (honestly)… 真係㗎,唔係呃你' (Honestly. I'm not lying to you). Here, however, the particular overtones of *Wallah* – swearing by Allah – locate the absence of fruit in a different discursive field. Such style shifts within Arabic, from the brusque functionality of the usual Arabic and English exchanges to this more congenial exchange, are occasioned it seems by the less common presence of a woman in this space (her role as a customer, as we have seen, does not necessarily engender politeness), her desire for strawberries and the language in which she pleads. Such style-shifting, therefore, involves interpersonal relations, the space and the colour and taste of fruit.

Red celery and the negotiation of meaning

Much is made in discussions of these kinds of multilingual to-ing and fro-ing of negotiation. Canagarajah (2013) identifies four different 'translingual negotiation strategies': *envoicing*, 'What mix of language resources to mesh, and where and when, involves strategic choices'(p. 80); *recontextualization,* people 'have to frame their talk in ways conducive to uptake and achieve the appropriate footing for meaning negotiation' (p. 80); *interactional*, the ways in which 'interlocutors adopt strategies that complement and/or resist those of the other for negotiation of meaning or rhetorical and social objectives' (p. 82); and *entextualization*, the ways 'speakers and writers monitor and manage their productive processes by exploiting spatiotemporal dimensions of the text' (p. 84). Clearly we could use such a framework to classify some aspects of the interactions already discussed here and elsewhere, showing how Nabil or Talib choose their language resources, frame what they have to say in relation to who they are talking to, make changes according to the dynamics of the conversation and control textual resources in various ways.

Nonetheless, we differ in our approach in various ways (aside from Canagarajah's focus on lingua franca English in multilingual contexts as opposed to our interest in multilingual contexts whether English is present or not), since our aim is not to classify but to diversify our understandings of metrolingual understandings, and our data seem to suggest a slightly less agentive approach to communication is needed: Interlocutors draw from the personal and spatial repertoires around them and in interaction with other people, objects and space, and in so doing, may not always operate in the strategic ways suggested. Above all, however, we also wish to draw attention to the ways in which interactions don't always work: In the rapid metrolingual multitasking of workplaces, language comes and goes, people interact, swear, turn away, do something else, and often it's not clear that meaning ever is established. An example comes from New Year's Eve in *Petit Paris*.

Excerpt 6.8 (Na: Nabil, C: Customer)

Japanese: *italics*; (translations in brackets)
[Nabil brings a dessert dish to a regular customer seated on his own at the counter chatting with the chef and other staff (from other conversations with Nabil, he appears connected to Italian food or restaurants)]

1. Na: *Kore … mashu serori. Ni serori.* (This … mashed celery. Celery stew.)
2. C: *Ni serori.* (Celery stew)
3. Na: *Ni serori.* (Celery stew)

Here, using the Japanese words for celery (*serori* [セ ロ リ]) and stew (*ni* [煮]), Nabil and his customer appear to have arrived at a reasonable agreement about what is being served and eaten, even though a celery stew seems a slightly unlikely dish, especially as a dessert. But then the customer becomes puzzled, noticing the colour of the supposed celery stew.

Excerpt 6.9 (Na: Nabil, C: Customer)

Japanese: *italics*; French: **bold**; English: plain (translations in brackets)

1. C: *Pinku. Serori. Ehhh?* (Pink. Celery. Ehh?)
2. Na: Pink?
3. C: (…) *Serori.*
4. Na: Eh?
5. C: *Ahh*
6. Na: *Nani* **betterave** (What beetroot)
7. C: *Eh?*
8. Na: **Betterave**, no? Ahh. **Céleri rémoulade**, you know? (Beetroot, no? Ahh. Celery remoulade).

At this point things have become rather confused. Also puzzled by the pink colour, Nabil now explains that it's beetroot, using the French term, **betterave** (line 6, with his distinctive apical [r] and shift from word-final stress). The French word for beetroot does not appear to be of much help to his customer, however, and in any case, Nabil quickly (line 8) rejects this in favour of another option, *céleri rémoulade,* a common dish using grated celery root (also known as celeriac) and a remoulade sauce (a mayonnaise-based sauce also used to accompany fish). *Céleri rémoulade* is a common dish (a cousin in some ways to coleslaw), which might also be served with other *crudités* (traditional French appetizer), such as beetroot, hence possibly the connections for Nabil between the pink dish he has served, celery and beetroot. But a celery remoulade seems unlikely (it is a fairly ordinary dish even for a bistro, and in any case it's neither pink nor a dessert).

There is no obvious relation between his two offerings (*céleri rémoulade* and beetroot) – or only to the extent that they might both be part of a plate of *crudités* – nor between either of these and the dish he has served, especially as dessert. Not surprisingly, the customer continues in confused persistence.

Excerpt 6.10 (Na: Nabil, C: Customer)
Japanese: *italics*; French: **bold**; English: plain (translations in brackets)
1. C: *Pinku pinku pinku kore … Serori serori serori serori.* (pink pink pink this … celery, celery, celery, celery)
2. Na: *Pinku?* (pink?)
3. C: *Pinku pinku* (pink pink)
4. Na: *Pinku::* (pinnnk)
5. C: (??)
6. Na: Ahh.
7. C: *Serori serori serori* (celery celery celery)
8. Na: **Céleri rouge?** (Red celery?)
9. C: no no.
10. Na: [Referring to another customer's question about his meal] *Chicchai? Koko?* … Sorry? *Koko?* (Small? This? … Sorry? This?)
11. Na: Chef! Chef! **C'est quoi céleri rouge en France**? (What's red celery in France?)
12. Na: [referring to the other customer's query about the size of the portion he has been served] **Il dit c'est grand.** (He says it's big.)

Here, while as always dealing with several things at once (a comment by another customer about the size of a dish), and using his array of linguistic resources, Nabil finally seems to sense something is wrong with both celery and beetroot as descriptors of the dish. Recognizing the customer's confusion, Nabil accommodates with a more Japanese sounding '*pinku*' and even the exaggerated version '*pinku::*' (lines 2 and 3) by inserting a vowel after the consonant. The word 'pink', which occurs in both English and Japanese [ピンク], and is pronounced in this data section in both styles, is another of those terms that seems to hover between languages. Here Nabil clearly attempts to accommodate to his customer with his extra emphasis on the final vowel of *Pinku::*. In response to the customer's rejection of Nabil's attempt to convince him that it is **céleri rouge**, he then turns to the chef (line 10) to ask what 'red celery' (**céleri rouge**) is in French/France. After a brief pause, both cooks (Patrick: chef 1 and Pierre: chef 2) chime in with 'rhubarb'.

Excerpt 6.11 (Na: Nabil, Ch1: Chef1, Ch2: Chef 2)
French: **bold** (translations in brackets)
1. Ch1: **Ah! Rhubarbe!**
2. Na: **Rhubarbe! Rhubarbe!**
3. Ch2: **Rhubarbe.**
4. Na: **Ahh rhubarbe. Ahh rhubarbe. C'est pas céleri. Oui oui rhubarbe.** (It's not celery. Yes yes rhubarb.)

At first sight, the ability of the cook to correctly decode Nabil's question about 'red celery' is a remarkable piece of interpretation: **Céleri rouge**/red celery is not a very obvious term for rhubarb (red celery does in fact exist in its own right as a type of celery). At second glance, however, we might suggest that the cooks' quick interpretation here has been assisted by the fact that they prepared the rhubarb dish to start with, and may also have overheard some of this confused conversation. Rather than translating **céleri rouge** as **rhubarbe** with only linguistic clues, they have worked out that Nabil's odd question about red celery in fact refers to the rhubarb tart he has just passed to the customer. The spatial arrangements, cooking practices, and spatial repertoire contribute here to the naming of this red dish.

Now that the missing term **rhubarbe** has finally been established, Nabil turns to the cook, Pierre (chef 2) to ask if he knows what the Japanese for rhubarb is since it is not clear that **rhubarbe** – like the earlier and mistaken **betterave** – has clarified things for the customer: '**Rhubarbe**, *nihongo wa*. **J'ai oublié. Pierre**?' (Rhubarb, in Japanese, I've forgotten, Pierre?).

Nabil's Japanese question ('*nihongo wa'*) is taken up by the other chef, Patrick. Pierre by then has moved onto another task.

Excerpt 6.12 (Na: Nabil, C: Customer, Ch1: Chef1)
Japanese: *italics*; French: **bold;** English: plain (translations in brackets)
1. Ch1: **Rhubarbe** nihongo no namae:: (Rhubarb in Japane::se)
2. C: *Serori. Serori.* (celery. celery.)
3. Na: No no no.
4. Ch1: *Aka serori*? (Red celery?)
5. C: *Serori serori.*
6. Na: *Nihongo wa*? (In Japanese?)
7. C: *Nihongo mo serori.* (Also celery in Japanese.)
8. Na: *Ahh honto desu ka*? (Ah really?) *Aka-serori*? (red celery?)
9. C: *Serori.*

While the customer continues almost to chant his confused '*Serori*' refrain in the background – he does not appear to have picked up on the revelation that it is in fact rhubarb – the chef tries to recall the Japanese for rhubarb, and offers, a little uncertainly, a Japanese translation (line 4) – *aka-serori* (red celery) – of Nabil's earlier **céleri rouge** (red celery). Nabil, apparently not picking up on the customer's continued chanting of '*Serori*' and assuming instead that the customer now knows this is in fact rhubarb, asks him to confirm the chef's '*aka-serori*' (red celery) (line 6), getting the reply in line 7 that it's the same in Japanese. The customer, however, who is still puzzling over the idea of celery, appears to be commenting only that the word for celery is more or less the same in English or French and Japanese. But Nabil appears to think that he has received confirmation of his cook's claim that the Japanese for rhubarb is *aka-serori* (line 8).

So finally, although Nabil has finally worked out what it is he has served the customer – rhubarb tart – he now appears to believe that rhubarb is *aka-serori* in

Japanese (not commonly known, the term ルバーブ [rubābu] would be used). Fortunately, they return to the safer ground of discussing the taste.

Excerpt 6.13 (Na: Nabil, C: Customer)

Japanese: *italics*; French: **bold**; English: plain (translations in brackets)

1. Na: *Aa, soo. Tarto sugoi oishii desho?* (Ah, right. The tart is really tasty, isn't it?)
2. C: *Oishii. Kore oishii.* (Tasty. This tastes good)
3. Na: **Tarte à la rhubarbe. C'est très très bon.** (Rhubarb tart. It's very, very good.)

Although from the outside we can work out more or less what is going on, and although we can see various multilingual strategies at work, they generally misfire, with a number of terms – **betterave**, *aka serori* – not registering with some of the participants; with Nabil suggesting terms in French that don't seem to make much sense (from **céleri rouge** to **céleri rémoulade,**) and now possibly believing that *aka-serori* is the Japanese for rhubarb (which it isn't), and the customer still confused (though happy enough with the dish). Such is the way that meaning gets negotiated across and against languages. Finally, Nabil settles the interaction both by returning to a discussion of the taste of the food, and by employing his subtle metrolingual accommodation strategies, where in the first line in Japanese, 'tart' is made more Japanese with its added ending '*tarto sugoi oishii desho?*' and then uses the capital afforded by French and referring to French cuisine: '**Tarte à la rhubarbe. C'est très très bon**'.

There are several implications of this exchange. It should come as no surprise that the negotiation of meaning in metrolingual contexts may be unsuccessful, or partially successful, or just remain rather foggy (it is New Year's Eve, after all). The particular foods under discussion also clearly play an important mediating role here: they are part of the action. Such foods and tastes not only mean different things to the participants as they move in and around their attempts to establish what is on the plate, but they also have very different meanings according to the different culinary backgrounds of participants. Rhubarb is an 'exotic' vegetable (or perhaps a fruit, depending on how it is cooked) in Japan and therefore has a very different meaning to how it may be understood in France. This customer, however, who is also in the restaurant industry, is persistently curious about the ingredient of the dessert dish. In the same way that the origin of the *moussaka* matters and generates the conversation during the lunchtime conversation in the basement (Excerpt 6.3), identification of the unfamiliar 'foreign' ingredient matters in the conversation. The mobility of ingredients and meanings and people and linguistic resources thus come together in this place as part of its spatial repertoire. These combinations of food and talk are essential ingredients of metrolingual practices.

Relocalization

This multidimensional relocalization of rhubarb in *Petit Paris* – as ingredient, as dish, as *aka serori* (red celery) – brings us to the ways in which food and language are reworked in different places. Like the lunchtime *moussaka* discussed earlier – cooked by Macedonians in Australia, but introduced to Macedonia through its proximity to Turkey and Greece (like the Serbian term *vala* (вала -'wave'), derived via the Ottoman Empire from the Arabic *Wallah* (I swear) used by Talib in Excerpt 6.7) – these foods and their linguistic labels, the way they are cooked and eaten, and the way they are discussed, invoke histories of mobility. For *Petit Paris*, these patterns of relocalization – where elements of Algerian life are transplanted via Paris in Tokyo, and where different culinary and linguistic elements intertwine – occur along lines of connection that reflect the long histories of colonialism, postcolonial relations and migration. When Nabil organizes a '*Soirée Couscous au Petit Paris*' (クスクスパーティ) – featuring *couscous agneau et merguez* (couscous with lamb and *merguez*, a spicy North African sausage now also common in France and elsewhere) – as part of the repertoire of a French restaurant in Tokyo, this may reflect not so much his own Algerian background as that history that has made *couscous* a common part of French cuisine.

Just as the Dutch enjoy a *rijsttafel* ('rice table', a meal consisting of many small dishes based on Sumatran *nasi padang*), so curry has seeped into British cuisine and been relocated and reinvented. The most famous example is *chicken tikka masala*, described by former British Foreign Secretary Robin Cook as

> a true British national dish, not only because it is the most popular, but because it is a perfect illustration of the way Britain absorbs and adapts external influences. Chicken Tikka is an Indian dish. The Massala [sic] sauce was added to satisfy the desire of British people to have their meat served in gravy.
>
> (Robin Cook, 2001)[4]

This dish is now also served in India, especially in regions where British tourists are common. Likewise, couscous has become a staple part of French food: As the owners of *Carthago* suggested (Chapter 3), like *curry rice* (カレーライス) in Japan, *couscous* is an everyday, casual, domesticated food. As the chef puts it, part of his motivation for opening the restaurant – which Nabil calls 'the couscous restaurant' from the time when he used to eat there regularly – was to reproduce the *couscous* and Northern African food that he used to eat every day when he was living in Paris (he used to live in a Tunisian precinct and the cook in the school canteen was Algerian). On their menu they use *Cousksi* rather than *couscous* with the explanation '*Cousksi* はチュニジアの発音表記' (*Cousksi* is a phonetic description of a Tunisian word). From *kesksu* in Berber, to *cousksi* in Tunisian Arabic, to *couscous* in French, this food now comes to represent Frenchness in a Tokyo restaurant.

These processes of relocalization, however, are far more complex than the mere domestication of food, involving the deliberate and casual recombinations of histories, signs and locations. *Petit Paris* is located in Kagurazaka, renowned for its mixture of old traditional Tokyo and French culture. The establishment of l'Institut Franco-Japonais de Tokyo and the Lycée Franco-Japonais de Tokyo's primary section[5] brought French food, language and people to this area. The small, sloping cobbled streets dating from the Edo (seventeenth to nineteenth century) period are often said to recall Montmartre in Paris (Tauzin, 2009). Nabil, the owner of *Petit Paris*, was born in the small city of Tipaza in Algeria (made famous, in part, by Albert Camus' *Noces à Tipasa*: Camus himself was a displaced *pied noir* with his own complex relation to colonial history, different again from his fellow French Algerian, Jacques Derrida) to a Moroccan mother and an Algerian father. At the age of about 16, he moved to Paris where he worked in various restaurants.

Like the Italian pizzeria run by a Greek migrant in Sydney, with its Polish and Nepalese cooks, Thai and Indian floor staff, such restaurants are part of the remaking of space and neighbourhood, as 'France', 'Paris' and 'Italy' are relocalized and reproduced through the traffic of people, linguistic resources and cultural artefacts. This relocalization is achieved by the 'throwntogetherness, the unavoidable challenge of negotiating a here-and-now (itself drawing on a history and a geography of thens and theres); and a negotiation which must take place within and between both human and nonhuman' (Massey, 2005, p. 140). Thus, what constitutes *Petit Paris* in Tokyo is this complex historical (postcolonial) and geographical coming together of people, language and objects ('non-humans'). The logo (Image 6.1) shows elements of 'throwntogetherness' that go into the making of the 'wine bazar', *Petit Paris*.

Image 6.1 Petit Paris logo.

Nabil notes that while one element was to 'make this logo with a spoon and a fork and a glass and a bottle of wine', the idea of the bazaar (here playfully combined with 'bar' as 'bazar') is also a reference to his home town of Tipaza in Algeria: 'This city, between us, people from Tipaza, we call it bazaar. [...] Old memory, nice memory from my life. From France, from Algeria, everything.' Ludic multimodality can also be observed in the two Ps made with a spoon, fork, wine glass and a bottle that resembles the first character in 巴里 (Paris) in Japanese characters. The complex process by which *Petit Paris* is produced thus leaves open the question of which trajectories and mobilities are at play here as we move from Tipaza to Paris, to *Petit Paris* and Kagurazaka. In this space a range of different meanings of Paris, Tipaza and Kagurazaka are all interacting as the restaurant goes through its busy day.

During the two years of our observations, the staff comprised a number of chefs (Jean: from France, worked in Cuba, Lebanon, Italy and Greece as a chef before moving to Tokyo 11 years ago; Pierre: from Réunion, lived in Paris before coming to Tokyo; and more recently chefs from Montreal and Togo), a Japanese manager from Tokyo and two floor staff (Nabil and Stéphane: French background, born in Côte d'Ivoire and grew up in Morocco and New York as a child, his early mobility a result of his father's job with Renault). In an interview with the writer Takano, Nabil explained: 'プチ・パリという名前を背負っているので、今後もスタッフはフランス人かフランス語圏の人にしたい' (Because it carries the name Petit Paris, I want to keep having French or French speaking staff) (Takano, 2012, pp. 145–146; our translation). The linguistic, cultural and gastronomic coming-together at *Petit Paris* thus entails a complex traffic and interaction of multiple trajectories, temporalities, historicities and mobilities, linking the postcolonial Francophone world rather than referring to an imagined immobile Paris. Like the 'circuits of flow' in hip hop that connect Marseille, Dakar and Montreal (Pennycook, 2007), these trajectories are often tied to the postcolonial in and around language, so that this restaurant in Tokyo with its '*Soirée Couscous*' has staff who can maintain the Francophone ambience Nabil wants to create, but whose trajectories draw together Algeria, Réunion, Côte d'Ivoire, Montreal and Togo.

A few blocks away from *Petit Paris*, a chicken rotisserie, *Yves Terrace* – described by its owner, Yves, as a 'casual French café' – has a different philosophy. Unlike Nabil's Francophone-oriented selection criteria for staff, Yves seems more relaxed about the staff selection: 'フランス語しゃべってから働いていいよじゃなくて、何か友達の紹介で' (not because you speak French you can work here, but it's like ... my friends' introductions). According to Yves, people speak in whatever language comes to mind – English, French, Japanese – and although Japanese is the main language of the kitchen, it is not uncommon for Japanese staff to pick up some French (cf Chapter 4). Being West African (Yves is originally from Togo, but studied rotisserie cooking while in Paris), he does not serve couscous but instead presents dishes from West African countries such as Ghana, Benin, Togo and Senegal. Here, African dishes are relocalized under the name of a casual French café, providing a diversity of possibilities of 'French-ness' in Kagurazaka.

Meanwhile, *Maison Bretonne* (in Sasazuka), with its smell of *crêpes* and *galettes* (*crêpes* made from buckwheat), Breton music, the heavy rustic door relocated from a country house in Brittany, a picture of a lighthouse in the middle of wild seas, works a different kind of relocation. Owned by Denis, the *crêpier*, born and bred in Bretagne and his Japanese wife, Eriko, who studied cooking in Belgium for three years, the focus here is often on the sea and climate of Brittany. When the weather is gloomy, Eriko often writes on the restaurant Facebook page that it reminds her of Brittany, and continues '手軽なブリターニュは笹塚にあります' (Bretagne is accessible in Sasazuka), suggesting customers come and have coffee and crêpes in such inclement times (Image 6.2):

> A sudden rain, I can almost hear people saying 'my laundry~!' and 'they are drenched'. Well, then here is the sea of Bretagne soaked in the rain. This is a typical landscape of Bretagne and the ripples are beautiful. […] why don't you relax and have some coffee and dessert crêpe as you listen to the rain drops? Wouldn't it make you feel happy? Bretagne is accessible in Sasazuka.
> (Facebook posting from June 23, 2013; our translation)

From rural Brittany to West Africa and the Maghreb, these 'French' restaurants in Tokyo relocalize the meanings, tastes and images of France. A different orientation to this Francophone circuit is seen in the Vietnamese-run *Paris Bakery* in Marrickville, Sydney (Image 6.3). Unlike other Vietnamese bakeries in the area, it has no *bánh mì* (Vietnamese pork roll) counter but rather concentrates on French-style and Australian pastries and sweets. The owner, originally from South Vietnam – 'Saigon. Freedom. Saigon. Not the communists [laughs]' – explains that the name *Paris Bakery* comes from their French style of making croissants: 'Because in here we make the bread like the croissant like Paris, like the French-style.' She is adamant that this is different from the other Vietnamese bakeries in the area: 'No, no, they do different way. When you taste it you can tell. But our croissant is the French-style, we learned from our country.'

突然の大雨！

洗濯物が〜！とか、びしょぬれになっちゃった〜！
とか、聞こえてきそうです。

という訳で、雨に濡れるブルターニュの海。
水面を打つ雨模様が美しい、ブルターニュらしい風景
です。

コートダルモール県（Côte d'Armor)の北に浮かぶ小
さな島、ブレア島（Île de Brehat)の小さなお家。
雨の音を聞きながら、ゆっくりコーヒーとデザートク
レープを。

幸せな気持ちになれそうですね♪

あ、手軽なブルターニュは笹塚にあります☆

Image 6.2 Maison Breton Facebook page.

Image 6.3 Paris bakery.

Here, French styles of making croissants are learned in Vietnam (but only in the 'free south') and relocated to Sydney. While Nabil's *Petit Paris* (with chefs from the wider Francophone circuit) relocates already-relocated (French) couscous in his Tokyo menu, the *Paris Bakery* relocates French croissants from Saigon, where they learned how to cook them, in a Sydney suburb. These processes of relocalization, of the remaking of locality in different places, involve both prior histories of relocalization (couscous in Paris, croissants in Saigon) and the 'slippage' and 'excess' that Bhabha (1994) suggests are always part of mimicry and cultural translations. Thus as things are repeated, they are never the same: as croissants are remade in Sydney based on the south Vietnamese ways of making French pastries, their relocalization always makes them slightly different (good, nonetheless; we bought some there the other day). Just as we can never step in the same river twice (Pennycook, 2010), so the recreation of Brittany, a *couscous soirée,* a Senegalese dish, a croissant, is always a different redoing.

Multitasking and participatory research

Among the challenges we faced in gathering data for this project was the question of how to engage people, how to gain trust so that they would be happy to participate, how to dissolve those relations of the researcher and researched so that we could enter their worlds more successfully. As we suggested in Chapter 5, in order to get a chance to hear the stories of Ben's family's migration from PNG,

Wafiq's chicken story, Yama-san's account of how he established his restaurant and how he cooks *ramen,* or Igor's tragic migration from Bosnia, we had to find ways to interact with people that put them at ease. In many cases, this was a result of multiple visits, of going back again and talking and establishing a relationship, allowing us to develop long-term relations, as well as to capture a better sense of the rhythms and spatial repertoires of research sites.

A first obstacle in many contexts was the question of how and why we were interacting with people. In a busy market, for example, it was difficult to engage people in conversation, let alone try to turn this towards a more specific set of questions. We soon realized that we needed to be buying things too, to be looking at the mangoes, discussing the price, negotiating a deal. When we returned from some fieldtrips, therefore, we had not only field notes and recordings but also bags of fruit and vegetables (we got a great deal on a box of artichokes and broad beans at the Produce Market, and provided bowls of fruit for colleagues after working at the Central Market). By seriously engaging with the business of the market, we were able to start up conversations as we looked at fruit, and money exchanged hands.

Metrolingual multitasking thus became not only something we observed in these research sites but also extended into our participatory research methodology. We stocked up on supplies of *mugicha* (Japanese barley tea) at Ishikawa-san's grocery shop. Emi became a regular customer at *Petit Paris* during the data collection and started introducing her friends to the quirky 'wine bazar'. On our second visit to the *Mad Coffee and Nuts Shop*, we got a handwritten recipe from Wafiq for *ful,* a common Arabic dish made from mashed fava beans.

Excerpt 6.14 (W: Wafiq, R: Researcher)
1. W: OK. Tomato. One or two. One will be enough, you know, just a small cut. Small cuts.
2. R: Do you cook it in with it, or just fresh?
3. W: Nah nah nah nah, just raw. Small cuts. [Sigh] Herbs and spices ... you can put, uh ... I put too many. You can use sumac.
[...]
4. W: So. How do you do it. You do the ful til it's ready, very soft. Ah, you crush the garlic, you put it together and crush it all together. You crush this too. You make ready the parsley and the mint. OK? And the tomato. Put them together and just stir it all together. Put the cumin, bit of salt, sumac, all that together. Lemon. One lemon would be alright. Put olive oil ... as much as you like. 'Cause it's nice. And make it so soft, you know, just crush them. So it will go ... everything will go together. The sumac, the olive oil, everything. And after that, you put it in the bowl ... I've got it here, I think, you know [shows a shallow terracotta bowl]. Put it here and put the olive oil again on the top and get the parsley and the mint and sprinkle over top.

Through this exchange, this everyday Arabic dish became part of Astrid's kitchen repertoire. But this exchange is also significant because it allowed us to see different aspects of Wafiq from the interview and to get a better understanding of his animated way of speaking, gestures (showing the terracotta bowl, another part of the spatial repertoire of his shop), the importance of the many spices in his shop (see Chapter 7) and his passion and knowledge for food. Unlike a written recipe from the Internet, here we could smell the spice, touch the terracotta bowl and have a glimpse of Wafiq's wider world.

A typical example of this type of research site engagement was at the Vietnamese beautician (Chapter 2). Having struggled to engage her in conversation, it became clear to Emi and Astrid that they needed to participate. So they got their eyebrows done. Once seated and with their eyebrows being attended to, they had entered the normal conversational space of this worker: This is when and how she talked to customers. There was a shift in the relationship as Emi and Astrid became more vulnerable, lying on the massage table, bearing the pain (for Emi in particular since this was her very first experience of getting her eyebrows plucked). The Vietnamese beautician started leading the conversation as the power dynamics changed. So when Emi and Astrid finished the day's fieldwork, they had not only newly shaped and fashionable eyebrows, but also a long and intriguing recorded discussion with the Vietnamese beauty salon worker.

Emi got to know Lyn, the owner of the café near one of the construction sites, when she wandered in with a large case of beer over her shoulder. Having left an audio recorder in the basement lunch room of the construction site, Emi had noticed the café and liquor store nearby. A case of beer seemed an excellent way to thank the workers for their help in making the lunchtime recordings, so with this on her shoulder, she decided to stop for a coffee. Surprised by the sight of this Japanese woman carrying a case of beer, Lyn helped Emi with the heavy box. Soon, after Emi commented on the interesting coffee spoons (bought from a small market in Lyn's home village in China), they started a longer conversation. Lyn turned out to have a quite precise knowledge of the construction sites, workers and rhythms of the area. It was Lyn that gave us the lead to the other construction site where most of the workers were fasting during Ramadan (the beer, obviously, was for the workers of Serbian and Fijian background at another site). Carrying the beer once more, Emi stopped off to talk to Len – the supervisor of Lebanese background who we later went back to talk to – before returning to the basement of the other building. The lunch break was almost over: 'Oh my god', exclaims Marko, 'they're going to think we're alcoholics here.' They laugh. 'Oh, thank you. How do you say "thank you"?' asks Marko. 'Arigato', Emi explains, putting the beer on the table. 'Arigato! Arigato', Marko exclaims.

There were numerous stories similar to this.[6] As this chapter suggests, a lot of research ideas emerged through commensal moments among the researchers, when Alastair, Astrid and Emi sat drinking coffee at the coffee shop in the convivial Japanese alley, or sharing a plate of sumac bread at five o'clock in the morning at Joseph's café at the Produce Market, or drinking vodka with the Polish 'boys' from *Patris* (Alastair and Emi have since sworn off vodka). Drinking, talking, buying, eating – all those everyday activities – brought us closer onto the lives of the people we were working with, crossing the boundaries of researcher and researched. And just as these were ways into research sites, and ways of staying engaged with these sites, so they have also become parts of our lives. Astrid's partner became so addicted to *mugicha* that we have had to keep returning to Ishikawa-san's for more. One of Emi's Japanese friends, a French- and English-speaking tour guide, has become a regular customer at *Petit Paris*, and takes her customers there when they want to try 'Western' food in Japan. Emi's balcony wall, which was repaired by Vukasin, Igor and Zlatan, workers of Serbian and Bosnian backgrounds, is now covered with the Japanese wild yam plant, which grew out of one of the neglected potatoes that she bought from the Japanese organic backyard farmer (Abe-san – see Chapter 7). When research sites involve many layers of participation, as we try to enter parts of people's lives, their worlds also start to enter ours.

Notes

1　This is presumably a reference to *Fanta Shokata*, a version of Fanta based on elderberry (*soc* in Romanian) common in the Balkan region.
2　Gordon Ramsay in *The F Word*, Series 2, Episode 6, July 26, 2006.
3　Spellings of terms such as *moussaka* varied quite widely. The use of katakana versions in Japan also complicated the picture. In *Carthago*, the Turkish spelling musakka was used.
4　According to Madhur Jaffrey (2014), Marks & Spencer claim to sell 18 tonnes of it every week and an estimated 23 million portions are sold in Indian restaurants in the UK each year.
5　Lycée Franco-Japonais de Tokyo has moved to Kita-ku area in Tokyo in 2012.
6　We should also clarify that while a few working lunches and breakfasts and minor expenses are appropriate research project costs, we are aware that cases of beer, bottles of vodka, fruit and vegetable shopping, while sometimes essential for the research, are less easily justifiable. These are all items we end up paying for, which is why we remain committed but impoverished researchers.

7 Layers, spaces, signs, networks

Out-of-place texts

The front window of the grocery store in the Japanese alley is full of community messages, and another brick wall inside has more, advertising a Japanese vet, and yoga and karate classes (Image 7.1). At the back of the store, however, past the bags of *mugicha,* the bottles of *Kikkoman* soy sauce and *Kyūpī mayonēzu*, the home-made Japanese sweets (*sakura mochi, daifuku*), the fridge with *natto* and *bento,* the *bigen* hair dye and *hokkaron* hot patches, the *daikon* radishes and rice cookers, is a glassed-in store room, a space created to protect the writing on the wall (Image 7.2). In large white letters on the painted red brick wall is written: 'P R Cook & Co Estate Agents.' Below that in different lettering: 'The South British Insurance Co Ltd, Fire, Accident, Workers Compensation.'[1] These advertisements date from an era when white-letter signs on brick walls were a common mode of advertising. This building was constructed in 1924 – along with the other surrounding buildings – by Phillip Robert Cook, who used it as an estate agent's premises until 1944 (Heritage Report, 1998).

In a picture taken of this street in 1924 (Image 7.3), shortly after the construction of these buildings, we can see the small building that is now the Japanese grocery store (to the right of the two central buildings, one of which was then a chemist, now the Japanese second-hand book store) with the PR Cooke Estate Agent advertising just visible below the eaves. In the foreground is a building with painted advertising for Bushells Tea. These advertisements are clearly oriented to the railway line (from where the photograph appears to have been taken). While these painted signs on walls bring echoes of the discussion in Chapter 5 of graffiti and the ownership of space, our focus here is on the layering of the city, the city as palimpsest as different texts in different languages are written over each other as the populations of different areas change. The P R Cook & Co Estate Agents text written on the back wall of the Japanese grocery shop in the little Japanese alley in the northern suburbs of Sydney (Chapter 2) sits now among other preserves – pickled radishes and ginger – at the other end of the shop from the Japanese community notice boards.

Image 7.1 Japanese community notices.

Image 7.2 P. R. Cook & Co.

Image 7.3 Wilkes St 1924.

At the same time, layers are not about the mere overlapping of texts on flat surfaces; rather, they need to be seen in terms of sedimented activities and practices that are still in motion. The picture taken in 1924 was initially found on the Facebook posting of the newly opened coffee shop in the avenue. The young owners posted the picture to show the location of their shop in the old photo: 'Our joint is the one next to the chemist' (Facebook post by the owners, December 28, 2012). The picture was passed on to the owners by Carolyn from a local not-for-profit community group that conducts archival research and has extensive historical data of the area, aiming to promote and protect the intellectual, physical and cultural welfare of the suburb.

> There was a chemist there for a long, long time. There was a doctors', and where Ben [the Coffee shop] is now, he had the doctor's surgery and then there was a garage next door. And the garage was converted into the waiting room at one stage. And then … they used to drive cars up the Avenue. There was a taxi rank at the end. It was very rough and potholey, there were documents somewhere about it being so bad, and the taxi driver writing to council and saying, you know, 'I'm getting all these all this damage done to my car because of the rough surface on the Avenue'.
>
> (Carolyn, interview, March 4, 2013)

Indeed, while the young owners were renovating the shop, they found traces of the past underneath the surface of the wall: 'this is what we found under the render. We also got told by our local Heritage Member that it used to be a garage with a lane way beside it. Makes sense' (Facebook post by the owners, December, 2012). From a taxi depot and a garage, to a doctor's surgery, where particular types of people and traffic converged and diverged, now the avenue that for a while had a reputation as a pretty dodgy area is closed off to traffic and has turned into a convivial Japanese precinct (Chapter 5). These traces on the walls speak of a history of mobility. The brick walls of the coffee shop are now covered with a metal grid to protect the surface from directly hanging objects such as the backboard menu and other items (Image 7.4) forming another textual layer of activity. Such menus themselves, with their *Croque Madame, Black Forest Gypsy Ham, Gruyère and Dijon, Rabbit Terrine, Dutch Carrots, Smoked Wagyu, Quinoa,* present another layering of the modern globalized eating space. Like the protected P R Cook & Co Estate Agents sign at the back of the Japanese grocery store (two doors down, next to the second-hand book store) the menu on the metal grid protecting the old brickwork, shows the layers of sedimented activity in this building.

Image 7.4 Coffee shop menu.

The historical layers of cities

As we shall see later, where part of the history of Haymarket has been deliberately preserved on the old brick walls, this layering of the city, this sedimented history of ownership, mobility and writing tells a central tale about languages and the city. Cities vary across time and space, each part of a city being distinct from other parts, but also changing in different times of the day as commuters, shoppers, workers, people in search of a drink or some food, street cleaners and construction workers come and go (see the discussion of city rhythms in Chapter 3). Cities, as Wood and Landry (2008) note, 'should be seen less as places of distinct communities marked by clear and fixed boundaries but rather as local public spheres with multidimensional connections that overlap and conflict' (p. 251).

Cities need to be understood historically. The growth of the city has been central to the development of humans, demanding new forms of cooperation between people: 'it was this close contiguity', notes Watson (2005, p. 100), 'this face-to-face style of cohabitation, that explained the proliferation of new ideas, particularly in the basic tools for living together – writing, law, bureaucracy, specialized occupations, weights and measures'. The growth of the city, therefore, was both an outcome of changing social and economic practices (climate change bringing about the need for communal irrigation, for example) and also a great driver of new changes in terms of social cooperation, cultural practices and forms of communications. 'Cities have been the forcing houses of ideas, of thought, of innovation, in almost all the ways that have pushed life forward' (Watson, 2005, p. 130). Hall (1998) argues that 'the biggest and most cosmopolitan cities, for all their evident disadvantages and obvious problems, have throughout history been the places that ignited the sacred flame of the human intelligence and the human imagination' (p. 7).

'Golden ages' have always been urban ages, as Hall (1998) remarks, charting the dynamic flowering of cultural, intellectual, economic and architectural activity in Athens in the fifth century BC, Florence in the 14th, London in the sixteenth, Vienna in the eighteenth and nineteenth centuries, Paris at the end of the nineteenth and Berlin in the early part of the twentieth century. There are of course many other candidates for this list, depending in part on how such activity is classified. Tokyo in the 1960s might be one such city. While there are many and complex reasons why cities at particular times are at the centre of a flourishing technological and artistic development, a more general reason for their role in human development is that they present many problems that need to be solved. Cities require vast amounts of organization and movement, of workers, food, water, sewerage, and more: 'It takes effort to keep cities going' (Byrne, 2001, p. 15). In order to solve the basic and mundane problems that a city poses – 'aqueducts and sewers and subways, asylums and workhouses and gaols, laws and regulations' (Hall, 1998, p. 6) – cities have been at the forefront of human innovation.

The growth of cities was a crucial stage of human development, with close relations developing between the city and agriculture, technology and industrialization: 'The industrial revolution was and is also the urban revolution' (Byrne, 2001, p. 14). A historical lens helps us see the ways in which cities have become layered palimpsests of different eras of settlement, migration and industry, the ways in which signs and street names, churches and mosques (and particularly when one has changed into the other) reveal a sedimented history of movements of people. A historical view also helps us see the very particularity of each city. In an age when the global city (Magnusson, 2000; Sassen, 1998; 2005) seems potentially disentangled from its locality, it is nonetheless important to see how cities differ. While Sydney shares the common feature of a great natural harbour and a colonial past with many large cities, its development as a convict settlement in the eighteenth century makes it very different from other cities with longer histories. Similarly, Tokyo on the one hand shares common features with other large Asian cities such as skyscrapers and densely populated city centres, yet on the other hand its historical and natural conditions also make it distinct. In particular the traces from the era of seclusion (the Edo government closed its door to both local Japanese and foreigners leaving or entering Japan), the feudal system during the Edo period, the destruction of WWII, the rapid post-WWII economic growth in the 1960s and the frequency of earthquakes, among many other factors, leave their marks on Kagurazaka (*Petit Paris*), Nakano (*Carthago*) and Sasazuka (*Maison Bretonne*) (see previous chapters).

Cities shift from season to season. In cold climate cities, from Chicago and Toronto to Moscow and Harbin, the winter sends people indoors, into underground shopping malls, heated transport systems and places of worship. In the summer, the streets are taken over again, with cities such as Montreal becoming pedestrian precincts once again, filling with festivals, street parties and open-air dining (while the *Fête des Neiges* [snow festival] may be held between January and February, it is in summer that the jazz festival, *le mondial de la bière* [world beer festival], *les weekends du monde* [weekends of the world] hit the streets and parks). In hotter climate cities, such as Hong Kong, people also seek the enclosed mall and the covered walkway for the air-conditional cool they provide. And in warm seaside cities, such as Rio and Sydney, people head to the beach in summer, and to other water sports through the year. City parks and public spaces – the Venice *piazza*, the Mexico *zocalo*, the Paris *square*, the Havana *malecon*, the Shanghai *Bund* (外滩) – empty and fill with the changing times of day and shifting seasons.

Ever since it became the first government-authorized park in 1873, Ueno Park in central Tokyo has been a space of diversity and change, with its shrines, concert halls, museums, art galleries, zoological park and Tokyo University of the Arts within the vicinity. It was also for a time (many of the temporary residences were recently removed by force by the local administration) home to a large population of homeless people, constructing an inner city of cardboard boxes and plastic sheets. During the Iraq-Iran war, Ueno Park was a hub for Iranian refugees to exchange information amid the flow of young and old, Japanese and foreigner, middle class and homeless, who ebb and flow with the rhythms of the city. During *hanami* (cherry blossom viewing) in April, people sit under the trees, drinking *sake*, eating *obento* (lunch boxes) and enjoying the soft pink of cherry blossoms falling gently through the spring air. Movement and mobility are thus central for any understanding of the city. As Canut (2009) notes, in order to understand city spaces, we have to appreciate that people are always moving between places, and thus 'the urban condition exists insofar as it is predicated on the space between these places' (p. 89). As we move through the city, we feel its size, diversity, difference.

Cities also change over longer time periods, as new areas are built and new transport systems open up (and others close down). Much of the data collected from construction sites was gathered in areas under gentrification. In the next block to the building where the colour of *Fanta* in Serbia as well as the history of *moussaka* and the Ottoman Empire were discussed (see Chapter 6) is a new trendy pub. The whole street and area is in transition from an inner-city suburb with a history of urban poverty and its attendant problems of crime and violence to a trendy, middle-class suburb of shops and apartments. One of the local newspapers comments on this suburb: 'When cafés and tapas bars move in, you know your suburb is on the move' (Gentrification, 2011). It is the construction workers, with their mixed trades and ethnic affiliations (see Chapter 2), that help build these changes.

Areas of a city change in terms of migration patterns, so that formerly White working-class areas of British cities such as London or Leeds gradually filled with South Asian and Caribbean arrivals. This is true of both religious and commercial properties. The brick building on the corner of Fournier Street and Brick Lane in Spitalfields, London, for example, is now the *Jame-e-masjid mosque*, frequented by a largely Bangladeshi local community. The building (*La Neuve Eglise*) was originally built by the Huguenots in 1743, fleeing persecution in France. In the early nineteenth century, it became a Methodist (Wesleyan) chapel with a focus on converting the large local Russian and Middle European Jewish community to Christianity. This project was presumably not as successful as hoped, since the building's next incarnation was as the *Spitalfields Great Synagogue*. As the Jewish population moved on from the garment industry and dispersed across the city, new migrants arrived from Bangladesh (particularly the Sylhet region), eventually turning this building into the mosque it is today. Cities have historical layers – here a building that has housed French-speaking Calvinists, English-speaking Methodists, the Yiddish and Hebrew of the Synagogue, the Bangla, Sylhetti and Arabic of the mosque (Eade, Jahjah & Sassen, 2004; Multicultural London, 2003).

Kagurazaka, where *Petit Paris* is located, is similarly historically layered. Old cobbled streets and houses in Kagurazaka, as well as the park to commemorate the birth place of *Karyūkai* (the geisha district) in front of *Petit Paris* show the historical layers of different practices. Since the relocation of *Bishamonten* temple in 1791, towards the end of the Edo period, people and businesses have flourished around this treasured Kagurazaka landmark (Taniguchi & Murozawa, 2011). Originally founded to protect and pray for the prosperity of the first Shogun of the Edo period, Ieyasu Tokugawa, *Bishamonten* has, since 2007, become a sacred place for the popular boyband *Arashi* (the temple was used to shoot a television program featuring one of the *Arashi* members) (Taniguchi & Ito, 2011). Like love locks hanging on bridges to wish for a happy relationship, *Bishamonten* has produced new layers of text on *Ema*, wooden votive tablets on which people write wishes before hanging at the designated area in the temple (the origin of *Ema* dates back to as far as Heian Period: eighth-twelfth century). The temple now has layers of hand-written *Ema* from young *Arashi* fans, making wishes to go to their concerts and hoping for the welfare of the group member. These form a new type of layered language practice, integrated into the history and Buddhist practices of the temple, alongside the *Karyūkai* (geisha district) and French restaurants (including the logo of *Petit Paris*, see localization of French in Chapter 6). New layers will emerge for they are but sedimented social and linguistic practices.

We are interested in this chapter in the layers and networks of these cities, which link to those crucial urban categories of space, rhythm and contiguity (Mac Giolla Chríost, 2007). Contiguity refers to that quality of cities, and particularly those sites of social interaction and commercial transaction such as markets, that bring people into constant close proximity. For Massey, cities are 'peculiarly intense, and probably heterogeneous, constellations of social trajectories' (2000, p. 226). From this point of view 'cities are particularly dense spatial formations containing a complex mix of multiple, heterogeneous social interactions, materialities, mobilities and imaginaries' (Edensor, 2011, p. 190). We have already discussed here and in Chapter 3 the rhythms of the city. Once we consider cities in terms of time, movement and space, then any human passing through them is 'one mobile element in a seething space pulsing with intersecting trajectories and temporalities' (p. 190).

Over time, therefore, cities become layered, places of linguistic sedimentation, with buildings, walls, streets and signs carrying the traces of the past, and present stories of migration, movement, worship and successful and failed businesses. It is these local manifestations of the global, the ways global cities 'are the terrain where a multiplicity of globalization processes assume concrete, localized forms' (Sassen, 2005, p. 40), this globalization from below, these local language practices that occur because these are global cities, these ways in which people in such major conurbations get by linguistically, that interest us. A lot of recent work in Europe has taken up Vertovec's (2006) account of superdiversity (e.g. Blommaert, 2010; 2013a) to account for what is assumed to be the increasing diversity of European cities. As Noble (2009) points out, however, such diversity has long been part of Australian cities. It is against the backdrop of an age of nationalism, monoculturalism and uniformity that we need to see 'today's seeming increase in multilingualism' (Yildiz, 2012, p. 3). While it is evident that European cities are going through major transformations, a current focus on superdiversity runs the danger of obscuring the ways in which such cities have always been diverse.

There is a certain irony that Blommaert's (2013a) captivating ethnographic account of the complexity of the linguistic landscapes of a suburb of Antwerp, an account that insists on the importance of understanding '*different historicities*' (p. 11) in the exploration of superdiversity, potentially overlooks the history of diversity of that very city. As Simon (2012) points out, there is good evidence to suggest that Pieter Bruegel the Elder's famous 1563 painting of the Tower of Babel (perhaps the best known of the many images of that tower) is based on Bruegel's city, Antwerp, which at the time 'was the largest, richest, and most international city of its day, the center of European trade and finance, the host to large communities of merchants from Italy, France, Germany, Spain, Portugal and England' (p. 152). The city sustained a 'vigorous humanist polyglot culture and, like Venice and Amsterdam, a flourishing publishing industry in an astonishingly wide range of languages' (p. 152). While Blommaert tellingly illustrates the shifting diversities of Oud-Berchem, with its Polish and Turkish stores and restaurants, small businesses changing hands from Dutch to Turkish to Gujarati (akin to the layering we have also been drawing attention to here), its mosques, new African churches and much more, it is important that we do not lose sight at the same time of the history of diversity, of the fact that Antwerp may already have been the model for one of the longest-lasting images of diversity.

Port cities

The development and expansion of cities have concerned not so much close-knit communities growing to fill a larger space, but rather the bringing-together of different communities. The necessity of close cohabitation and cooperation and the contiguous living arrangements of cities have therefore always been about living with others, dealing with outsiders. The growth of the city has entailed cooperation not only between specialized workers – relying on farmers and shopkeepers to supply food, for example, while others produce metal artefacts – but also cooperation with people of different backgrounds. Trade and market places have been central to this process. The buying and selling of goods was integral to the development of cities, which therefore always emerged along trade routes. Water transport was a significant part of trade and nowhere has the development of diverse, contiguous trading centres been more evident than in the development of port cities. From Antwerp to Sydney, from Malacca – Lee Su Kim (2010) notes the extraordinary diversity of the Baba/Nyonya/Peranakan culture that grew up there – to other cities on the spice routes such as Cochin (see Nandy, 2006; Pennycook, 2012a) and cities such as Istanbul, Cape Town or Rio de Janeiro, complex diversity has always been the everyday norm.

Simon (2012) notes Smyrna (Izmir, in Anatolia, Western Turkey), along with Istanbul, Beirut and and Alexandria, as one of the 'multilingual port cities which contained, in addition to significant populations of conquered Ottoman peoples, enclaves of Europeans' (p. 154). In his account in *Middlesex* of the burning of Smyrna (by the Turks in 1922: multilingual port cities were also often the focus of violence), Jeffrey Eugenides notes both its multicultural diversity as well as its linguistic cosmopolitanism: 'In Smyrna, East and West, opera and *politika,* violin and *zourna*, piano and *daouli* blended as tastefully as did the rose petals and honey in the local pastries' (2002, p. 57). Everyone in the city, he suggests, 'could speak French, Italian, Greek, Turkish, English and Dutch' (p. 61). While this fictional account is by no means a reliable description, and while it may be more useful to think in terms of spatial repertoires (Chapter 4) – of available language resources in particular places, rather than people speaking lists of languages – it gives a sense of the cultural and linguistic diversity (while missing Armenian and many others) of such port cities.

Smyrna, as with so many cities, also had a sizable Jewish population, who themselves brought their own linguistic repertoires to the city. It is the Jewish population of Odessa that interests Edmund de Waal in his book, *The Hare with the Amber Eyes.* The Ephrussi family, the subject of de Waal's book, spread out across Europe from Odessa, a city famous for its rabbinical schools and synagogues, rich in literature and music, a magnet for the impoverished Jewish shtetls of Galicia. It was also a city that doubled its population of Jews and Greeks and Russians every decade, a polyglot city full of speculation and traders, the docks full of intrigues and spies, a city on the make.

(p. 24)

The language patterns of this family changed as their wealth increased and they took up residence in the great cities of Paris and Vienna, exchanging the casual polyglottism of the port city for the cosmopolitan multilingualism of the wealthy (Latin, Greek, German, French and English): 'With languages, you can move from one social situation to another. With languages, you are *at home anywhere*' (p. 31).

The metrolingual repertoires of these port cities are part of the ethos of the *Carthago* restaurant, with Turkish, French, Persian, English, Japanese, Arabic and occasionally Spanish part of the repertoire of the restaurant. Like the description of the restaurant on the website, アラブ・トルコ地中海料理店 (Arab-Turkey Mediterranean restaurant), it is a hub for people from the region. Mama, the co-owner who works as floor staff explains this further.

聞こえてくるのはやはり英語とフランス語が多いです。多国籍のグループや、日本人と来ている外国人は母国語ではないと思われる特徴のある英語で会話していることが多いですね。サウジの学生がグループで来るときは、やっぱりアラビア語で会話していてエキゾチックです。中東の人がいる場合は、アラビア語圏とわかった時点でアラビア語で挨拶をし、どちらの国か伺い、その国の方言でもう一言何かいうようにしています。イスラエルの人だったらヘブライ語で挨拶します。昔ほどイスラエルの人は多くありませんが。あ、たまにスペイン語も聞こえてきます。中南米のスペイン語のほうが多いです。レバノン出身とか多いからでしょうね。

(email correspondence, October 14, 2013)

English and French are the languages I hear a lot. Multinational groups or foreigners who are accompanied by Japanese are often speaking in English with non-native accent. It is exotic when a group of students from Saudi Arabia visits and speaks in Arabic. When we have guests from the Middle East and when I notice that they have an Arabic language background, I greet them in Arabic and ask which country they are from. And then I will try to say something in the dialect of the country. If the customers are from Israel, I greet them in Hebrew. We do not have as many Israelis as we used to though. Oh, and occasionally we can hear Spanish. More from South America. Perhaps it is because there are many people from Lebanon.

(Our translation)

The Mediterranean influences of *Carthago* attract people connected by oceans, languages and mobilities, including the South American Lebanese diaspora. In the blog on their website (November 29, 2013), the chef writes '羊肉にこだわった おかげで、インドのお客様も多いんですよ' (Due to our persistence in using lamb, we have lots of Indian customers, too), adding that the primary philosophy of the restaurant is to provide food for those people who can only eat out in such places (unable to eat beef, for example). Thus, serving Middle Eastern food to Japanese 'cosmo-mulitculturalists' (Hage, 1997) engaged in 'eating the other' (Flowers & Swan, 2012), according to the chef, is secondary to providing food for those 'others' in Tokyo.

Foods of the Mediterranean, such as *moussaka* – from Arabic *musaqa'h* via Turkish *musakka* and Greek *mousakás* (μουσακάς) – with its layers of eggplant, or aubergine (from Arabic *(al-)bāḍinjān* باذنجان. via Catalan *albergínia*), potato, tomato and minced lamb – also of course turn up in such places. 'Krzyś, Ravioli Moussaka!' calls out Polish cook Aleksy in *Patris* to his brother, Krzysztof (who replies 'Co?' [Polish: what?]). '**Iki** no **musaka**'[2] (moussaka for table 2, using the Turkish 'iki' for two) calls out the chef in *Carthago*. The spread of moussaka through the Ottoman Empire was also a topic of conversation between Macedonian and Serbian workers during a lunch break in a construction site (see Chapter 6). Couscous (see Chapter 6) also becomes part of this network. Nabil (the owner of *Petit Paris*, of Algerian background) knows *Carthago* as a couscous restaurant – 'I know another restaurant, couscous restaurant in Nakano' – confirming in some ways the chef's mission to provide food to people from the Mediterranean region. He knows the chef – 'a Japanese guy' – and has eaten at his restaurant 'many times', confirming too that the *Carthago* chef 'has Tunisian style'. Here the layers of food and language that are remade in *Carthago* become part of a wider Mediterranean network. On the wall in *Carthago* a large map of the Mediterranean Sea and surrounding countries, surrounded by tiles, plates and pictures speaks of these layers and connections, of port cities, Phoenicians, Greeks, Turks, Romans, Arabs, foods, languages, layers and links.

Port cities give us insights into contemporary diversities, for in an era of airports, every city becomes a port city. Much is made of current urban diversity brought about by increased levels of immigration, but port cities have always been places where people of many backgrounds came to trade and live. The denial of diversity that was part of the modernist settlement has meant that the current focus on superdiversity runs the risk of overlooking the ubiquity and ordinariness of diversity (Higgins & Coen, 2000). As Gilroy (2004) puts it, by understanding the 'everyday patterns of heterocultural life' we can reduce 'the exaggerated dimensions of racial difference to a liberating ordinariness' (p. 131). Above all, however, we need to appreciate that the claims to a new diversity, a superdiversity, in modern times as a result of increased migration to European cities, is also a return to the cities of old.

Commenting on the changes to Istanbul after the fall of the Ottoman Empire, Orhan Pamuk notes that the 'cosmopolitan Istanbul' he knew as a child had disappeared by the time he was an adult, as the neighbourhoods were emptied of Jews and Greeks and 'the city was losing its vernacular diversity' (Simon, 2012, p. 154). 'The association of Istanbul with a time now past', suggests Simon, corresponds to a pattern of 'then' and 'now' in the life of cosmopolitan cities. 'Then' was the time of the pre-national city. Nationalism came with a call for translation: the modernity of the Turkish language was announced by the purging of Eastern words, just as the Turkish nation itself was purged of ethnic minorities.

(pp. 154–156)

It is this purging of diversity, and the continued efforts to purge diversity by assimilation, that needs to be set against the new modes of diversity, lest we forget that port cities, and indeed all cities, were founded on diversity.

Layered languages

Part of our understanding of metrolingualism includes this layering of the city, the sedimentation of current and historical linguistic practices in relation to the network of activities of ever-changing cities. Just as we argued in Chapter 3 that we need to understand the rhythms of the city, the ways in which the city breathes in and out as workers and families and students and consumers head across the city in their different directions and waves, so here we want to focus on time and space over longer historical periods, and particularly on the signs and traces left on the urban environment. This takes us into the territory of linguistic landscapes, an approach to understanding the role of language as part of the physical environment. Research studies of linguistic landscapes 'offer fresh perspectives on issues such as urban multilingualism, globalization, minority languages, and language policy' (Gorter, 2013, p. 205).

At least in urban contexts – as Coulmas (2009) points out, a better term might indeed be *linguistic cityscape* – language surrounds us, directs us, hales us, calls for our attention, flashes its messages to us. Linguistic landscapes take us into the spatiality of language; we are invited to explore what Scollon and Scollon (2003) called *geosemiotics*: 'an integrative view of these multiple semiotic systems which together form the meanings which we call place' (p. 12; see also Chapter 4). As Shohamy and Gorter (2009) explain, linguistic landscape (LL) 'contextualizes the public space within issues of identity and language policy of nations, political and social conflicts ... LL is a broader concept than documentation of signs; it incorporates multimodal theories to include sounds, images, and graffiti' (p. 4). From these beginnings, attention to the linguistic landscape has now become not only a focus in itself but also part of a broader sociolinguistic toolkit to study anything from graffiti (Jørgensen, 2008c; Pennycook, 2010) to Welsh teahouses in Patagonia (Coupland, 2013), the semiotic landscape of airports (Jaworski & Thurlow, 2013) or the Corsican tourist scene (Jaffe & Oliva, 2013).

In order to avoid the trap of linguistic landscape studies becoming as superficial as the textual surfaces they record (the ease of digital imaging and the assumptions about numerical linguistic presence can lead to a lack of depth), Blommaert (2013a) argues for the importance of an ethnographic and historical understanding of the complexity around signs: We need to understand their physical emplacement, their intended audiences, their histories, the things they point to in the world, their take up and interpretation and their changing patterns over time. Linguistic landscapes 'are not just indicators of a particular demographic composition, and they are even less interesting as rather evident pointers towards (stable) societal multilingualism'. Rather, they are 'historical documents, layered-simultaneous outcomes of different histories of people, communities and activities in ever-changing compositions – they become uniquely informative chronicles of complexity' (Blommaert, 2013a, p. 120).

Two big wall pictures greet you as you enter the library of the University of Technology, Sydney: a young man pushing a trolley-load of vegetables on the wall to the left (Image 7.5) and another image of the old market to the right. They are there because these walls were built on the old Sydney haymarket, a layer on top of the old brick walls. This is another place where the layers of the city have been deliberately preserved. The market was originally established in the 1830s to provide hay and animal fodder alongside the nearby cattle market. Haymarkets were common parts of expanding cities as the need for horse and cattle fodder grew. Many have become major landmarks in the city: Haymarket in London dates from the fifteenth century and is now part of the theatre district, and the Chicago Haymarket was the site of the 'Haymarket Affair' in 1866, an important influence on the May Day observance of workers' rights.

Image 7.5 Market worker.

Chicago, with its Haitian/French origins in the fur trade, through its waves of immigrants from Europe (German was the dominant language in the nineteenth century), more recent Spanish-speaking workers from Mexico and Puerto Rico, and Asian migrants from China and Korea and the Philippines, 'has been plurilingual since its inception' (Farr, 2011, p. 1162), growing up haphazardly like most cities, as its trade routes moved from the shipping on Lake Michigan to the railroads of the nineteenth century. Chicago 'came to possess a certain intensity that defines cities, not only with regard to its sheer size, including in terms of both the built physical environment and population, but also regarding its capacity to compress both time and space' (Mac Giolla Chríost, 2007, pp. 11–12). But the role of beef in its development made its haymarket central.

As in Chicago, the old name 'Haymarket' has stuck in Sydney (and now describes the district), though the market had already changed by the 1860s once hay and grain were transported by train to the Darling Harbour and Redfern rail yards. Instead, a diverse market – also known as Paddy's Market, a name still used today and probably imported from the Irish market of the same name in Liverpool, England – with entertainment and a diversity of products had established itself. In the early twentieth century, however, the market changed again with the construction of new buildings and a clock tower (where the university library is now), becoming the central produce market for Sydney (Christie, 1988). The old market shop signs, built around 1910, have been preserved as remnants of the old traders there (James Slater Pty Ltd; A Yee Pty Ltd [Image 7.6]), even though the

Image 7.6 Haymarket stores.

main produce market has now been moved to another part of the city (see Chapter 1) and Paddy's Market has moved into a newer building next door. Old Uncle Tony provides continuity between them, having started work in Haymarket in 1938 at the age of 16 fresh off the boat from his home in Zhongshan, Guangdong, China. He still remembers the times when potatoes and carrots from Tasmania were unloaded from horse-drawn carts that came up from the docks at Darling Harbour.

Uncle Tony recalls the Italian and Maltese workers at Haymarket (Chapter 2) and the much smaller numbers of Chinese (because of the White Australia policy; see Chapter 5) but today it has a strong Chinese presence. Haymarket is now synonymous with Chinatown in Sydney. The old signs on the wall are a remnant of that earlier market history but are now integrated into the everyday life and signage of both Chinatown and the UTS faculties of law and business, with their own multilingual layers. In 2013, 46 per cent of UTS students were from a language background other than English, with 48 per cent born outside Australia. The largest language groups after English being Cantonese, Vietnamese, Arabic and Mandarin, it is now varieties of Chinese, as well as Vietnamese and Arabic that are commonly heard in the café next to the pillars. The building walls are covered with signs in many languages: Chinese scribbles on toilet doors and desks, multilingual student notice boards. The ever-changing cityscape lays down its layers of languages.

Marrickville's (see Chapter 2) metrolinguistic landscape, meanwhile, is characterized not only by a particular demographic composition represented in the linguistic landscape of signs (Image 7.7) but also by a range of other culinary, sensory and linguistic layers. Scattered across the table in the Vietnamese-run hairdresser's shop are various Vietnamese magazines (Image 7.8). At the front of the Bangladeshi-owned video and spice store, which, along with its small travel agent business at the back, sells spices, pots and pans, cosmetics and DVDs of Bangladeshi films, an assortment of Bangla and Nepali papers (Image 7.9) is spread across the floor.

There is the 'Bengali Newspaper' *SadaKalo* (White and Black), the 'Most popular and highest circulated Bangla newspaper in Australia' *Desh Bidesh* (Home and Away), next to the 'Most circulated Bangla newspaper in Australia' *The Bangla Barta* (Bangla News), 'The largest newspaper in Australia for Bangladesh and Kolkata Community' *Muktamancha* (Open Theatre) and 'The leading Australian Bangladesh Monthly Community Paper' *Shuprobhat Sydney* (Good Morning Sydney).[3] This diversity of newspapers, almost entirely in Bangla, points to the common use of Bangla in the community, the different political affiliations within the community, and the wide number of local services available, from travel agents to money transfers, clothing and jewellery stores to restaurants, estate agents to tax accountants. The Nepali offerings are more moderate, including only the *Nepalipatra* and the *Nepali Times*. These piles of community papers, spread across the floor, like the Vietnamese papers at the hairdressers, are part of the layered linguistic landscape of the suburb.

Image 7.7 Marrickville streetscape.

Image 7.8 Vietnamese papers.

Image 7.9 Bangla and Nepali papers.

As with the scent of the Indian spices that waft out onto the street from this video and spice store, each of these shops presents a range of smells, products and languages. This sensory landscape (Landry, 2012) or more particularly here the urban smellscape (Henshaw, 2013) or odourscape, is an unmissable part of any such street. Returning to Wafiq's store down the road, one meets the rich smells from the bags of spices (labelled in English and Arabic) (Image 7.10) – sumac, ground aniseed, coriander powder, 'Morroccan spice', 'souvlaki seasoning', sweet paprika, *ras-el hanout* (North African spice mix – حانوت رأس – implying the best spices from the shop) – mingle with the smells of coffee, homemade halva and preserved lemons. At the family-owned Greek delicatessen down the road, it is the salami and cheese at the counter by the door that first greet the customer – like the cheery 'Yassou brother' from a departing customer – followed beyond the olive counter by layers of products, from Serbian *Ajvar* (ajвар) to pickled gherkins, peppers and other vegetables from Germany, the Czech Republic, Macedonia and Greece, *Rot Kohl* or *Rode Kool* from Germany and the Netherlands, Spanish *paella* spice mix, Italian *polenta* mix, Vietnamese rice paper, cans of *dolmathakia* (stuffed Greek vine leaves), Israeli *matzo* (מַצָּה) and Greek rusks (παξιμάδι), bottles of *Mayasan* dairy drinks and pomegranate juice from Turkey, pomegranate and blueberry juice from Georgia, *Sciroppo di Orzata* from Italy, and on and on. There are layers of languages, tastes, smells, labels, products (Image 7.11).

Image 7.10 Lebanese spices.

Image 7.11 Shelves.

The entrance to the gaming room of a nearby bar, meanwhile, formalizes its multilingual approach with a sign (Image 7.12) wishing luck to potential customers in multiple languages (English, Chinese, Vietnamese, Thai, Greek, Portuguese, Arabic, Italian, Korean), and the local chemist has a sign stating 'we speak Greek, English, Portuguese, Mandarin, Spanish, Cantonese, Vietnamese, Arabic'. Here we see the intertwined-ness of historical migrations and everyday practices of multiplicity through eating, shopping, entertaining, consulting and grooming. The layers of linguistic landscapes need to be understood not so much in terms of static physical emplacements, but rather as the mobilization of history through everyday practices.

Image 7.12 Good luck.

Researching networks: the multilingual cucumber

'ぱりぱりだよ (*Pari pari dayo*)' calls Ueki-san, the owner of a Japanese grocery store in the shopping complex in North Sydney to Emi as she walks past. He is signalling the crunchiness (*pari pari*) of his *kyūri,* Japanese cucumbers. 'やっぱ り違うんだよね、　ぱりぱりなんだよね' (After all, they're different, you know, crunchy), he continues, commenting further on how quickly the cucumbers sell. As Emi touches and feels the spiky skin of the cucumber, she can already feel the crunchy, yet juicy texture in her mouth, a taste and texture for which Lebanese cucumbers were no substitute. With excitement, she shares her experience by putting a photo of the cucumbers on Facebook, to which there was an immediate response from a non-Japanese friend who is a frequent traveller to Japan: 'Fantastic! I love the crunchy Japanese cucumbers too ... and have wondered why the cucumbers I usually buy in Sydney, though they *look* the same, aren't pari pari.' It is this '*pari-pari*'-ness of cucumbers that led us into a wider exploration of networks and cucumbers, also drawing attention to the ways in which research projects, however well planned and laid out, also start to both follow and describe these networks.

An important element of the way the city is both understood and produced is through the networks that interlink people, places and precincts. We have already seen in Chapter 2 the ways in which people of different backgrounds affiliate along particular lines of connection, and in Chapters 3 and 6 how the rhythms of the city are created by patterns of commuting and consuming. Here we want to show how the city's networks also became important channels of investigation in our research. The research on which this book is based can be understood as a multisite linguistic ethnography. Multi-sited ethnography, as Marcus (1995) notes, involves 'following connections, associations, and putative relationships' (p. 97). Thus, although we originally set out with a quite clear plan of action to conduct research in specific sites in Sydney and Tokyo, it was often the chance encounters ('*pari pari dayo*'), the connections and networks and relationships that sent us in particular directions.

The networks between people and markets and restaurants and workplaces, or the connections made between markets by Uncle Tony (introduced to us by Joseph who runs the café at the Produce Market, who knows Jean, who runs the grocery store in a northern suburb of Sydney, from where Ueki-san gets various products), the connections we found between growers and sellers, also became the networks of unexpected associations we followed. Several parts of this research project developed through unexpected networks: following construction workers from site to site, as well as at the café near the site (and see Chapter 6), conversations in markets and shops. Research from this perspective has parallels with certain approaches to critical language education as 'the quiet seeking out of potential moments, the results of which we don't always know. It's about the everyday and unexpected futures' (Pennycook, 2012a, p. 149). The networks of people and vegetables, growers and sellers, also became our networks of research. Networks are established through exchange and sharing of objects, space and practices (religious, ethnic, cultural, culinary and business). Linguistic and ethnic networks play a crucial role in finding a job in the building industry while culinary networks around the Mediterranean linked various people in Tokyo.

If the layers of signs gave us, in a sense, a vertical ordering of the city in terms of people and migrations, the networks give us a horizontal set of connections. In a northern suburb of Sydney, the networks in and beyond the (33-year-old) shopping plaza where the Japanese cucumbers turned up, follow a variety of lines of affiliation. The middle-class area where the complex is located is one of cosmopolitan rather than domestic multiculturalism (Hage, 1997), where 'eating the other' (Flowers & Swan, 2012) and sampling different cuisines is common. The shopping complex has restaurants from various culinary cultures that include Ethiopian, Japanese, Himalayan, Singaporean, Malaysian and Indian. It also has Japanese and Indian grocery shops, a hairdresser (the owners are of Japanese background, as are many of the customers), a Vietnamese beauty salon, a Chinese massage and acupuncture clinic, greengrocer, butcher (Anglo Australian owned), news agency (ethnic Chinese owned) and a picture frame shop.

The space is full of different languages, smells, sounds and artefacts ostensibly harmoniously co-existing. The oldest shop in the complex is the fruit and vegetable store run by a Lebanese family, which is as old as the plaza. Jean, an acquaintance of Joseph from the Produce Market (they are both of Christian Lebanese background), supplies vegetables to various shops within the complex and the local community. Every day for the last 33 years, except Sundays, he has gone to the market and purchased various fresh vegetables and flowers and had a casual chat with Joseph (see Chapter 1). Meanwhile, Jean's sister-in-law, who runs a little Lebanese bread and sweet kiosk opposite his greengrocer's shop, suggests these networks do not necessarily always run along obvious lines.

Excerpt: 7.1 (J: Jean, A: Angela [Jean's sister in law], R: Researcher)
1. R: Do you always go to the Lebanese growers?
2. J: No. Not much … doesn't matter no, I don't have to go Lebanese. Because in the market, you got all the international. You got the Greek, Lebanese, Italian, Spanish … everything
3. R: Maltese and Chinese,
4. J: Yes, yes. Most of the vegetables … the herbs, the radish, shallot, all Chinese. All Chinese.
5. A: Nothing beats them. It's funny, because I live in Bexley and I buy my parsley, shallots 'cause they come straight from the farm … to a Chinese lady … and I tried to go the farm in Brighton and they were dearer, more dear, than hers.

While the produce sold by Jean is mainly from the Produce Market, Angela buys the parsley and herbs (*gwai lou coi*) for her *tabouli* from local Chinese grocers, who in turn source their goods from Chinese market gardens similar to those discussed in Chapter 2. Meanwhile, a range of networks connect people in this mall to each other and to others elsewhere. Before he opened his own *ramen* restaurant in the Japanese alley (Chapters 3 and 5), Yama-san used to work in the *ramen* shop in this mall. The Himalayan restaurant in the same complex receives vegetable supplies from Jean, meat from the butcher and soy sauce from the Japanese grocery: 'We have got a relationship with fruit market down there … Jean's one yeah. As well as the Japanese, you know the grocer, a supermarket [referring to the supermarket upstairs in the complex]' (Himalayan restaurant owner, interview, November 20, 2012). The Japanese grocer, Ueki-san, supplies plastic containers to Jean, and gets special boneless thigh cutlets with the skin on (not available in local supermarkets) for Japanese customers from the butcher.

The Japanese cucumbers, we learned, were sourced from an organic vegetable grower located near the market gardens discussed in Chapter 2. So began our story of the mobile, multilingual, multicultural cucumber. Cucumbers, it turns out, have both a long history and an intriguing contemporary life in modern Sydney. Among the first market gardeners at what was then known as Kissing Point (later Putney) on the Parramatta River – the river that leads west from the great expanse of Sydney Harbour (Port Jackson) – one of the first farmed areas of the colony and the main source of fresh fruit and vegetables for Sydney in the early-nineteenth century, was a certain Thomas Chadwick. 'This green-fingered thief had been transported for stealing seven cucumber vines', and there was a certain irony in the fact that having been transported to Australia for stealing cucumber plants, he was given cucumber seedlings to grow 'by the same government that originally sentenced him' (Christie, 1988, p. 34).

From these early origins of English cucumbers being grown on the banks of the river by a convict transported for stealing cucumber vines, cucumbers eventually started to diversify as different market gardeners, fruit and vegetable sellers and culinary tastes started to change the possibility of what it meant to be a cucumber. And, along with ethnic affiliations, there also appeared to be cucumber affiliations.

Excerpt 7.2 (J: Jean, R1: Researcher 1, R2: Researcher 2)
1.   R1: … So do you have cucumbers as well?
2.   J: Everything.
3.   R1: Do you have Lebanese cucumber?
4.   J: And telegraph cucumber. Longer. Before you used to use Aussie cucumbers … nobody buys them anymore.
5.   R2: Too bitter!
6.   R1: Telegraph one is the long
7.   J: The long, with the plastic, covered in the plastic. But the popular one is the Lebanese cucumber.
8.   R1: I had a Japanese cucumber from that shop [referring to Japanese shop] the other day.
9.   J: Yeah yeah?

As with our discussion of food and eating (Chapter 6), such conversations around food constantly take place across cities such as Sydney. The terms of this conversation also echo in interesting ways the ethnic labelling discussed in Chapter 5. Here we have Aussie cucumbers (out of fashion these days), the popular Lebanese cucumbers (connected in obvious ways to the networks and affiliations of market gardens, and shops), telegraph cucumbers (long and covered in plastic, also known as English or Continental, and referred to by Talib in the Produce Market as 'tele cu') and indeed Japanese cucumbers.

Emi's moment of pleasure at the *'pari pari'*-ness of the Japanese cucumbers recalls a story told by a Lebanese woman (in Hage, 1997) about first finding Lebanese cucumbers in Sydney. As Hage notes, apart from cucumbers grown in back gardens, Lebanese in Australia had been deprived of their smaller, crunchier cucumbers until the 1970s, when they started to be grown on a larger commercial basis. As Nayla reports:

> It was incredible. I was visiting my sister who lived on the other side of the station. On the way back, I stopped to get some beans for dinner and here they were ... I touched them ... I held them in my hands. They were firm. It was like touching my mother [her mother lived in Lebanon]. Shawki, the shopkeeper, saw me, smiled and nodded: 'yes ... there's Lebanese farmers growing them down near Liverpool. No more mushy stuff.' That's how we refer to the Australian cucumbers. I bought two kilos, although we were poor then, and they were very expensive. I ate one on the spot in the shop. Adel [her husband] used to say, almost everyday, how much he missed the taste of Lebanese cucumbers.
>
> (p. 109)

As she goes on to explain, she made a cucumber salad with garlic and lemon and placed it on the table in front of her husband, telling him to close his eyes and taste what she had found. It took him a while before he finally realized what was in the salad, but then 'he got up, he kissed me and he started dancing and singing something like ya 'ayni 'al khyar!' (Oh I love you cucumbers!). These cucumbers, she explains, 'really made us happy. It was like reuniting with a close relative' (Hage, 1997, p. 110).

This moment of pleasure is recapitulated – with related emphasis on that particular crunchiness that only one's own cucumbers can bring – as we started to explore the Japanese cucumber network that had finally emerged many years after the Lebanese cucumber networks. Cucumbers connect people and businesses through many levels, from growing to distribution and consumption. Having tasted her Japanese cucumber from Umeki-san, Emi later on also purchased more from Ishikawa-san in the Japanese alley, and we discovered that many of the Japanese cucumbers available in Sydney seemed to emanate from one grower. The cucumber network emerged and expanded as we dug deeper. So we headed back down to Botany Bay, near the market gardens (see Chapter 2) to talk to Abe-san.

The front door of his house is almost invisible, obscured by the verdant foliage of the vines and bushy plants from his *myoga* (Japanese ginger) and *jinenjo*

(Japanese wild yam) plants. Walking along a narrow path down the side of the house, surrounded by buckets of organic fertilizer mix he creates himself, we entered a small back yard full of so-called 'Japanese vegetables' such as Japanese burdock, *yuzu* citrus, *mitsuba* and *shiso* (Japanese mint) and *satoimo* (Japanese sticky taro). This is where Abe-san spends most of his spare time, a side job, he explains, to make pocket money for buying cigarettes and alcohol. Unexpectedly, the supply of Japanese cucumbers in Sydney is grown and dispatched from a small backyard of Abe-san's private residence and the location of his backyard adjacent to the Chinese market gardens turns out to be a coincidence.

'日本の土が作れるかがポイント' (the key is whether you can produce Japanese soil), he explains, and the key for good soil is worms: 'their poo is good soil' (Interview, March 19, 2013). So he feeds his worms with vegetable scraps while talking to them in Japanese: '子孫繁栄させてね' (Please produce lots of descendants for your prosperity). Each time he moved, he explained, he transferred the fertilized soil in a truck with the help of his bike-rider friends. Japanese vegetables would get food poisoning if you use the commercial Australian soil, he explained. 'Japanese' was therefore not just a label for language and cooking styles, but for the food itself – Japanese cucumbers, Japanese strawberries (which would become Australian strawberries after three generations in Australian soil) – as well as the soil and the worms. The soils in his garden are layered, with 'Japanese soil' on top of the 'Australian' local soil, to optimize the condition for the Japanese vegetables to stay 'Japanese' – and the soil is produced by the worms, which are spoken to in Japanese (worms might also turn from Australian to Japanese after a few generations).

Perhaps the *pari-pari*-ness of Japanese cucumbers (Image 7.13) has to be nurtured by Japanese worms, fed Japanese food, in Japanese soil and spoken to in Japanese. And yet Abe-san's intense Japaneseness is one part of a wider cosmopolitanism that is not limited to his Japanese and English resources. His travels for 18 months on his motorbike through parts of Africa – including Zimbabwe, Tanzania and Uganda – before riding on up through Spain and other parts of Europe, have left him with a repertoire of resources that includes words and phrases from various languages such as Swahili, Spanish (which he says he found useful in Yugoslavia), French and German. It was on his return from this trip, when he was writing a local newspaper column about his travels, that he found that growing vegetables seemed to help him overcome his writer's block.

As we interviewed Abe-san, various networks surfaced. Ishikawa-san had encouraged him to start the side business as a grower rather than just as a hobby when she tried his *shiso* (Japanese mint) at the Japanese school fest. Ishikawa-san and Yama-san are examples of what Wise (2009, p. 24) calls 'transversal enablers': people who produce 'intersectional gossip, knowledge and inter-ethnic information networks'. Abe-san supplies *pari pari* cucumber to Ueki-san (now his best client), Ishikawa-san and a *ramen* shop in another suburb. He also has an extensive list of private clients that includes the owner of the second-hand book shop on the Japanese alley, where he used to take his three children after Japanese Saturday school to buy *manga*. They are still regular customers, apparently.

Image 7.13 Japanese cucumbers.

This cucumber network opened up several important dimensions for our research. However good our plans and proposals for what we will research – and how and where – we always have to be ready to follow unexpected pathways, to be ready to take up leads, to see where connections may take us. Sometimes, of course, following up these connections takes us nowhere (such non-networks are not reported here) but often these traces pushed us back and forth across the city in fascinating ways. For research purposes, this also means more than just expecting the unexpected, since it also entails unexpecting the expected (Pennycook, 2012a); that is, not merely being ready to go in unexpected directions but also constantly scrutinizing our expectations to see what they may be blinding us to.

The cucumber – a rather mundane artefact we had not considered important when we started some of our metrolingual explorations – turned out to have many dimensions (beyond size, firmness, and crunchiness). Cucumbers had important histories in Sydney, from one of the early crops grown by European settlers (invaders) – indeed grown by a convict transported for stealing cucumber vines – to a layered history of ethnicity and vegetables (from English to Lebanese to Japanese). The ordinariness of Abe-san's backyard and the simplicity of the cucumber also reinforced our focus on the everyday. Like Wise's (2009, p. 25) interest in backyard exchanges (in another Sydney suburb) of fruit and vegetables – as some of Fran's 'large box of oranges, peaches, cucumbers or whatever' end up with Lakshmi, to be reciprocated by a gift of 'her latest chilies or limes', followed by some of Tony's tomato seedlings, and later curry leaves from another backyard tree and lemons and rosemary from another garden – our interest is in the ordinary ways in which people in cities connect and get along. The convivial and commensal backyard relations connect ethnic, linguistic and culinary affiliations. Abe-san's backyard tells us how a seemingly insignificant everyday event, such as buying and eating cucumbers, entails connections, mobility and histories of people and the city.

Our cucumber networks revealed several further dimensions to these patterns. The networks of cucumbers were not only quite widely dispersed – this was not passing vegetables across the fence (as had long happened in many communities) but transporting across the city – but also interlinked with other types of network (Abe-san got into the business partly because he took his children to the second-hand Japanese book store). This brings us back to language and the ways in which these vegetables operate as mediating artefacts in people's repertoires. As with other foods (see Chapter 6), cucumbers invoked both desire and talk: certain tastes and textures brought about linguistic reactions ('*ya 'ayni 'al khyar*' – Oh I love you cucumbers! – or 'やっぱり違うんだよね，　ぱりぱりなんだよね' – After all, they're different, you know, crunchy). They also, at least for some people (including Emi, who now talks to the Japanese wild yam on her balcony – grown from one of Abe-san's yams – in Japanese), invoke not only culinary and gustatory responses, but linguistic ones as well.

Here too we saw that pull of the fixity of metrolingual relations – as Abe-san talked to his Japanese worms in their Japanese soil in Japanese – but also their fluidity: This Japaneseness turned out to be only one part of his wider repertoire, and as his cucumbers moved across the city and became part of the multilingual plaza in north Sydney, their Japaneseness was reconfigured in relation to other people, and foods, and languages and places. If we view these cucumbers as Japanese Australian (in terms of the soil, the growers, the eaters, the localities), we also need to address all the complexity of these terms – the diversity of all that is Australian and the changing mixtures that make up Japaneseness. As researchers, we need to be attentive not only to the possibilities these networks present but also to the ways in which they are always contingently constructed, made along certain lines of affiliation at certain times in certain places.

Notes

1   The company was originally established in 1872 as the South British Fire and Marine Insurance Company of New Zealand, before being incorporated in 1907 and changing its name to the South British Insurance Company Ltd.
2   The spelling here follows Japanese *romaji* conventions based on the Japanese phonetic system (see Chapter 3 for discussion of the transcript systems we have used for Japanese).
3   Our thanks to Shaila Sultana for help with these papers and an understanding of their role in the broader community. For more on the Bangladesh film industry, see Sultana, Dovchin and Pennycook (2013).

8 Metrolingua francas

Languages and the market

Although the Central Market still carries its preserved history of layered signs (see Chapter 7) suggesting a range of owners and workers, it is now in the heart of Sydney's Chinatown. When the young Uncle Tony started work there in 1938 at the age of 16, he was a minority among the Irish, Italians, Maltese and others, but now it is varieties of Chinese that dominate the fruit and vegetable market. Just as a cursory glance at a section of a fruit and vegetable stall might suggest only 'apples' or 'potatoes' while a more careful exploration reveals much greater variety (Granny Smith, Pink Lady, Braeburn, Fuji, Golden Delicious; Charlotte, Desiree, King Edward, Nicola, Romano), so this Chinese market is also a place of great diversity. It was in conversation with two young men of Indonesian background who were husking corn over a large bin that the situation was perhaps best explained. When asked what languages are used in the market, the response was '乜language都有㗎!' (all kinds of languages are spoken here!). The conversation continued in Cantonese.

> **Excerpt 8.1 (R: Researcher, C: Corn husker)**
> Chinese: (Cantonese) characters (translations in brackets)
> 1. R: 係呀! 咁你自己呢? (Really! What about yourself?)
> 2. C: 我呀? 我又福建話, 又印尼話, 又客家話.
>   (Me? I speak Hokkien, Indonesian and Hakka.)
> 3. R: 咁勁! (Oh wow!)
> 4. C: 乜都有, 撈埋一齊. (all sorts of languages mixed together.)

Later on in the conversation, he added Mandarin and English to the list, and since the conversation was in Cantonese, we need to assume this young worker's repertoire includes Hokkien, Hakka, Cantonese, Mandarin, Indonesian and English. Of course, as we have argued elsewhere, such lists of languages do not tell us a great deal about what kind of knowledge is implied for each language. As we saw in the lists of languages in *Patris* (Chapter 4), these are loosely identified linguistic resources. But this list of resources and the proposition that they use 乜 都有, 撈埋一齊 (all sorts of languages mixed together) points us in two directions:

First, how do we understand the *market value* of such languages, and second, how do we understand the ways in which 'all sorts of languages' become part of a spatial repertoire that workers and customers can draw on?

In dealing with the first of these questions, it is important to observe that these workers, with their extensive language repertoires – Hokkien, Hakka, Cantonese, Mandarin, Indonesian and English – are not highly paid; indeed, they are working at the lower end of a poorly resourced informal economy. Why does this multilingualism not bring financial benefits? There are several ways we can address the question of values accorded to languages, through a lens of language policies and hierarchies, a focus on language commodification and an emphasis on local practices. A first possible answer to this question comes via an understanding of the ways in which languages are socially and politically valued. A brief detour via Luxembourg and its rare bi/trilingual *Luxemburger Wort* newspaper sheds some light on this.

For many formally bilingual states, such as Canada, newspapers are not so much bilingual (in French and English) as a choice between English – *The Globe and Mail*, *The Vancouver Sun*, *Toronto Star* or *The Gazette* (the Quebec English language paper) – or French – *Le Devoir* or *La Presse*. There are of course also local 'community' papers (like those we saw piled up in doorways in Chapter 7), though these similarly often offer a choice between languages. The *Australian Chinese Daily* [澳洲联邦], for example, one of five Chinese papers in Sydney, has minimal text in English (a few titles, terms and announcements). Of the four popular Japanese community papers and magazines, only one (JENTA Sydney; Bridging Medium for Australia and Japan) is 'bilingual', with nearly equal numbers of pages dedicated to both English and Japanese articles. Such papers, however, might be better classified as bi-monolingual, aimed as they appear to be at two different audiences: Japanese readers and English readers interested in Japan. Elsewhere, some local, bilingual papers, such as the *Spanglish Times* produced in Phoenix, Arizona, make a more overt statement about bilingualism, having a 'general philosophy' to confront 'the hegemonic dominance of monolingual English by contrasting it with an "ideal" bilingualism' (Sebba, 2012, p. 106). As internet-based publications have proliferated, there are now many more publications that take a more open attitude towards the languages of publication.

Yet national bi/tri-lingual papers are something of a rarity. One example is *The Vanuatu Independent/L'independant Du Vanuatu*, a weekly newspaper that has articles in English, French and Bislama, also reflecting (though not proportionally) the official language policy in the country: Bislama is the widely used lingua franca of these islands, both the national language as well as one of the three official languages (with French and English). Absent, however, is any sign of either the common language mixing or the many indigenous languages that are 'vital expressions of Vanuatu's social and cultural identity' (Nasonal Lanwis Polisi of Vanuata, 2010, np). Amid the similarly linguistically regulated domains of the *Luxemburger Wort*, it is harder to find the third language of this triglossic nation, Luxembourgish (*Lëtzebuergesch*) (Horner & Weber, 2008; Sebba, 2012).

It is only when the national and international news are finished (in German, which is widely used in media, and French, which has the highest status as a dominant language of the service sector and government), and we get to the local news and events, that Luxembourgish (a Franconian variety of German and the common language of local people) starts to peep through.

It turns up in personal messages (death announcements – *avis mortuaires*), which are in either Luxembourgish or French (but rarely in standard German), or in quotes of spoken language. A report of a local food festival ('Kommt kucken a schmaachen', 2010) – 'Der vom lokalen "Syndicat d'iniative" organisierte "Lëtzebuerger Weekend"' (The Luxembourg weekend organized by the local development council) – is in German (Der vom lokalen … organisierte), French (Syndicat d'iniative) and Luxembourgish (Lëtzebuerger Weekend) (or French or English, depending on how one classifies 'weekend'). Here, bits of the local language emerge as people start to talk about food (and note, as discussed in Chapter 6, the significance of language and food relations): 'Lëtzebuerger Weekend, mir hunn am Ländche gudd Saachen, kommt kuchen a schmaachen' (Luxembourg weekend, we have good things in our little country, come have a look and taste)[1] and 'sou schmaacht Lëtzebuerg' (this is how Luxembourg tastes).

Here at last, then, in this rare bi/multilingual paper, which nonetheless is generally resolute in its separation of languages, the third local language shows through the cracks when food and local taste come to the fore, when the everydayness of local language use is allowed a space. In simple terms this reflects a common set of language ideologies in which so-called standard, prestige varieties are given 'symbolic value in public institutions, facilitating access to global rather than local resources' while 'vernacular language practices', which may have symbolic value in local communities, struggle for recognition in the wider domain (Farr, 2011, p. 1162). In the most pernicious version of this stance, state authorities may even ascribe a state of *zerolingualism*, where students' first languages (such as Moroccan or Turkish) are dismissed and their supposed lack of proficiency in a standard variety is deemed to produce a total of 'zero' (Jaspers, 2011, p. 1267).

This first account of language policies, ideologies and hierarchies, then, gives us one way of thinking about why the languages of these multilingual corn-huskers are not accorded much value: their linguistic resources, even though they come from a variety of sources, and even though they include resources that might be deemed high-status varieties (English and Mandarin), are largely vernacular resources that only get to peep through the cracks of regulated language hierarchies on occasions (and sometimes, like the indigenous languages of Vanuatu, or the Portuguese and Cape Verde Creole of immigrant populations in Luxembourg not to appear at all). These are spoken resources, picked up through life trajectories, whose value is considered low in the broader linguistic ideological context.

Another approach to this question is to focus more on the question of language commodification. Under late capitalist modes of production language comes to play 'an increasingly central economic role' both as 'the means through which work is accomplished' and as 'a product of labor' (Heller, 2010, p. 104). Looking at the ways in which multilingual skills are valued in a tourism call centre (2009) and a Swiss airport (2011), Duchêne argues that the the structures of the neoliberal market and the ideologies and practices of late capitalism give value to certain languages while exploiting the linguistic competencies of migrant workers. Multilingualism (*plurilinguisme*) is thus recognized as adding value for the institution (*un apport pour l'entreprise*), though this value is differentially recognized: the multilingualism of staff dealing with customers is differently valued from the multilingualism of baggage handlers, whose skills may nevertheless be called on when the need arises. Central to Heller and Duchêne's (2011; Duchêne, 2009; 2011) position, therefore, is an argument that under late capitalism, we see not only continued capitalist expansion and saturation of markets but also new ways in which language is valued and devalued within new forms of capitalist enterprise (including areas such as tertiary education which have moved inexorably from the state to capital spheres).

As Duchêne (2009) explains, 'institutionalized language choices remain strictly market-driven and do not incorporate languages that are considered to be of no economic or national value to tourism companies' (p. 47). This process, therefore, not only favours certain languages and speakers over others but also reproduces global inequalities 'by choosing languages that are already highly valued or by choosing languages which allow them to enter a new market' (p. 47). More broadly we can clearly see several related phenomena: the global spread of languages such as English closely linked to the global economy; the valorization and devalorization of certain languages and multilingual skills in different institutional and work settings; and the regulation of linguistic styles, irrespective of the language in which they occur, in sectors of the global market such as call centres and fast food outlets (Cameron, 2003; Friginal, 2009; Hultgren, 2011).

From this point of view, then, we can observe the value that accrues to languages through the functions of the market. The markets we are discussing in this book, however, clearly function at very different levels: while this local fruit and vegetable market is operating within a global city, and is inevitably subject to the forces of global capital, it nonetheless also has a relative autonomy. Urban space has been both a catalyst for capitalist expansion and site of struggles against capital. The combination of capitalism and growing industrial urbanization (the birth of the urban factory through changed steam, coal and technological changes) was essential to the growth of the city as a site of a densely concentrated and exploitable labour force 'whose lives were and are subject to the constant flux of capitalist development and consequent change and uncertainty' (Byrne, 2001, p. 167). Indeed, the very design and construction of the city 'has produced a space amenable to the ongoing accumulation of capital' (Millington, 2011, p. 5); and yet, as Sassen (2005) and Millington (2011) show, the city is multilayered and of vast complexity, and once we try to understand not only the role of global capital in relation to the city but also how non-hegemonic globalization from below works (Mathews & Vega, 2012), how the interwoven networks, layers and practices of the city operate, we cannot assume that any given language or language practice is at the service of, or a victim of, global capital.

A focus on local language practices within such markets can therefore help us understand the distribution of value. As Park and Wee (2012) note in their related 'market-theoretic perspective' on the 'ideologies and practices that shape and negotiate the value of language varieties as they are perceived in social context' (p. 6), we need to go beyond a focus only on 'market relations, such as the 'demand' for English under globalization' (p. 124), lest we confound value and price by viewing the value of English as a commodity in terms only of 'the economic mechanisms of supply and demand' (p. 124). The value attributed to English or other languages is a product not only of the market place but also of all the other social and cultural spheres in which it is seen as having value. Thus, once we take on board Bourdieu's (1984; 1991) understanding of capital, field and market, we need not only to question the reification of languages demanded by a language commodification perspective (Block, Gray & Holborrow, 2012; Block, 2014), but also to appreciate how languages and language practices – 'dynamic, flexible, and locally contingent competence' (Kramsch, 2009, p. 199) – achieve symbolic value in different fields (Kramsch & Whiteside, 2008).

As long as we stay at a broad and generalized level of social, economic and linguistic explanation – talking in terms of the value that accrues to languages under late capitalism – we will inevitably miss the dynamics of how value is gained and distributed. For people buying and selling in a multilingual market, language is important, but so are the freshness of the zucchini, the price of parsley, the availability of strawberries and the colour of the mangoes. We are interested in both multilingualism and markets from below, in the ways in which languages, artefacts and people rub up against each other in the everyday workings of small trade. We also therefore need to think not so much in terms of the commodity value of 'languages', but rather the constellation of language practices, local economies, gender relations, discrimination and types of work that lead to the ways in which language practices gain value.

Language identifications, as we saw in Chapter 2, are one of the key conduits for ethnic job channelling. From Serbian construction workers to Chinese market gardeners, these lines of linguistic identification and solidarity create positions within labour markets that produce particular forms of language-linked class formations. The ways in which languages and multilingualism are valued – the value accorded to the Hokkien, Hakka, Cantonese, Mandarin, Indonesian and English repertoire of the corn-husker – need to be understood not so much through an analysis that assumes a priori infrastructural determinants of capital and thereby accepts the logic of commodification by market forces to attribute value to languages, but rather through an analysis that takes language practices and their regulation, linguistic identification and exclusion, as crucial to the construction of class positions themselves.

When, in the early morning at Flemington Market, Muhibb shouts '*Yallah yallah* shītake, shītake […] Let's go, come on', for example, we need to consider several things.

Excerpt 8.2 (M: Muhibb, W: Worker, C: customer. T: Market trader)
Arabic: *italics*; English: plain; Japanese: **bold**

1. M: At the front Bob, the black fungus is at the front. How many oysters do you need?
2. C: Where's the black fungi?
3. M: At the front of the stand. Right at the front of the stand. Get 'em.
4. W: Fifty-five … forty-five,
5. M: Fifty-five *el box el abyad.* Forty-five *haydekeh.* (Fifty-five for the white box. Forty-five for the other one.) No worries. [to the customer]
    [inaudible]
6. M: [shouting] Black fungi? [to another trader in the distance]
7. T: How many you want? [shouting back]
8. M: Ten kilo?
9. T: Ten kilo? Black fungi? [surprised]
10. M: I mean ah **shītake.**
11. T: Ah, **shītake.** I thought the black fungi, [T is closer now]
12. M: *Yallah yallah* (come on, come on) **shītake, shītake.**
13. W: **shītake::** ten kilo::
14. M: Let's go come on.
15. T: over here.
16. M: I was going to take in the morning but you weren't here.
17. T: Ok, Thank you.
18. M: Ten kilo yeah? Thank you very much. [friendly voice]

Muhibb's instuction to his worker (line 5) regarding the boxes of black fungi – 'Fifty-five *el box el abyad.* Forty-five *haydekeh* (Fifty-five for the white box. Forty-five for the other one)' – suggests that it is not always the case that Arabic is used for numbers. Unlike other examples, such as the negotiated price of yellow zucchini in front of the customer of Maltese background (Chapter 1, excerpt 1.3) – 'Tell him **arba wa ashreen** (Tell him *twenty-four*)' – here his use of English appears to include the customer in the understanding of the price while the Arabic clarifies the difference to the worker. His friendly 'no worries' also shows another side of his capacity to rapidly shift styles. After the confusion over black fungi and shītake, and the other trader's apparently differently-paced readiness to discuss this further, Muhibb picks up the pace again, urging them to get moving (lines 12–14): '*Yallah yallah* (come on, come on) **shītake, shītake** [...] Let's go, come on', before gently thanking the trader at the end of the episode (line 18).

To classify this as trilingual – Arabic '*yallah*' (come on); Japanese '**shītake**' (mushrooms); English 'let's go' – does not seem a particularly helpful move. To then assume certain levels of commodification for each language would be to abstract these resources from their contexts of use. The Arabic here is a local (Lebanese Australian) Arabic that is used for getting some of their business done, and here for giving orders to other speakers of Arabic (including those who perhaps only know this phrase from its repeated use). It matters who is saying it: the phrase used by the bearded, Lebanese Australian Muhibb to hurry things up in the hectic dawn trading is very different from the ACE foreman Phillip's learned use on construction sites: 'but I know how to, um, I know how to say "hurry up" in Arabic: "*yallah yallah*". And "*pali pali*" is Korean for hurry up'(Phillip, interview, October 31, 2012). When Muhibb uses it, it is a sign of authority: because his family runs the business; he is a large, bearded man; this is the 'Lebanese end' of the market floor; his employees are casual workers from immigrant backgrounds; this is the busiest time of the early morning; his capacity to shift styles allows him to speed up and slow down interactions and because his voice and its rhythmic instigation – '*yallah yallah*, **shītake, shītake** [...] Let's go, come on' – is one of command.

As for **shītake**, whose Japanese origins might suggest a wider set of linguistic resources, in this context of use it is surely little more than a common term for anyone dealing with fruit and vegetables (no more Japanese than *carpaccio* or *formaggio* are necessarily Italian – see Chapter 4). The restaurants to which they are sending these items, furthermore, are by no means upmarket Japanese restaurants; indeed shītake have now been adapted to a wide variety of cuisines, including 'Modern Australian'. The English 'let's go, come on' – more or less a repetition of the Arabic '*yallah yallah*' – is also here not necessarily a resource of high value. Although the brothers' ease in English, their capacity to switch registers and styles with different customers and vendors and their ability to carry on multiple tasks across English and Arabic is of great importance to their business, here its use is tied both to its previously uttered Arabic equivalent and to the work relations between Muhibb and the workers responsible for shifting and stacking fruit and vegetables. The value of these linguistic resources as they are deployed in this early morning market are always therefore contingent: Languages themselves do not have value; rather semiotic resources in action gain value in relation to who is using what with whom.

We therefore need to take into account the relations between the language practices, linguistic capital, speakers and type of labour. The market value of the corn-huskers' diverse linguistic resources is relatively low (the relativity is important here – they may be at the bottom of a low-paid, informal economy but they may also be better off than others from similar backgrounds) because the work these resources are used for and the vernacular style of these resources are devalued within the broader market. In *Petit Paris*, Nabil's resources – his French, Japanese and English repertoire, more than his Arabic – gain a different level of capital because of the work they do (ordering bread, serving dishes, attending to customers, talking to the chef) and the way a language such as French ('*bon appétit*') may be viewed in this context.

The very question posed at the beginning of this section – why doesn't their multilingualism deliver greater assets? – is one based in particular language ideologies. To assume that multilingualism may be linked to wealth (or cognitive development or many other supposed advantages) is to presuppose an understanding of multilingualism as the combination of certain forms of language linked to work, wealth, literacy and education. Yet many people are multilingual because they are poor (not poor because they are multilingual): You need multilingual skills to get by in the informal global economy, and while this may bring some better living conditions than non-participation, the material benefits may be limited. For these workers, like Nischal's language list in *Patris* (Chapter 4), these are resources that get things done. While the commodification of languages affects certain language workers, and the language policies and ideologies that place languages in hierarchies influence the way languages are perceived, it is not some abstracted form of commodifiable multilingualism that such workers possess but rather an ability to engage in a range of metrolingual practices, which, like the language affiliations across construction sites, gives them access to the food and employment networks of this market and beyond.

'乜language都有㗎!': from niche to metrolingua francas

Perhaps more interesting than the listing of languages by the corn husker – Hokkien, Hakka, Cantonese, Mandarin, Indonesian and English – is this young man's observations first that '乜language都有㗎!' (all kinds of languages are spoken here!), and second that these are '乜都有, 撈埋一齊' (all sorts of languages mixed together), for this comes closer to our understanding of how such markets, such everyday multilingualism, actually operate. Rather than trying to map languages by place, person or percentage, what we actually need to appreciate are the *manifold multilingualisms* that emerge in all those moments of *metrolingual multitasking* (Chapter 4) that make up the daily interactions across this space. The spatial repertoires of these markets include a wide range of linguistic resources, depending on who is talking to whom, during what activity, in what transaction, at what point in which personal trajectory.

Our analysis of the metrolinguistic market place, like many of the other sites we have looked at, suggests we have to incorporate an understanding of the multilayered dynamics of the spatial repertoires – the activities, objects, place and semiotic resources – as integral to metrolinguistic practices. While remaining attentive to the ways in which the shifting linguistic resources of these workplaces are a product of the social and economic conditions that govern such workforces, our focus centres on the everydayness of such linguistic exchanges, 'the dimensions and practices of globalization from below' (Mathews & Vega, 2012, p. 1), the everyday forms of exchange that 'produce capacities for the recognition or acknowledgement of otherness in situational specificity' (Wise, 2009, p. 35).

Excerpt 8.3 (FS: female fruit seller, MC: male customer)
Chinese (Cantonese): characters (translations in brackets)
1. FS: 呢呢呢呢...係呀, 係呀.呢個色好食.
    (Look look look look … yeah, yeah. This colour tastes good.)
2. FS: 唔係呃你㗎! (I'm not lying to you!)
3. MC: 信你! (I believe you!)
4. FS: 你唔信呢, 就一樣買一隻返去試吓!
    (if you don't believe me, then buy one and try it at home!)
5. FS: 真係, 越黃嘅越好食. 我都想話自己拾返啲去.
    (Honestly, the more yellow the better the taste. I was just saying I want to take some home to try it.)

6. FS: 試吓. 真係㗎,唔係呃你. 因為佢呢喺樹熟先.
   (Try it. Honestly, I'm not lying to you. Because these ripen on the tree.)
7. MC: 哦 … 樹上熟. (oh … ripen on the trees.)
8. FS: 唔係呃你㗎 … 真係唔係呃你㗎.
   (I'm not lying to you … really I'm not lying to you.)
9. MC: 試吓先. (let's try it then.)
10. FS: 甜好多㗎, 嗰啲呢, 嗰啲生啲嘅嗰酸啲.
   (it's much sweeter, this one, that one is less ripe and so is very sour.)

As with the earlier interactions at the Produce Market (see for example Chapter 1), this interaction needs to be understood in relation to the place, the surrounds, the tasks and the type of interaction (Image 8.1). At the centre of the action are the mangoes themselves, the fruit that sit between the two interactants and make up the constant focus of negotiation (including colour, taste, tree-ripening, price). As we argued in Chapter 4, we can usefully expand on Thrift's (2007) *associational* view of space with the addition of a linguistic dimension, drawing attention to the

Image 8.1 Central Market.

interrelated roles of space, language practices, and objects. Thus we are trying to grasp the ways in which spatial repertoires (the linguistic resources available in particular places, as well as artefacts and objects) form part of the communicative activity of particular places. As we have argued at many points in this book, metrolingualism focuses not only on the linguistics of interaction but also on the city, the surrounds, the artefacts, all those other things that are equally part of the action. Along with the multitasking that frequently accompanies such transactions – simultaneous interactions with other customers, manipulating fruit, money and bags – these mangoes, their colours, textures, tastes and smell, are part of the action and become part of the spatial repertoire. This interaction may be in a more-or-less shared Cantonese code, but it is also part of a much wider process of metrolingual multitasking drawing on wider spatial repertoires.

This interaction is dominated by the insistence by the fruit seller that she is not lying (lines 2, 6 and 8), that her mangoes are sweet (lines 1, 5 and 10) and that she is offering the deal (not much of a deal, in fact) that he can buy them and try them at home (Lines 4 and 5), as she was about to do herself. It matters too that it is the yellowness of the mangoes that is part of their selling point: Unlike the yellowing zucchinis in Chapter 1 (which brought the price down) or the yellow *Fanta* in the construction site (Chapter 6) (which made the Serbian workers long for the green *Fanta* back home), here the ripening from green to yellow is the significant selling point (it is also a strategy to avoid having to cut one open to taste it). The sales pitch is thus characterized by two main moves: the insistence on the sweetness of the fruit as evidenced by their yellow colour – '呢個色好食' (this colour tastes good); '越黃嘅越好食' (the yellower the better) – and the insistence that she is telling the truth – '唔係呃你㗎…真係唔係呃你㗎' (I'm not lying to you … really I'm not lying to you).

There is, then, a constant movement back and forth between the appeal to the colour and taste of the material object and the appeal to the honesty of the seller, a movement echoed as a set of relocalized linguistic practices (see Chapter 6) in all those other transported Chinese markets in San Francisco, Kuala Lumpur, or London. As discussed in Chapter 6, like Talib's '*La wallah*' (no, I swear) (Excerpt 6.7), similar claims to honesty occur in many markets: 'Yoruba speakers, especially Moslems, often use the expression "Wallahi" when they wish to convince a listener that they are speaking the truth' (Ayoola, 2009, p. 396). Like the many other strategies of haggling, from humour to insult, from cajoling to flattery, these market strategies are both common across the world yet particular to the language, products and locality.

The central question we want to focus on here, however, is where this language use sits within the larger set of manifold multilingual market language use, the spatial repertoires of the Central Market. Here, the customer and seller have settled on a fairly shared code of Cantonese (though hers is a more rural Guangdong variety). In this market, Cantonese is a common language of interaction, but scratch the surface and it inevitably gets more complicated. A common picture from interviews with workers here is that English is the default language of commercial transaction, and Cantonese the language of social interaction. This picture is complicated in a number of ways. Mandarin Chinese also plays a role here. Indeed one informant asserted that Mandarin was in fact the lingua franca of the market, though this claim appears to be a result of the widespread use of various Mandarin resources, and this speaker's limited Cantonese resources. The fact that he was able to use Mandarin relatively successfully across the market suggested that it was more widely spoken than seemed to be the case. Like Nischal's view that Polish was the language of the *Patris* kitchen, and Aleksy and Krzyzstof's view that it was English (Chapter 4), we need to be able to accommodate the different perspectives of who speaks what to whom and what is therefore assumed to be a common language.

Mandarin Chinese is also a useful language alongside English for selling, and certainly the cheap sales at the end of the day are often done in varieties of English and Mandarin: 'One dollar! One dollar! *Yi kuai quan! Yi kuai quan!*' Among the Cantonese speakers, furthermore, there was great variety, including not only Hong Kong and Mainland, rural and urban, but also a range of histories, locations, backgrounds and other language uses. At one fruit and vegetable stall, where we had noted the different Cantonese accents, we discovered that the four women who work there are from Mauritius, Hong Kong, Vietnam and China. Their recognizably different Cantonese styles cannot be reduced to easy labels such as 'Vietnamese Cantonese' but rather reflect the far more complex life trajectories of these women: None of them was simply 'from' these places since all had travelled complex routes, physically, socially and linguistically, to end up at this market stall.

There is also a range of workers of other language backgrounds, as a young second-generation Lebanese stallholder explained.

Excerpt 8.4 (S: stallholder, R: Researcher)
1. S: Um, I speak a bit of, I dunno, like, Chinese or something.
2. R: Right, so you've picked that up working here?
3. S: Yeah, I've picked it up here, because there's a lot of Chinese people, so I speak like, maybe the numbers and that.

As with our discussion in Chapter 4 of the ways in which languages were identified, here too it was more important to do things with words rather than identify the code in which these were done. As well as Thai, Nepalese and Korean workers, we also spoke to a young man at a spice stall who explained he uses English, Portuguese and Arabic at home (his mother is Portuguese and father Lebanese) but English, Portuguese and Spanish at the market when Portuguese- and Spanish-speakers come to the stall for spices. According to him, there is far less Arabic spoken at this market than Spanish or Portuguese, once again, perhaps pointing to the perspectival nature of any understanding of a lingua franca. It is interesting to note, however, that immediately following the interaction shown in Excerpt 8.3, two (Latin American) Spanish speakers come into the recorded soundscape by this fruit stall. They are talking to each other (if they bought at this stall, they would presumably use English), which also points to another feature of such linguascapes: It is not only a question of the languages of stall-holders and their transactions with customers but also of all the other languages that customers use in the in-between spaces. Such observations show once again the impossibility of any easy linguistic mapping amid the dynamic metrolinguistic practices of the market.

This also raises the question of what we should consider the spatial repertoire of this market to include. As we argued in Chapter 4, the idea of spatial repertoires is concerned with the available and sedimented resources in particular places. It does not therefore include all and every linguistic soundbite that may occur, but rather draws attention to both the availability of a range of resources as well as the ways in which these become regularized. These Spanish resources, although at this juncture being used while passing a Cantonese-dominant interaction, may be seen as part of the spatial repertoire surrounding the spice stall. How these repertoires are taken up in the lingua francas of the market is part of the wider question we wish to pursue here.

One approach to understanding the complexity of multilingual urban language use has been to talk in terms of what Block (2007) calls *niche lingua francas* – second languages that are not the dominant language but are used for localized communication in a particular domain. The idea of *lingua francas,* however, needs some further discussion, particularly since this has been rather muddied by the intense focus in recent years on the notion of English as a lingua franca (Jenkins, 2006; 2009; Mackenzie, 2014; Pennycook, 2012b). The original lingua franca was a language that developed for trading purposes across the Mediterranean, using vocabulary from Arabic, French, Greek, Italian, Spanish and Turkish (to the extent that these were namable entities) (Ostler, 2005; 2010). The term *lingua franca* (Italian for 'Frankish tongue') originated in the Mediterranean region in the Middle Ages among crusaders and traders of different language backgrounds. The term itself comes from the Italian, but is based on the Arabic view that all Europeans were 'Franks' (*Faranji/farengi*). The original *lingua franca*, or *Sabir*, suggests Walter (1988), 'served its purpose perfectly in commercial exchanges because of its particular quality that each user thought that it was the other's language' (p. 216, our translation).

Referring to the current use of English as a lingua franca, Phillipson (2009) suggests a certain historical irony here that the language of the mediaeval crusaders has now become the term affixed to 'English as the language of the crusade of global corporatization, marketed as "freedom" and "democracy"' (p. 167). Among other things, this points to the shift in meaning from a lingua franca as an emergent contact language for trade to its common current use: 'all language deliberately acquired outside the home environment is a kind of contact language, consciously learned for social or pragmatic reasons' (Ostler, 2010, pp. 36–37), or a common language between people who do not share a mother tongue[2] (Kirkpatrick, 2011). Indeed, Kachru (2005) has objected to this notion of English as a lingua franca largely on the grounds that the term is inaccurately used: there is a big difference between a contact language emerging through trade and the learning of an existing language, such as English, for international communication.

While there is little to be gained from an insistence on the original meaning of lingua franca, there is nonetheless an important linguistic ideological distinction to be made here. If we view lingua francas through the lens of modernist language ideology, where a lingua franca becomes a *learned object*, we have put language as an entity before the process of communication. If, however, we view a lingua franca as an emergent mix that is always in flux, that indeed should not be predefined as 'English' or any other pregiven language, then we can place the processes of interaction before an assumption about the medium. This is why Canagarajah (2007) opts for the idea of Lingua Franca English (LFE) rather than ELF, since from this position LFE is emergent from its contexts of use: speakers 'activate a mutually recognized set of attitudes, forms, and conventions that ensure successful communication in LFE when they find themselves interacting with each other' (p. 925). LFE is 'intersubjectively constructed in each specific context of interaction. The form of this English is negotiated by each set of speakers for their purposes' and thus 'it is difficult to describe this language a priori' (Canagarajah, 2007, p. 925). This 'translingual perspective' takes 'diversity as the norm' and 'challenges the assumption of other models of global Englishes that sharedness and uniformity of norms at different levels of generality are required for communicative success' (Canagarajah, 2013, p. 75).

The *Carthago* kitchen (see Chapters 4 and 7) locates itself as part of the flow of Mediterranean languages and people (in Tokyo), thus linking with the development of the first lingua franca, and shows how emergent lingua francas may develop out of a range of languages being used: French-speaking customers may drop by the kitchen to chat with the chef, for example, though Mama, working as floor staff, notes she herself is more likely to respond in Japanese to a French comment. When Mama says to the chef '*poason* mitai dake do, **dajaj** dakara' (it looks like fish but it's chicken you see), using the French for fish and Arabic for chicken (she also uses the Arabic word, *samak*, for fish), this mixing of words ('いろんな単語が入り乱れています' – various vocabularies are jumbled together) is always, as she explains, about getting things done. The language between the chef and Mama (Chapters 3 and 7) – their 共通用語 (common terminology) as she calls it – is an emergent and sedimented product of the trajectories of people through the restaurant. From the Turkish numbers picked up from a Turkish restaurant where they both used to work to the Arabic from one of the floor staff (who was studying Arabic), to the French the chef learned during his time in Paris to the Spanish Mama learned in Granada, and the bits of other Mediterranean languages they picked up travelling, these linguistic resources become part of the spatial repertoire of *Carthago* and thus become available as an emergent lingua franca.

Although Block's (2007) focus on niche lingua francas sheds light on the use of languages other than dominant and expected ones, it potentially reinforces the assumption that these are nonetheless extant objects rather than negotiated codes. Instead we want to develop the notion of *metrolingua francas* as emergent from spatial repertoires. By *metrolingual franca*, then, we are referring not to the choice of a language from among a list of linguistic options (Cantonese, Vietnamese, English etc.) but rather to the particular linguistic practices at any moment that draw on the available spatial repertoires. There may often be little agreement on what the local lingua franca is: as we saw from previous comments in this largely 'Chinese-speaking' market, it rather depends who you ask, and for what purposes the language is used. People use and identify languages (they 'lingo' as Joseph puts it in Chapter 1) according to a range of perceptions about their interlocutors, their own languages and the transactions they are engaged in. While there was sometimes agreement that Cantonese was the language of social interaction between many stall keepers, and English was more often the default language of market transaction at the stalls, others suggested Mandarin was the lingua franca, while at a more local level Hokkien, Indonesian, Vietnamese, Thai and Spanish all emerged as languages used across areas of work.

More detailed analysis of interactions in that market, furthermore, showed that while Cantonese was a common language of social interaction, this was also a diverse Cantonese, sometimes rural Cantonese with hints of languages such as Teochow or Hakka, sometimes city Cantonese from Hong Kong or Guangzhou (which may be quite 'Mando' – Mandarin-influenced – as one research assistant put it) and at other times Cantonese as spoken by Chinese Malaysians, Vietnamese or Indonesians. Just as Muhibb's '*yallah, yallah*' was used to Lebanese and Egyptian Arabic speakers as well as people of Somalian and other backgrounds, and the workers at ABC construction site spoke a variety of types of Arabic, so the Cantonese of this market is of many types. While Cantonese and English were common working languages, Mandarin was also used, albeit a fairly Cantonese version and in simple form ('one dollar, one dollar! *yi kuai qian, yi kuai qian!*'). This seemed in response to both interpretations of the likely language of passers by, as well as a general sense that Mandarin was a more useful language for wider use. Such contexts, then, are characterized by high levels of diversity within and across languages.

The ways in which people understand each other (or sometimes don't – see Chapter 6) can be many. They involve a range of linguistic and non-linguistic resources. In *Petit Paris,* things don't always work smoothly. Nabil explains how he communicates when only he and other francophone chefs are there with Japanese customers:

> Sometimes some Japanese people can speak a little French, or little English, or ... then it's OK for me. If they don't speak, I just feel what they say. I don't understand, really 100 per cent, but I can feel them because it's my business, it's 25 years in a restaurant, and I feel Japanese customers sometimes what they want, even [if] I don't understand.
>
> (Interview, December 27, 2011)

Likewise, sometimes when the Japanese manager (Hata-san) and the chef need to communicate, it just seems to happen. Nabil states: 'Chef don't speak Japanese, don't speak English, but he can express himself. I mean ... But in general, of course, communication between them is good. But few words in English, few words in Japanese, few words in French'; and later: 'Even just Hata and Chef they can communicate. Sometimes with heart, sometimes with international language.' When words fail, it is the knowledge of the business that counts, the 'feeling' for what is going on, the heart. This is not so much about a shared, common language operating in the kitchen but about how people manipulate the resources (including expertise and knowledge) available in the space they are in, and the development of shared, sedimented resources, including 'heart', over time, as they engage in shared activities. As Blommaert notes, some transactions can occur without being 'competent' in the local vernacular; instead bits and pieces of languages may be mobilized as an 'emergency lingua franca' (Blommaert, 2010, p. 8). These interactions may also be achieved cooperatively, involving a range of people and repertoires.

In contexts of complex multilingual interaction a lingua franca is not some pregiven language but rather a constantly emergent (rather than emergency) set of linguistic possibilities. Markets are sites of layered multilingualism in which different language resources are mobilized within a flow of other practices. If we ask what the lingua franca of such markets, restaurants, kitchens, shops and constructions sites is, expecting an answer that identifies a recognizable code such as 'English', 'Cantonese', Arabic' and so on, we are looking in the wrong direction. As Makoni and Pennycook (2012; Makoni, Makoni & Pennycook, 2010) argue, a strategy similar to the nonpluralization strategy of metrolingualism is to think in terms of multilingua francas, where mixed but varied language use is the norm, resulting in what we are calling *metrolingua francas* that are never fixed, stable or shared but rather sets of linguistic and non-linguistic resources that can be drawn on in different moments.

This takes us back to the original sense of lingua franca – as a trade language, as a language flexible enough to believe you are always speaking the others' language (Walter, 1988), as interactionally constructed in each specific context of interaction (Cangarajah, 2007; 2013), contexts that also include the practices and objects that are part of the action: the looks, the clothes, the gestures, the mangoes, the movements. When we asked stall-holders how they decided how to address different customers, clothes took on a larger role than we had expected: There is a domain of interpretation of appearance – shirts, shoes, eyewear, hairstyles, bags – that influenced decisions about language use; 'you just can tell' as one worker at a fruit stall put it. All these interactions need to be understood in relation to the intersecting domains of mobilities, practices, spaces and subjects (Cresswell & Merriman, 2011).

We have therefore stressed the need to understand that such interactions employ a range of semiotic resources drawn from the wider spatial repertoire. The repertoires of linguistic resources that people bring from their historical trajectories intersect with the spatial organization of other repertoires, while the practices of buying and selling, bartering and negotiating, husking corn and stacking boxes bring a range of other semiotic practices into play. None of these can sit outside any consideration of the spatial repertoires of these markets: yellowing zucchini (down goes the price) and yellowing mangoes (up goes the price), the linguistic repertoires, beliefs and expectations of interlocutors, the noise and urgency of market selling, the rhythm of the city (a mid-morning slow sale at Central Market is very different from flogging off the celery at the end of the afternoon – 'One dollar!! One dollar!! *Yi kuai qian! Yi kuai qian!*'), all play crucial roles in how various resources will be used and taken up, and therefore what constitute at any place and time the spatial repertoires from which the *metrolingua franca* may be drawn.

Metrolingual pedagogies and policies

From a language policy point of view, a focus on metrolingualism raises a number of points. Perhaps most obviously it urges language policy and planners to move their focus away from those beloved demolinguistic approaches to enumerable languages and to focus instead on language practices. On another level, a metrolingual approach to languages raises important questions for how we understand the idea of language contained in ideas such as language maintenance or language death. Substantial critiques have already been made of some of the reductionist discourses that equate 'one language' with 'one culture' and claim that the 'death' of one will cause the death of the other. As Heller and Duchêne (2007) make clear, such approaches to diversity are part of a continued attempt to 'maintain the language-culture-nation ideological nexus' (p. 7). We need to ask, they suggest, what interests are served by holding on to the linguistic ideologies that emerged from modernity:

> Rather than assuming we must save languages, perhaps we should be asking instead who benefits and who loses from understanding languages the way we do, what is at stake for whom, and how and why language serves as a terrain for competition.
>
> (p. 11)

Set against the discourses of language loss and preservation, we might also therefore note the growth and development of new languages, particularly urban vernaculars. Most announcements of newly discovered languages, such as the 'discovery' of a new language, Koro, in north-eastern India in 2010 (New Language Discovered, 2010), occur in remote communities that have never before been studied by linguists. Others, such as the recent announcement that a new 'mixed' language, 'Light Warlpiri' – which combines elements of Warlpiri, (Aboriginal) English and the English-based creole, Kriol – had been discovered in remote northern Australia (New Language Uncovered, 2013; O'Shannessy, 2013) acknowledge that these may also be recent, mixed and not necessarily linked to traditional ways of life. The growth of urban vernaculars, however, suggests both a need to rethink this approach to discovery and counting as well as rethinking more generally what we mean by languages.

As McLaughlin (2009) explains, the broad African context of 'profound multilingualism' is intensified in the city, with migration into the urban areas from diverse multilingual rural regions, and the growth of 'urban vernaculars' (p. 2). An outcome of the burgeoning growth of African cities, therefore, is 'an intensification of the linguistic environment and an increase in multilingualism' (p. 5). Because of the particular demographic and linguistic factors at play in African cities – 'the strong presence of young people under the age of 20 in African capitals, the extremely high levels of unemployment and poverty, the role of the informal economy, and the place of multilingualism' (Canut, 2009, p. 86) – it is not just the urban environment but also urban languages (Bokamba, 2009; Bosire, 2006; Kiessling & Mous, 2004; Kube-Barth, 2009; Makoni, Makoni & Pennycook, 2010) that are always under construction. These languages derive from multiple linguistic and cultural resources: an urban youth engagement with popular culture and a sense of global urban life. They are already mixed (to classify instances of mixed language as code-mixing is to miss the point), they are emergent from local interactions (these are never the fixed, standardized languages of statist dreams and educational syllabi) and are very hard to classify or describe (they are always in flux, always a use of whatever linguistic resources are at hand). These are the metrolingua francas of urban growth.

Once we look at online language use (from Facebook to YouTube comments) by participants loosely located in cities as different as Dhaka or Ulaanbaataar (Sultana, Dovchin & Pennycook, 2013; 2015), the diversity multiplies. But most importantly this metrolingual diversity suggests the need to stop talking in terms of languages as commonly understood. As Canut points out,

> Language mixing, linguistic overlap, and plural linguistic practices are all part of daily life and do not for the most part evoke any special metadiscourse, they simply are a reality, moreover speakers are always baffled by the importance researchers give to the topic.
>
> (Canut, 2009, p. 87)

For Canut, therefore, 'the only way of understanding the heterogeneity characteristic of cities is to focus the analysis on the subjective categories of each speaker' (2009, p. 89) and thus to avoid the imposition of external categories (language, ethnicity, identity) on these contexts.

This has of course presented a constant tension in this book: How to talk about languages in terms other than the pre-fixed terminology of both academic and popular discourse? How to both acknowledge and question Joseph's (Chapter 1) contention, for example, that the Produce Market workers 'use broken English and lingo in Lebanese'? If we wish to come to terms with contemporary language use, particularly of the young, particularly in cities, we cannot use the categories of old, the notions of language and culture that were nurtured under particular processes of modernity and state formation. As we have also argued, this is not just about the contemporary world, the 'superdiversity' of modern cities, the exchanges of young people in online environments. This is also as old as cities as themselves, as common as markets, as everyday as talking over food. We have thus proposed the notion of metrolingualism to capture some of the ways that language relates to the spatial organization of the city, the ways in which mixed language use is the norm.

It is not so much the case that 'a language' serves as a lingua franca in such contexts, but rather that a highly variable *multilingua franca* – or what we have here called a *metrolingua franca* – drawn from the spatial repertoire of places of diversity is always emergent. There are clearly cultural, culinary and ethnic ties that are part of the broader histories and networks of growers and sellers, particularly in relation to different waves of immigration (Italian, Maltese, Lebanese, Cantonese for example). These are linked to the need to grow one's own food (often for basic economic purposes, but also for culinary reasons) as part of a wider informal economy and a variety of forms of labour provided by market gardens and markets themselves. They are also embedded within processes of marginalization and discrimination faced by various groups of migrants. These broad affiliations, language practices, employment possibilities, discrimonations and interactions intersect in the *metrolingua francas* of such places. Any serious attempt to engage with language policy and education in the contemporary world has to start to grapple with these language realities rather than remaining locked into a vision of languages as fixed objects of modernity.

When García (2009) suggests that 'bilingual education is *the only way* to educate children in the twenty-first century' (p. 5), we need to ask what is this bilingualism of which she speaks? Bilingual education may be a national education programme to produce people competent in two languages. In Colombia, for example, the *National Bilingual Programme* is concerned not with various types of bilingualism, but rather 'with the aim of offering all students in Colombia the possibility of becoming bilingual in English and Spanish' (de Meija, 2012, p. 247). Bilingual in this context means little more than giving everyone access to the 'global language' English, largely, as with many such current programmes, with an eye to increased participation in the global economy. The recent English Education reform initiatives in Japan in response to globalization (Dec 13, 2013) – intended for full implementation by the 2020 Tokyo Olympics and Paralympics – are another acute version of such monoglossic bilingual education. MEXT (the Ministry of Education, Culture, Sports, Science & Technology) emphasizes the need for school children to acquire English skills to *transmit Japanese culture* ('日本の文化の発信') an idea based on nationalistic discourse and identity ('日本人としてのアイデンティティ').

Kubota (2014) points out that this initiative ignores the diversity of language used in the international community by uncritically assuming that English is the lingua franca of the world, thereby reinforcing a narrow, monolingual view of globalization. Such nationalistic bilingual campaigns that bifurcate the national (Spanish, Japanese) and the global (English) have more to do with the entrenched language ideologies of modernity than with contemporary language use (Nakane, Otsuji & Armour, 2015). As García goes on to explain, by contrast, what she means by bilingual education is not so much 'a monoglossic view of bilingual education' like a 'bicycle with two balanced wheels' but rather 'an all-terrain vehicle in its heteroglossic possibilities' (p. 17). For García, then, bilingual education is not an education in two separate languages but rather a practice of *translanguaging*, the '*multiple discursive practices* in which bilinguals engage in order to *make sense of their bilingual worlds*' (p. 45; García's emphasis). This is not, therefore, the bi/ multilingualism of the *Luxemburger Wort*, with its French and German sections and its Lëtzebuergesch peeping through now and then, but rather the translanguaging of '乜都有, 捞埋一齊' (all sorts of languages mixed together).

Blackledge and Creese (2010) argue for a *critical* perspective on multilingualism since 'public discourses and language policies in the United Kingdom, as elsewhere in the developed, English-speaking world, are frequently out of step with the plural linguistic practices of its population' (pp. 4–5). Popular and populist discourses about multilingualism portray the use of non-majority languages as a problem, as a lack of will to integrate, as a ghettoizing factor, as a factor in 'civil unrest, social segregation, family breakdown, educational failure and financial burden to the state' (p. 5). While Belgian children of Arabic, Berber and Turkish backgrounds may be disparaged as 'zerolinguals' because their home languages are discounted and their knowledge of standard Dutch is limited, they nonetheless fight back with their play around 'illegal Dutch' (Jaspers, 2011, p. 1267). In such framings of multilingualism, being able to speak languages learned in school – the learned and limited languages of schooled bilingualism, typically languages such as French, German, Spanish and Chinese – is to be praised, while the local multilingualism of minority communities is a problem; and these forms of multilingualism are indeed very different.

García points to the need for pedagogical practices 'firmly rooted in the multilingual and multimodal language and literacy practices of children in schools in the 21st century' (2009, p. 8). This *translanguaging* approach to education makes central 'the act performed by bilinguals of accessing different linguistic features or various modes of what are described as autonomous languages' (García, 2009, p. 141). Translanguaging thus 'requires an epistemological change in which students' everyday languaging and school languaging is expanded and integrated, and in so doing blends ways of knowing which are traditionally found in different spaces' (García & Li Wei, 2014, p. 69). Likewise, Blackledge and Creese (2010) advocate 'teaching bilingual children by means of a bilingual pedagogy' and argue for a 'a release from monolingual instructional approaches' (2010, p. 201) through translanguaging. Central to these proposals is an acknowledgement of the complex and mixed language practices of bilingual worlds and the need for our language classes to start to resemble these worlds more. In Canagarajah's (2013) view, pedagogy needs to

> be refashioned to accommodate the modes of performative competence and cooperative disposition we see outside the classroom. Rather than focusing on a single language or dialect as the target of learning, teachers have to develop a readiness in students to engage with the repertoires required for transnational contact zones.
>
> (p. 191)

Related *transglossic* approaches to language (Sultana, Dovchin & Pennycook, 2015), by incorporating elements of the *transgressive*, ensure that there is much more to this than merely mixing languages together. Conceived initially in opposition to the notion of diglossia to capture the way languages are blended and mixed rather than used in isolation (García, 2009, p. 304) this notion takes on a more dynamic, transgressive form in subsequent formulations where 'transglossia releases ways of speaking of subaltern groups that had been previously fixed within static language identities and are constrained by the modern/colonial world system' (García, 2013, p. 161). García here draws on Mignolo's (2000) notion of *bilanguaging,* which 'as a way of living in languages in a transnational world, as an educational and epistemological project, rests on the critique of reason, of disciplinary structures, and cultures of scholarship complicitous with national and imperial languages' (p. 273). There is far more at stake here, then, than a mixing of languages in the classroom; rather, this has to do with a much broader educational and epistemological challenge to the alliance between nations, languages and educational systems.

While a metrolingual approach shares much with these translingual approaches, it differs in various dimensions. Unlike the work of Blackledge, Creese, García, Li Wei or Canagarajah, we have not been looking at educational sites. Thus while they are able to draw more immediate implications from their observations of translingual practices in classrooms or student writing, the implications of metrolingualism are less direct. Certainly we should be clear that just because the various people we have focused on in these chapters – from Nabil in his restaurant to Talib and Muhibb at their market stall – use a range of linguistic resources to get things done, this does not necessarily mean that this is what we should teach. Nonetheless, our work asks us to question what language myths we perpetuate by the language ideologies we reproduce in our language classes, with our bounded entities 'French', 'German', 'Japanese', 'Chinese', 'Korean', 'Indonesian', 'Italian', 'English' or in our 'bilingual' or 'multilingual' language policies.

By viewing language use as profoundly bound up with space and activity, metrolingualism also raises questions about how we understand languages not only in relation to each other but also in relation to all that is going on in a particular place. The notions of *metrolingual multitasking, spatial repertoires* and *metrolingua francas*, following Thrift's (2007) *associational* understanding of space, draw attention to the interrelated roles of space, language practices, people and objects in motion. The challenge from an educational point of view is how then to get beyond a segregational view of languages towards a more integrated one and how to help students to 'integrate their own semiological activities with those of their interlocutor' (Harris, 2009, p. 75). Our focus on language as a local practice, rather than on languages as systems and learnable entities, suggests that an emerging goal of language education may be less towards mythical native-speaker-like users of mythical languages and more towards resourceful metrolingual speakers (Otsuji, 2011; Pennycook, 2012a) who draw on multiple semiotic resources and are good at accommodating, negotiating and being light on their feet and loose with their tongues.

If, as Canagarajah (2013, p. 175) argues, contemporary approaches to language education need to develop an understanding of the expansion of repertoires (rather than the learning of languages), the co-construction of terms of engagement or questions of positionality, negotiation and language practices, and if, as we have argued, we need to include a focus on the wider spatial repertoires, language practices, objects and activities, then we need to incorporate a multifaceted understanding of language, space and place into our approaches to education. As García and Li Wei (2014) make clear, the relations between classrooms and outside language use are complex. We cannot bring the spatial repertoires of the market, the construction site, the kitchen into the classroom (the very idea of space renders this impossible) and nor would we want to. Neither do we want to provide students only with the linguistic resources to barely function at the lower end of the informal global economy. But if we ignore this world of repertoires, resources, language practices and mobilities, we risk deepening even further the gap between the languages of school and the languages of life, the fixed codes of schooled multilingualism and the fluidity of everyday metrolingualism.

Conclusion: writing it all together

At the heart of this book have been language and the city (metrolingualism). We have tried to show, both in our descriptions of shops and cafés and markets and construction sites, and in our ways of writing, how the city is a place of diversity, of rhythms and layers. Central to the city are the contiguity and commensality of daily life, the proximity of lives lived together and the importance of food and talking. These close interactions, these mobilities and materialities, are so often bound up with language. We have tried therefore to show how the way we think about the city has major implications for any consideration of language: If we cut the city up into ethnicities and numerical accounts of languages, we miss the dynamics of metrolingual practices. So the way we think about languages also has major implications for how we understand the city. Both are deeply involved in each other, in a constant exchange between people, architecture, urban landscapes, linguistic resources, movements across the city, meals, buying, selling, telling stories and expressing desires.

In order to evince the complexity of language and the city, we have needed ways of writing that can catch some of this dynamism. As our late colleague[3] Alison Lee (Aitchison & Lee, 2006; 2010) reminded us, writing about research in fields such as sociolinguistics and applied linguistics is not so much a process of 'writing up' a research report, but is intimately part of the research itself. Just as ethnography has to be understood as process and as writing (see Blommaert & Dong, 2010; Chapter 2), so writing has to be seen not as the translation of data into text, but as another part of that process of knowledge construction. This has several implications. As in other publications (Otsuji & Pennycook, 2010; 2014), we have placed data excerpts early in the text, thereby transgressing various norms of academic writing. This is not just to entice a reader in, or to avoid leaving the examples of research till after a couple of chapters of literature review, but also to suggest that these standard approaches to social scientific writing and research have always been flawed.

In empirical, social scientific research, it is often stated that the data should be central, that themes and implications need to emerge from the analysis, and yet when it is written, the account of the research all too often places a stack of recycled ideas in the way. It is almost impossible to start with data before moving to a discussion (and we have struggled with peer reviews that have objected to our approach). This is not to say that research writing needs to replicate the research process, but it is to suggest that a closer relation between the two may shed light on how we get to our interpretations and conclusions, and may help us to see that the way we write plays a crucial role in relation to what we write. It is for these reasons that we have, for example, tried to capture the noise and repeated calls of the market traders in this chapter by repeating phrases such as 'One dollar!! One dollar!! *Yi kuai qian! Yi kuai qian!*' We sought a more performative rather than merely descriptive way to write the market.

The themes in this book emerged in the process of the research and the writing. They developed from reading about cities and languages, and from talking in and about cafés, and from writing things down and then writing them up. We hoped, as this project progressed, to create an interwoven text, with extracts from our data, ideas from our readings, multiple contexts and examples, interwoven in a layered, sedimented text that related to the ways we were starting to understand metrolingualism. This also therefore involved not only writing down and writing up but writing over and over. Like the writing on the city walls (Chapter 7), this text has been written on top of other versions, with hints of earlier attempts peeping through. Like the movement of people in and out of the breathing city (Chapter 3), the text has gone back and forth, back and forth. Like the changing patterns of cities as people and jobs and restaurants and places of worship come and go, the organization and shape of this text has constantly changed, with new data inhabiting new sections, new sections waiting for new ideas to move in.

The data changes too. While some images of data may suggest a static set of collected realities, the complexity of our data has also led to its instability, as we go back and listen again, rethink an exchange, ask participants what was going on. Different day, different data. Although we placed our data early in chapters and the book, although we tried to work from our data, it nonetheless had no meaning prior to its entextualization. As we wrote, the data changed its identity; it talked to us differently at different stages of writing. The data and the textual organization, like the city, are only temporary arrangements. As we talked and annotated and changed, our texts and excerpts often replicated the metrolingual surfaces of the city with their multilingual scribbles and scripts and comments. The writing processes themselves became metrolingual as the city and its sounds and smells interacted with our writing.

So finally this has always been a writing together, a complex, collaborative endeavour, where texts change, disappear, move and intertwine. Like the convivial yet contested relations of multicultural suburbs (Chapter 5), this textual production has had moments of pleasure and dispute. Our hope is that this text carries the traces of the many people we worked with on this project, their conversations, transactions and ways of living, the places we worked in, with their noise and

Image 8.2 Market sketch.

smells and atmosphere, and the layers of writing together, with all the frustrations, pleasures and greater possibilities that can bring. There comes a time when we reach the limits of our writing, and turn to other means to capture what we are doing, hence Emi's attempts to capture the feeling of the market in a different mode (Image 8.2). Drawing becomes another part of the research process, and a possible mode to try to capture the importance of space, the simultaneity of action and rhythm, a different approach to sensing the smells and noises and feelings of a market place that our texts can only start to portray.

Notes

1 Thanks to Jean-Jacques Weber for checking and correcting our translations, and for further comments on triglossia in the *Luxemburger Wort*. These extracts from the *Luxemburger Wort* for Monday 6th September, 2010, p. 23.
2 This view draws in part on Kirkpatrick's (2011) peculiar assertion that the term *lingua franca* derives from the Franks' adoption of the local language after their invasion of Gaul in the 5th century. Like Phillipson's assertion that *lingua franca* refers to 'the language of the Franks' (2009, p. 167), this seems to miss the point that the term derives from the generalization of Franks as Europeans not from the language spoken by the Franks.
3 We have lost a number of inspirational colleagues during the research and writing of this book, and the many conversations and interactions with them have left deep traces in our work. We want particularly to mention Jens Normann Jørgenson, whose work on polylanguaging was crucial for our development of metrolingualism; Leo van Lier, whose thinking on language ecologies has helped us understand the complexity of language and context: Michael Higgins, who helped us understand the ordinariness of diversity; and our UTS colleague Alison Lee, whose work on writing and research has long informed our thinking. We hope that their ideas live on in some ways in our own attempts to understand the many things that interested them.

Appendix
Transcription conventions

Modified from the work of Jefferson (2004).

[...]	material omitted
(??)	unclear
?	rising or question intonation
!	animated tone or exclamation
::	prolongation of the immediately prior sound
...	a brief interval within or between sentences
.	falling intonation
,	unfinished intonational contour
[word]	paralinguistic features and situational descriptions
( )	English translation for utterances for languages other than English

References

Agnew, J (2011) Space and place. In J Agnew and D N Livingstone (Eds) *The SAGE handbook of geographical knowledge*. Thousand Oaks: SAGE, pp. 316–331.

Aitchison, C and A Lee (2006) Research writing: Problems and pedagogies. *Teaching in Higher Education* 11(3): 265–278.

Aitchison, C. and A. Lee (2010) Writing in, writing out: Doctoral writing as peer work. In M Walker and P Thomson (Eds) *The Routledge doctoral supervisor's companion*. London: Routledge, pp. 260–269.

Ali, M (2003) *Brick Lane*. New York: Scribner.

Alim, H Samy (2004) *You know my steez: An ethnographic and sociolinguistic study of styleshifting in a Black American speech community*. Durham: Duke University Press.

Alim, H S and G Smitherman (2012) *Articulate while Black: Barack Obama, language and race in the US*. Oxford: Oxford University Press.

Allatson, P. (2001) Beyond the hybrid: Notes against heterophilic authoritarianism. *Genre* 22: 191–207.

Ang, I (2001) *On not speaking Chinese: Living between Asia and the West*. London: Routledge.

Ang, I, J Brand, G Noble and J Strenberg (2006) *Connecting diversity: The paradoxes of Australian multiculturalism*. Artarmon: Special Broadcasting Services (SBS).

Appadurai, A (1996) *Modernity at large: Cultural dimensions of globalization*. Minneapolis: University of Minnesota Press.

Appadurai, A (2001) Grassroots globalization and the research imagination. In A Appadurai (Ed.) *Globalization*. Durham: Duke University Press, pp. 1–21.

Australian Bureau of Statistics (2011) www.abs.gov.au/ [last accessed 21 October, 2014].

Ayoola, K (2009) Haggling exchanges at meat stalls in some markets in Lagos, Nigeria. *Discourse Studies* 11(4): 387–400.

Bailey, B (2007) Heteroglossia and boundaries. In M Heller (Ed.) *Bilingualism: A social approach*. New York: Palgrave Macmillan, pp. 257–274.

Bakhtin, M (1981) *The dialogic imagination: Four essays* (C Emerson and M Holquist, Trans.). Austin: University of Texas.

Bakhtin, M (1986) *Speech genres and other late essays*. Austin: University of Texas Press.

Bamberg, M and A Georgakopoulou (2008) Small stories as a new perspective in narrative and identity analysis. *Text and Talk* 28(3): 377–396.

Barni, M and G Extra (Eds) (2008) *Mapping linguistic diversity in multicultural contexts*. Berlin: Mouton de Gruyter.

Belasco, W (2008) *Food: The key concepts*. Oxford: Berg.

Bell, D (2007) The hospitable city: Social relations in commercial spaces. *Progress in Human Geography* 31(1): 7–22.

Benor, S B (2010) Ethnolinguistic repertoire: Shifting the analytic focus in language and ethnicity. *Journal of Sociolinguistics* 14: 159–183.

Bhabha, H (1994) *The location of culture*. London: Routledge.

Blackledge, A and A Creese (2010) *Multilingualism: A critical perspective*. London and New York: Continuum Press.

Block, D (2006) *Multilingual identities in a global city: London stories*. Basingstoke: Palgrave Macmillan.

Block, D (2007) Niche lingua francas: An ignored phenomenon. *TESOL Quarterly* 41(3): 561–566.

Block, D (2014) *Social class in applied linguistics*. London: Routledge.

Block, D, J Gray and M Holborow (2012) *Neoliberalism and applied linguistics*. London: Routledge.

Blommaert, J (2008) *Grassroots literacy: Writing, identity and voice in Central Africa*. London: Routledge.

Blommaert, J (2010) *The sociolinguistics of globalization*. Cambridge: Cambridge University Press.

Blommaert, J (2013a) *Ethnography, superdiversity and linguistic landscapes: Chronicles of complexity*. Bristol: Multilingual Matters.

Blommaert, J (2013b) Complexity, accent, and conviviality: Concluding comments. *Applied Linguistics* 34(5), 613–22.

Blommaert, J and A Backus (2013) Super diverse repertoires and the individual. In I de Saint-Georges and J-J Weber (Eds) *Multilingualism and multimodality: Current challenges for educational studies*. Rotterdam: Sense Publishers, pp. 11–32.

Blommaert, J and J Dong (2010) *Ethnographic fieldwork: A beginner's guide*. Bristol: Multilingual Matters.

Blommaert, J, S Leppänen and M Spotti (2012) Endangering multilingualism. In J Blommaert, S Leppänen, P Pahti and T Räisänen (Eds.) *Dangerous multilingualism: Northern perspectives on order, purity and normality*. London: Palgrave Macmillan, pp. 1–21.

Bokamba, E G (2009) The spread of Lingala as a lingua franca in the Congo Basin. In F McLaughlin (Ed.) *The languages of urban Africa*. London: Continuum, pp. 50–70.

Bosire, M (2006) Hybrid languages: The case of Sheng. In O F Arasanyin and M A Pemberton (Eds) Selected proceedings of the 36th annual conference on African linguistics (pp. 185–193). Somerville: Cascadilla Proceedings Project.

Bourdieu, P (1984) *Distinction*. Cambridge: Harvard University Press.

Bourdieu, P (1991) *Language and symbolic power*. Oxford: Polity Press.

Bruner, J (1991) The narrative construction of reality. *Critical Inquiry* 18(1): 1–21.

Bucholtz, M (2000) The politics of transcription. *Journal of Pragmatics* 32: 1439–1465.

Burgess, E W (1924) The growth of the city: An introduction to a research project. *The American Sociological Society* 18: 85–99.

Busch, B and J Schick (2007) Educational materials reflecting heteroglossia: Disinventing ethnolinguistic differences in Bosnia-Herzegovina. In S Makoni and A Pennycook (Eds) *Disinventing and reconstituing languages*. Clevedon: Multilingual Matters. pp. 216–232.

Busch, B (2012a) *Das sprachlige Repertoire oder Niemand ist einsprachig*. Vorlesung zum Antritt der Berta-Karlik-Professur an der Universität Wien. Klagenfurt: Drava.

Busch, B (2012b) The linguistic repertoire revisited. *Applied Linguistics* 33: 503–523.

Busch, B (2013) *Mehrsprachigkeit*. Wien: Facultas Verlags.

Byrne, D (2001) *Understanding the urban*. Houndmills: Palgrave.

Cameron, D (2003) Globalizing 'communication'. In J Aitchison and D Lewis (Eds) *New media language*. London: Routledge, pp. 27–35.

Canagarajah, S (2007) Lingua Franca English, multilingual communities, and language acquisition. *Modern Language Journal* 91: 923–939.

Canagarajah, S (2013) *Translingual practice: Global Englishes and cosmopolitan relations*. London: Routledge.

Canut, C (2009) Discourse, community, identity: Processes of linguistic homogenization in Bamako. In F McLaughlin (Ed.) *The languages of urban Africa*. London: Continuum, pp. 86–102.

Chiaro, D (2013) Passionate about food: Jamie and Nigella and the performance of food talk. In C Gerhardt, M Frobenius and S Ley (Eds) *Culinary linguistics: The chef's special*. Amsterdam: John Benjamins, pp. 83–102.

Christie, M (1988) *The Sydney Markets 1788 – 1988*. Flemington: Sydney Market Authority.

Chun, C (2014) Mobilities of a linguistic landscape at Los Angeles City Hall Park. *Journal of Language and Politics* 13:4 653–74.

Chun, C (2015) *Engaging with the everyday: Power and meaning making in an EAP classroom*. Bristol: Multilingual Matters.

Clyne, M (2005) *Australia's language potential*. Sydney: UNSW Press.

Coad, D (2008) *The metrosexual: Gender, sexuality, and sport*. Albany: SUNY Press.

Collins, J and P Kunz (2009) Ethnicity and public space in the city: Ethnic precincts in Sydney. *Cosmopolitan Civil Societies: An Interdisciplinary Journal* 1(1): 39–70.

Collins, J (2009) Sydney's Cronulla riots: The Context and Implications. In G Noble (Ed.) *Lines in the sand: The Cronulla riots, multiculturalism and national belonging*. Sydney: Institute of Criminology Press, pp. 27–43.

Cook, R (2001) Robin Cook's chicken tikka masala speech. www.theguardian.com/world/2001/apr/19/race.britishidentity [last accessed 21 October, 2014].

Coulmas, F (2009) Linguistic landscaping and the seed of the public sphere. In E Shohamy and D Gorter (Eds) *Linguistic landscape: Expanding the scenery*. London: Routledge, pp. 13–24.

Coupland, N (2007) *Style: Language variation and identity*. Cambridge: Cambridge University Press.

Coupland, N (2012) Bilingualism on display: The framing of Welsh and English in Welsh public spaces. *Language in Society* 41(1): 1–27.

Coupland, N (2013) Welsh tea: The centring and decentring of Wales and the Welsh language. In Sari Pietikäinen and H Kelly Holmes (Eds) *Multilingualism and the periphery*. Oxford: Oxford University Press, pp. 133–153.

Crang, M (2001) Rhythms of the City: Temporalised space and motion. In J May and N Thrift (Eds) *Timespace: Geographies of temporality*. London: Routledge, pp. 187–207.

Creese, A (2008) Linguistic Ethnography. In K A King and N Hornberger (Eds) *Encyclopedia of language and education*, 2nd ed. New York: Springer, pp. 229–241.

Creese, A and A Blackledge (2011) Separate and flexible bilingualism in complementary schools: Multiple language practices in interrelationship. *Journal of Pragmatics* 43: 1196–1208.

Cresswell, T and P Merriman (2011) Introduction: Geographies of mobilities – practices, spaces, subjects. In T Cresswell and P Merriman (Eds) *Geographies of mobilities: Practices, spaces, subjects*. Farnham: Ashgate, pp. 1–15.

Cummins, J (2000) *Language, power and pedagogy: Bilingual children in the crossfire*. Clevedon: Multilingal Matters.

Daveluy, M (2011) War, peace and languages in the Canadian navy. In A Duchêne and M Heller (Eds) *Language in late capitalism: Pride and profit*. London: Routledge, pp. 142–160.

de Mejía, A-M (2002) *Power, prestige and bilingualism: International perspectives on elite bilingual education*. Clevedon: Multilingual Matters.

de Mejía, A-M (2012) English language as intruder: The effects of English language education in Colombia and South America – a critical perspective. In V Rapatahana and P Bunce (Eds) *English as Hydra: Its impacts on non-English cultures*. Bristol: Multilingual Matters, pp. 244–254.

Derrida, J (1996) *Le monolinguisme de l'autre ou la prothèse d'origine*. Paris: Editions Gallilée.

Derrida, J (1998) *Monolingualism of the Other; or the prosthesis of origin* (Trans P Mensah). Stanford: Stanford University Press.

Derrida, J (2005) *Sovereignties in question: The poetics of Paul Celan* (T. Dutoit and O. Pasanen, Eds). New York: Fordham University Press.

Derrida, J and A Dufourmantelle (2000) *Of hospitality*. Stanford: Stanford University Press.

De Waal, E (2011) *The hare with the amber eyes*. London: Vintage.

Duchêne, A (2009) Marketing, management and performance: Multilingualism as a commodity in a tourism call center. *Language policy*, 8(1): 27–50.

Duchêne, A (2011) Néolibéralisme, inégalités sociales et plurilinguismes: l'exploitation des ressources langagières et des locuteurs. *Langage & Société* 136: 81–106.

Duruz, J, S Luckman and P Bishop (2011) Bazaar encounters: Food, markets, belonging and citizenship in the cosmopolitan city. *Continuum: Journal of Media & Cultural Studies* 25(5): 599–604.

Dvorak, P (2012) Forcing Frederick County's immigrants to speak English: Dubious motives, obvious benefits. *The Washington Post* 24 February, 2012. www.washingtonpost.com/local/forcing-frederick-countys-immigrants-to-speak-english-dubious-motives-obvious-benefits/2012/02/23/gIQAxXzlWR_story.html [last accessed 1 March, 2012].

Eade, J, D A Jahjah and S Sassen (2004) *Identities on the move*. London: British Council.

Eckstein, S and T-N Nguyen (2011) The making and transnationalization of an ethnic niche: Vietnamese manicurists. *International Migration Review* 45(3): 639–674.

Edensor, T (2011) Commuter: Mobility, rhythm and commuting. In T Cresswell and P Merriman (Eds) *Geographies of mobilities: Practices, spaces, subjects*. Farnham: Ashgate, pp. 189–204.

Ehlich, K (2011) Stadt/ Sprachen/ Spektrum: Von der sprachligen Folge der 'Globalisierung' in urbanen Raum. In M Messling and D Läpple and J Trabant (Eds) *Stadt und Urbanität. Transdisziplinäre Perspektiven*. Berlin: Kadmos, pp. 131–145.

Eugenides, J (2002) *Middlesex*. New York: Picador.

Evans, N (2010) *Dying words: Endangered languages and what they have to tell us*. Chichester: Wiley-Blackwell.

Evans, M (2012) The sociolinguistics of schooling: The relevance of Derrida's *Monolingualism of the Other or the Prosthesis of Origin*. In E Esch and M Solly (Eds)

The sociolinguistics of language education in international contexts. Bern: Peter Lang, pp. 31–46.

Extra, G and K Yağmur (2008) Immigrant minority languages in Europe: Cross-national and cross-linguistic perspectives. In G Extra and D Gorter (Eds) *Multilingual Europe: Facts and policies.* Berlin: Mouton de Gruyter, pp. 315–336.

Extra, G and K Yağmur (2011) Urban multilingualism in Europe: Mapping linguistic diversity in multicultural cities. *Journal of Pragmatics* 43: 1173–1184.

Farr, M (2011) Urban plurilingualism: Language practices, policies, and ideologies in Chicago. *Journal of Pragmatics* 43 (2011): 1161–1172.

Fishman, J (1972) Domains and the relationship between micro- and macrosociolinguistics. In J Gumperz and D Hymes (Eds) *Directions in sociolinguistics: The ethnography of speaking.* New York: Holt, Rinehart and Winston, pp. 407–434.

Fitzgerald, J (2007) *Big White Lie: Chinese Australians in White Australia.* Sydney: University of New South Wales Press.

Flowers, R and E Swan (2012) Eating the Asian other: Pedagogies of food multiculturalism in Australia. *PORTAL Journal of Multidisciplinary International Studies* 9(2): 1–30.

Foucault, M (1977) A preface to transgression. In Donald F. Bouchard (Ed.) *Language, counter-memory, practice.* Ithaca: Cornell University Press, pp. 15–52.

Friedmann, J and G Wolff (1982) World city formation: An agenda for research and action. *International Journal of Urban and Regional Research* 6(3): 309–343.

Friginal, E (2009) Threats to the sustainability of the outsourced call center industry in the Philippines: implications for language policy. *Language Policy* (2009) 8: 51–68.

García, O (2007) Foreword. In S Makoni and A Pennycook (Eds) *Disinventing and reconstituting languages.* Clevedon: Multilingual Matters, pp. xi–xv.

García, O (2009) *Bilingual education in the 21st century: A global perspective.* Oxford: Wiley.

García, O (2013) From diglossia to transglossia: Bilingual and multilingual classrooms in the 21st century. In C Abello-Contesse, P Chandler, M López-Jiménez and R Chacón-Beltrán (Eds) *Bilingual and multilingual education in the 21st century: Building on experience.* Bristol: Multilingual Matters, pp. 155–175.

García, O (2014) Countering the dual: Transglossia, dynamic bilingualism and translanguaging in education. In Rani S Rubdy and Lubna Alsagoff (Eds) *The global-local interface and hybridity: Exploring language and identity.* Bristol: Multilingual Matters, pp. 100–118.

García, O and Li Wei (2014) *Translanguaging: Language, bilingualism and education.* Basingstoke: Palgrave Macmillan.

Gentrification (2011) News local. www.dailytelegraph.com.au/newslocal/city-east/ redferns-gentrification-continues-as-families-and-young-couples-flock-to-the-inner-city-suburb/story-fngr8h22-1226806547038) [last accessed 21 October, 2014].

Gilroy, P (2004) *After empire: Melancholia or convivial culture?* London: Routledge.

Gogolin, I (1994) *Der monolinguale "habitus" der multilingualen Schule.* Münster: Waxman-Verlag.

Goldstein, T (1996) *Two languages at work: Bilingual life on the production floor.* New York: Mouton de Gruyter.

Gorter, D (2013) Linguistic landscapes in a multilingual world. *Annual Review of Applied Linguistics* 33: 190–212.

Gumperz, J (1964) Linguistic and social interaction in two communities. *American Anthropologist* 66: 137–153.

Haberland, H (2005) Domains and domain loss. In B Preisler, A Fabricius, H Haberland, S Kjaerbeck and K Risager (Eds) *The consequences of mobility*. Roskilde: Roskilde University, Department of Language and Culture, pp. 227–237.

Hage, G (1997) At home in the entrails of the West: Multiculturalism, ethnic food and migrant home-building. In H. Grace, G Hage, L Johnson, J Langsworth and M. Symonds (Eds) *Home/world: Space community and marginality in Sydney's West*. Annandale: Pluto Press, pp. 99–153.

Hall, P (1998) *Cities in civilization*. London: Weidenfield & Nicholson.

Han, Chong-suk (2009) We both eat rice, but that's about it. Korean and Latino relations in multi-ethnic Los Angeles. In A Wise and S Velayutham (Eds) *Everyday multiculturalism*. Houndmills: Palgrave Macmillan, pp. 237–254.

Hardt, M and A Negri (2000) *Empire*. Cambridge: Harvard University Press.

Harissi, M, E Otsuji and A Pennycook (2012) The performative fixing and unfixing of subjectivities. *Applied Linguistics* 33(5): 524–543.

Harris, A (2013) *Young people and everyday multiculturalism*. London: Routledge.

Harris, R (2009) *After epistemology*. Sandy: Authors Online.

Harvey, D (2008) The right to the city. *New Left Review* 53 (Sept/Oct): 23–40.

Heller, M (2007) Bilingualism as ideology and practice. In M Heller (Ed) *Bilingualism: A social approach*. New York: Palgrave Macmillan, pp. 1–21.

Heller, M (2010) The commodification of language. *Annual Review of Anthropology*, 39: 101–114.

Heller, M (2011) *Paths to post-nationalism. A critical ethnography of language and identity*. New York: Oxford University Press.

Heller, M and A Duchêne (2007) Discourses of endangerment: Sociolinguistics, globalization and social order. In A Duchêne and M Heller (Eds), *Discourses of endangerment: Ideology and interest in the defence of languages* (pp. 1–13). London: Continuum.

Heller, M and A Duchêne (2011) Pride and profit: Changing discourses of language, capital and nation-state. In A Duchêne and M Heller (Eds) *Language in late capitalism: Pride and profit*. London: Routledge, pp. 1–21.

Henshaw, V (2013) *Urban smellscapes: Understanding and designing city smell environments*. London: Routledge.

Heritage Report (1998) Heritage Report: 1–9 Wilkes Plaza. Wayne McPhee and Associates. [Unpublished Report]

Higgins, M and T Coen (2000) *Streets, bedrooms, and patios: The ordinariness of diversity in urban Oaxaca*. Austin: University of Texas Press.

Hill, J (2008) *The everyday language of White racism*. Chichester: Wiley-Blackwell.

Hinchliffe, S and S Whatmore (2006) Living cities: Towards a politics of conviviality. *Science as Culture* 15(2): 123–138.

Holmes, J, M Marra and B King (2013) How permeable is the formal-informal boundary at work? An ethnographic account of the role of food in workplace discourse. In C Gerhardt, M Frobenius and S Ley (Eds) *Culinary linguistics: The chef's special*. Amsterdam: John Benjamins, pp. 191–209.

Horner, K and J Weber (2008) The Language Situation in Luxembourg. *Current Issues in Language Planning* 9: 69–128.

Hultgren, A K (2011) 'Building rapport' with customers across the world: The global diffusion of a call centre speech style. *Journal of Sociolinguistics* 15(1): 36–64.

Hutnyk, J (2000) *Critique of exotica: Music, politics and the culture industry*. London: Pluto Press.

Hutnyk, J (2005) Hybridity. *Ethnic and Racial Studies* 28(1): 79–102.

Hymes, D (1974) *Foundations in sociolinguistics*. Philadelphia: University of Pennsylvania Press.

Illich, I (1973) *Tools for conviviality*. London: Marion Boyars.

Inglis, D and D Gimlin (2010) Food globalizations: Ironies and ambivalences of food, cuisine and globality. In D Inglis and D Gimlin (Eds) *The globalization of food*. Oxford: Berg, pp. 3–42.

Jaffe, A and C Oliva (2013) Linguistic creativity in Corsican tourist context. In Sari Pietikäinen and H Kelly Holmes (Eds) *Multilingualism and the periphery*. Oxford: Oxford University Press, pp. 95–117.

Jaffrey, M (2014) Madhur's chicken tikka masala. www.sbs.com.au/food/recipes/madhurs-chicken-tikka-masala [last accessed 21 October 2014].

James, S (2008) Market gardens and McMansions: Contesting the concept of 'growth' on Sydney's peri-urban fringe. Online proceedings of 'Sustaining Culture' annual conference of the Cultural Studies Association of Australia (CSAA) UniSA, Adelaide 6–8 December, 2007. http://unisa.edu.au/com/csaa/onlineproceedings.htm

Janiszewski, L and E Alexakis (2003) California dreaming: The 'Greek cafe' and its role in the Americanisation of Australian eating and social habits. *Modern Greek Studies (Australia and New Zealand)* 11–12: 177–197.

Jaspers, J (2011) Talking like a 'zerolingual': Ambiguous linguistic caricatures at an urban secondary school. *Journal of Pragmatics* 43: 1264–1278.

Jaworski, A and A Thurlow (2013) The (de-)centring spaces of airports: Framing mobility and multilingualism. In S Pietikäinen and H Kelly Holmes (Eds) *Multilingualism and the periphery*. Oxford: Oxford University Press, pp. 154–198.

Jefferson, G (2004) Glossary of transcript symbols with an introduction. In G H Lerner (Ed.) *Conversation analysis: Studies from the first generation*. Amsterdam: John Benjamins, pp. 13–31.

Jeffrey, B and G Toman (2004) Ethnographic time. *British Educational Research Journal* 30(4): 535–548.

Jenkins, J (2006) Current perspectives on teaching World Englishes and English as a Lingua Franca. *TESOL Quarterly* 40(1): 157–181.

Jenkins, J (2009) Exploring attitudes towards English as a Lingua Franca in the East Asian context. In K Murata and J Jenkins (Eds) *Global Englishes in Asian contexts: Current and future debates*. Basingstoke: Palgrave Macmillan, pp. 40–56.

Jervis, J (1999) *Transgressing the modern: Explorations in the Western experience of Otherness*. Oxford: Blackwell.

Johnston, J and S Baumann (2010) *Foodies: Democracy and distinction in the gourmet foodscape*. New York: Routledge.

Jørgensen, J N (2008a) Polylingal languaging around and among children and adolescents. *International Journal of Multilingualism* 5(3): 161–176.

Jørgensen, J N (2008b) *Languaging: Nine years of poly-lingual development of young Turkish-Danish grade school students*. (2 Volumes). Copenhagen: University of Copenhagen.

Jørgensen, J N (2008c) Urban wall writing. *International Journal of Multilingualism* 5(3): 237–252.

Kachru, B (2005) *Asian Englishes: Beyond the canon*. Hong Kong: Hong Kong University Press.

Karrebæk, M S (2012) "What's in your lunch box today?": Health, respectability, and ethnicity in the primary classroom. *Journal of Linguistic Anthropology* 22(1): 1–22.

Kiessling, R and M Mous (2004) Urban youth languages in Africa. *Anthropological Linguistics* 46(3): 303–341.

Kirkpatrick, A (2011) English as an Asian lingua franca and the multilingual model of ELT. *Language Teaching* 44: 212–224.

Kral, I (2012) *Talk, text and technology: Literacy and social practice in a remote indigenous community*. Bristol: Multilingual Matters.

Kramsch, C (2008) Multilingual, like Franz Kafka. *International Journal of Multilingualism* 5(4): 316–332.

Kramsch, C (2009) *The multilingual subject: What foreign language learners say about their experience and why it matters*. Oxford: Oxford University Press.

Kramsch, C and S Thorne (2002) Foreign language learning as global communicative practice. In D Block and D Cameron (Eds) *Globalization and language teaching*. London: Routledge, pp. 83–100.

Kramsch, C and A Whiteside (2008) Language ecology in multilingual settings. Towards a theory of symbolic competence. *Applied Linguistics* 29: 645–671.

Kropp Dakubu, M E (2009) The historical dynamic of multilingualism in Accra. In F McLaughlin (Ed) *The languages of urban Africa*. London: Continuum, pp. 19–31.

Kube-Barth, S (2009) The multiple facets of the urban language form, Nouchi. In F McLaughlin (Ed) *The languages of urban Africa*. London: Continuum, pp. 103–114.

Kubota, R (2014) Orimpikku to eigo kyoiku: Hangurobaruteki kaikaku [The Olympics and English language teaching: An anti-global reform]. *Shukan Kinyobi* 975: 63.

Labov, W (1966) *The social stratification of English in New York City*. Washington, DC: Center for Applied Linguistics.

Labov, W (1972) *Language in the inner city: Studies in the Black English vernacular*. Philadelphia: University of Pennsylvania Press.

Lamarre, P and S Lamarre (2009) Montréal 'on the move': Pour une approche ethnographique non-statique des pratiques langagières des jeunes multilingues. In T Bulot (Ed) *Ségrégations et discriminations urbaines (Formes et normes sociolinguistiques)*. Paris: L'Harmattan, pp. 105–134.

Landry, C (2012) *The sensory landscape of cities*. Bournes Green: Comedia.

Lasagabaster, D (2010) Australia's language potential. *International Journal of Multilingualism* 7(2): 187–190.

Latour, B (1993) *We have never been modern*. Hemel Hempstead: Harvester Wheatsheaf.

Latour, B (1999) *Pandora's hope*. Cambridge: Harvard University Press.

Latour, B (2005) *Reassembling the social: An introduction to actor-network theory*. Oxford: Oxford University Press.

Lee Su Kim (2010) *Kebaya Tales*. Selangor: Marshall Cavendish.

Leeman, J and G Modan (2009) Commodified language in Chinatown: A contextualized approach to linguistic landscape. *Journal of Sociolinguistics* 13 (3): 332–362.

Lefebvre, H (1968) *Le droit à la ville*. Paris: Editions Anthropos.

Lefebvre, H (1973) *Espace et politique*. Paris: Editions Anthropos.

Lefebvre, H (1991) *The production of space*. (*La production de l'espace*. 1974). Oxford: Blackwell.

Legally Brown (2013) SBS (Special Broadcasting Service) Australia. www.youtube.com/watch?v=PffJ1BXjm90 [last accessed 21 October, 2014].

Li Wei (2011) Moment analysis and translanguaging space: Discursive construction of identities by multilingual Chinese youth in Britain. *Journal of Pragmatics* 43: 1222–1235.

Lin, A (2009) 'Respect for da chopstick hip hop': The politics, poetics, and pedagogy of Cantonese verbal art in Hong Kong. In H S Alim, A Ibrahim and A Pennycook (Eds) *Global linguistic flows: Hip hop cultures, youth identities, and the politics of language.* New York: Routledge, pp. 159–177.

Lin, J (2011) *The power of urban ethnic places: Cultural heritage and community life.* New York: Routledge.

Livingstone, D (2007) Science, site and speech: scientific knowledge and the spaces of rhetoric. *History of the Human Sciences* 20: 71–98.

Loosemore, M and D W Chau (2002) Racial discrimination towards Asian operatives in the Australian construction industry. *Construction Management and Economics* 20: 91–102.

Loosemore, M and P Lee (2002) An investigation into communication problems with ethnic minorities in the construction industry. *International Journal of Project Management,* 20(3): 517–524.

Loosemore, M, F Phua, K Dunn and U Ozguc (2010) Operatives' experiences of cultural diversity on Australian construction sites. *Construction Management and Economics* 28: 177–188.

Lorange, A (2014) *How Reading Is Written: A Brief Index to Gertrude Stein.* Middletown, Connecticut: Wesleyan Press.

Lorente, B (2011) The making of "workers of the world": Language and the labor brokerage state. In A Duchêne and M Heller (Eds) *Language in late capitalism: Pride and profit.* London: Routledge, pp. 183–206.

Mac Giolla Chríost, D (2007) *Language and the city.* Basingstoke: Palgrave Macmillan.

Mackenzie, I (2014) *English as a lingua franca.* London: Routledge.

Magnusson, W (2000) Politicizing the global city. In E F Isin (Ed) *Democracy, citizenship and the global city.* London: Routledge, pp. 289–306.

Maher, J (2005) Metroethnicity, language, and the principle of Cool. *International Journal of the Sociology of Language* 11: 83–102.

Maher, J (2010) Metroethnicities and metrolanguages. In N Coupland (Ed) *The handbook of language and globalization.* Malden: Wiley-Blackwell, pp. 575–591.

Makoni, S (2011) Sociolinguistics, colonial and postcolonial: An integrationist perspective. *Language Sciences* 33(4): 680–688.

Makoni, S and B Makoni (2010) Multilingual discourses on wheels and public English in Africa: A case for 'vague linguistique'. In J Maybin and J Swann *The Routledge Companion to English Language Studies.* London: Routledge, pp. 258–270.

Makoni, B, S Makoni and A Pennycook (2010) On speaking multilanguages: Urban lingos and fluid multilingualism. In P Cuvelier, T Du Plessis, M Meeuwis, R Vandekerckhove and V Webb (Eds) *Multilingualism from below.* Hatfield, Pretoria: Van Schaik, pp. 147–165.

Makoni, S and P Mashiri (2007) Critical historiography: Does language planning in Africa need a construct of language as part of its theoretical apparatus? In S Makoni and A Pennycook (Eds) *Disinventing and reconstituting languages.* Clevedon: Multilingual Matters, pp. 62–89.

Makoni, S and A Pennycook (2007) Disinventing and reconstituting languages. In S Makoni and A Pennycook (Eds) *Disinventing and reconstituting languages* Clevedon: Multilingual Matters, pp. 1–41.

Makoni, S and A Pennycook (2012) Disinventing multilingualism: From monological multilingualism to multilingua francas. In M Martin-Jones, A Blackledge and A Creese

(Eds) *The Routledge handbook of multilingualism*. New York: Routledge, pp. 439–453.

Marcus, G (1995) Ethnography in/of the world system: The emergence of multi-sited ethnography. *Annual Review of Anthropology* (24): 95–117.

Markus, A (1979) *Fear and hatred: Purifying Australia and California 1850–1901.* Sydney: Hale and Iremonger.

Martinovic, B (2011) *The Dutch city of Utrecht as a European hotspot and laboratory for multilingualism.* Department of Sociology, Utrecht University.

Massey, D (1991) A Global Sense of Place. *Marxism Today, 1991*(June): 24–29.

Massey, D (1994) *Space, place and gender.* Cambridge: Polity Press.

Massey, D (2000) Travelling thoughts. In P Gilroy, L Grossberg and A McRobbie (Eds) *Without guarantees: In honour of Stuart Hall.* London: Verso, pp. 225–232.

Massey, D (2005) *For space.* London: Sage.

Mathews, G (2012) Neoliberalism and globalization from below in Chungking mansions, Hong Kong. In G Mathews, G L Ribeiro and C A Vega (Eds) *Globalization from below: The world's other economy.* London: Routledge, pp. 69–85.

Mathews, G and C A Vega (2012) Introduction: What is globalization from below? In G Mathews, G L Ribeiro and C A Vega (Eds) *Globalization from below: The world's other economy.* London: Routledge, pp. 1–15.

Maybin, J and Tusting, K (2011) Linguistic ethnography. In J Simpson (Ed) *Routledge handbook of applied linguistics.* London: Routledge, pp. 515–528.

McGowan, B (2005) Chinese market gardens in southern and western New South Wales. *Australian Humanities Review,* 36(July): np. www.australianhumanitiesreview.org/archive/Issue-July-2005/10McGowan.html [last accessed 21 October, 2014].

Mc Laughlin, F (2009) Introduction to the languages of urban Africa. In F McLaughlin (Ed) *The languages of urban Africa.* London: Continuum, pp. 1–18.

McNamara, T (2012) Language assessments as shibboleths: A poststructuralist perspective. *Applied Linguistics* 33: 5.

McQuire, S (2008) *The media city: Media, architecture and urban space.* London: Sage.

Mesthrie, R (1989) The origins of Fanagalo. *Journal of Pidgin and Creole Languages* 4(2): 211–240.

Mesthrie, R (2014) Analyzing sociolinguistic variation in mutilingual contexts. In J Holmes and K Hazen (Eds) *Research methods in sociolinguistics: A practical guide.* Oxford: Wiley Blackwell, pp. 276–289.

Mignolo, W (2000) *Local histories/ global designs: Coloniality, subaltern knowledges, and border thinking.* Princeton: Princeton University Press.

Mikkelsen, B (2011) Images of foodscapes: Introduction to foodscape studies and their application in the study of healthy eating out-of-home environments. *Perspectives in Public Health* 131(5): 209–216.

Millington, G (2011) *'Race', culture and the right to the city: Centres, peripheries and margins.* Houndmills: Palgrave Macmillan.

Milon, A (2002) Tags and murals in France: A city's face or a natural landscape? In A-P Durand (Ed.) *Black, blanc, beur: Rap music and hip-hop culture in the Francophone world.* Lanham: The Scarecrow Press, pp. 87–98.

Mitchell, D (2003) *The right to the city: Social justice and the fight for public space.* New York: Guilford Press.

Modan, G (2007) *Turf wars: Discourse, diversity and the politics of place.* Oxford: Blackwell.

Modjeska, D (1999) *Stravinsky's lunch.* Sydney: Pan Macmillan.

Mohanty, A (2013) Multilingual education in India: Overcoming the language barrier and the burden of the double divide. In P Siemund, I Gogolin, M Schulz and J Davydova (Eds) *Multilingualism and language diversity in urban areas: Acquisition, identities, space, education.* Amsterdam: John Benjamins, pp. 305–326.

Mohr, R and N Hosen (2014) Crossing over: Hosts, guests and tastes on a Sydney street. *Law Text Culture* 17(1): 100–128.

Møller, J S (2008) Polylingual performance among Turkish-Danes in late-modern Copenhagen. *International Journal of Multilingualism* 5(3): 217–236.

Moore, R, S Pietikäinen and J Blommaert (2010) Counting the losses: Numbers as the language of language endangerment. *Sociolinguistic Studies* 4(1): 1–26.

Moriarty M and S Pietikäinen (2011) Micro-level language-planning and grass-root initiatives: A case study of Irish language comedy and Inari Sámi rap. *Current Issues in Language Planning* 12(3): 1–17.

Multicultural London (2003) Multicultural London: Changing shadows. *The Economist*, Dec 18th 2003.

Nakane, I, E Otsuji and W Armour (Eds) (2015) *Languages and identities in a transitional Japan: from internationalization to globalization.* New York: Routledge.

Nandy, A (2006) The return of the sacred, the language of religion and the fear of democracy in a post-secular world. Trans/forming Cultures Annual Lecture, 12 September, 2006, University of Technology Sydney. http://hdl.handle.net/2100/44 [last accessed 21 October, 2014].

Nasonal Lanwis Polisi of Vanuata (2010) www.vanuatuculture.org/documents/NasonalLanwisPolisi.doc [last accessed 6 March, 2012].

New Language Discovered (2010) New language discovered in India. www.abc.net.au/news/2010-10-06/new-language-discovered-in-india/2286464 [last accessed 12 November, 2013].

New Language Uncovered (2013) New language uncovered in indigenous Australian community. http://abcnews.go.com/blogs/headlines/2013/07/new-language-uncovered-in-indigenous-australian-community/ [last accessed 12 November, 2013].

Noble, G (2009) Everyday cosmopolitanism and the labour of intercultural community. In A Wise and S Velayutham (Eds) *Everyday multiculturalism.* Houndmills: Palgrave Macmillan, pp. 46–65.

Ochs, E and M Shohet (2006) The cultural structuring of mealtime socialization. *New Directions for Child and Adolescent Development* 111: 35–49.

O'Shannessy, C (2013) The role of multiple sources in the formation of an innovative auxiliary category in Light Warlpiri, a new Australian mixed language. *Language* 89(2): 328–353.

Ostler, N (2005) *Empires of the word: A language history of the world.* New York: HarperCollins.

Ostler, N (2010) *The last lingua franca: English until the return of Babel.* New York: Walker and Company.

Otsuji, E (2010) 'Where am I from': Performative and 'metro' perspectives of origin, in D Nunan and J Choi (Eds), *Language and culture: reflective narratives and the emergence of identity.* New York: Routledge, pp. 186–93.

Otsuji, E (2011) Metrolingualism and Japanese language education: linguistic competence across borders. *Literacies* 9: 21–30.

Otsuji, E and A Pennycook (2010) Metrolingualism: Fixity, fluidity and language in flux. *International Journal of Multilingualism* 7: 240–254.

Otsuji, E and A Pennycook (2014) Unremarkable hybridities and metrolingual practices. In R S Rubdy and L Alsagoff (Eds) *The global-local interface and hybridity: Exploring language and identity.* Bristol: Multilingual Matters, pp. 83–99.

Our Market Supply (1897) *The Daily News* (Perth, WA). Saturday 10 July, 1897, p. 5.

Panayiotopoulos, P (2010) *Ethnicity, migration and enterprise.* Hampshire and New York: Palgrave Macmillan.

Park, J S-Y and L Wee (2012) *Markets of English: Linguistic capital and language policy in a globalizing world.* New York: Routledge.

Paugh, A and C Izquierdo (2009) Why is this a battle every night? Negotiating food and eating in American dinnertime interaction. *Journal of Linguistic Anthropology* 19(2):185–204.

Pavlenko, A and B Malt (2011) Kitchen Russian: Cross-linguistic differences and first-language object naming by Russian–English bilinguals. *Bilingualism: Language and Cognition* 14(1): 19–45.

Pennycook, A (2007) *Global Englishes and transcultural flows.* London: Routledge.

Pennycook, A (2008) English as a language always in translation. *European Journal of English Studies*, 12(1): 33–47.

Pennycook, A (2009) Linguistic landscapes and the transgressive semiotics of graffiti. In E Shohamy and D Gorter (Eds) *Linguistic Landscape: Expanding the scenery.* London: Routledge, pp. 302–312.

Pennycook, A (2010) Spatial narrations: Graffscapes and city souls. In A Jaworski and C Thurlow (Eds) *Semiotic landscapes.* New York: Continuum International Publishing Group, pp. 137–150.

Pennycook, A (2012a) *Language mobility: Unexpected places.* Bristol: Multilingual Matters.

Pennycook, A (2012b) Lingua francas as language ideologies. In A Kirkpatrick and R Sussex (Eds) *English as an international language in Asia: Implications for language education.* NewYork: Springer, pp. 137–154.

Pennycook, A (2013) Language policies, language ideologies and local language practices. In L Wee, R B H Goh and L Lim (Eds) *The politics of English: South Asia, Southeast Asia and the Asian Pacific.* US: John Benjamins Publishing Company, pp. 1–18.

Pennycook, A and E Otsuji (2014a) Metrolingual multitasking and spatial repertoires: 'Pizza mo two minutes coming'. *Journal of Sociolinguistics* 18(2): 161–184.

Pennycook, A and E Otsuji (2014b) Market lingos and metrolingua francas. *International Multilingual Research Journal* 8:4, 255–70.

Perera, S (1994) Unspeakable bodies: Representing the Aboriginal in Australian critical discourse. *Meridian* 13(1): 15–26.

Phillipson, R (2009) *Linguistic imperialism continued.* New York: Routledge.

Pietikäinen, S (2012) Experiences and expressions of multilingualism: Visual ethnography and discourse analysis in research with Sámi children. In S Gardner and M Martin-Jones (Eds) *Multilingualism, discourse and ethnography.* New York: Routledge, pp. 163–178.

Pietikäinen, S (2013) Heteroglossic authenticity in Sámi heritage tourism. In S Pietikäinen and H Kelly-Holmes (Eds) *Multilingualism and the periphery.* Oxford: Oxford University Press, pp. 77–94.

Platt, J and H Platt (1975) *The social significance of speech: an introduction to and workbook in sociolinguistics.* Amsterdam: North-Holland.

Pratt, M L (1987) Linguistic utopias. In N Fabb, D Attridge, A Durant, and C Maccabe (Eds) *The linguistics of writing: Arguments between language and literature.* Manchester: Manchester University Press, pp. 48–66.

Probyn, E (2000) *Carnal appetites: FoodSexIdentities.* London: Routledge.

Purcell, M (2002) Excavating Lefebvre: The right to the city and its urban politics of the inhabitant. *GeoJournal* 58: 99–108.

Radice, M (2009) Street-level cosmopolitanism: Neighbourhood shopping streets in multi-ethnic Montréal. In A Wise and S Velayutham (Eds) *Everyday multiculturalism.* Houndmills: Palgrave Macmillan, pp. 140–157.

Rampton, B (2006) *Language in late modernity: Interaction in an urban school.* Cambridge: Cambridge University Press.

Rampton, B (2007) Neo-Hymesian Linguistic Ethnography in the UK. *Journal of Sociolinguistics* 11(5): 584–608.

Rampton, B (2009) Interactional ritual and not just artful performance in crissing and stylization. *Language in Society* 38: 149–176.

Rampton, B (2011) Style contrasts, migration and social class. *Journal of Pragmatics* 43: 1236–1250.

Redder, A (2013) Multilingual communication in Hamburg: A pragmatic approach. In P Siemund, I Gogolin, M Schulz and J Davydova (Eds) *Multilingualism and language diversity in urban areas: Acquisition, identities, space, education.* Amsterdam: John Benjamins, pp. 257–285.

Ribeiro, G L (2012) Conclusion: Globalization from below and the non-hegemonic world-system. In G Mathews, G L Ribeiro and C A Vega (Eds) *Globalization from below: The world's other economy.* London: Routledge, pp. 221–235.

Rojo, L M (2014) Taking over the square: The role of linguistic practices in contesting urban spaces. *Journal of Language and Politics* 13:4 623–52.

Sabre, C (2013) New images of Japan in France: A survey to Japan Expo. *Regional Studies* 7: 95–122.

Sassen, S (1998) *Globalization and its discontents.* New York: The New Press.

Sassen, S (2005) The global city: Introducing a concept. *Brown Journal of World Affairs,* X1 (Winter/Spring): 2, 27–41.

Sayahi, L (2014) *Diglossia and language contact: Language variation and change in North Africa.* Cambridge: Cambridge University Press.

Schatzki, T (2010) *The timespace of human activity: On performance, society, and history as indeterminate teleological events.* Lanham: Lexington Books.

Scollon, R and S Wong Scollon (2003) *Discourses in place: Language in the material world.* London: Routledge.

Sebba, M (2012) Multilingualism in written discourse: An approach to the analysis of multilingual texts. *International Journal of Bilingualism* 17(1): 97–118.

Shohamy, E and D Gorter (2009) Introduction. In E Shohamy and D Gorter (Eds) *Linguistic landscape: Expanding the scenery.* London: Routledge, pp. 1–10.

Simon, P (1997) Les représentations des relations interethniques dans un quartier cosmopolite. *Recherches sociologiques* 28(2): 5–37.

Simon, R (1992) *Teaching against the grain: Texts for a pedagogy of possibility.* Toronto: OISE Press.

Simon, S (2012) *Cities in translation: Intersections of language and memory.* London: Routledge.

Singer, P and J Mason (2006) *The way we eat: Why our food choices matter.* Emmaus: Rodale.

Skutnabb-Kangas, T (1981) *Bilingual or not: The Education of Minorities*. Avon: Multilingual Matters.

Skutnabb-Kangas, T (1988) Multilingualism and the education of minority children. In T Skutnabb-Kangas and J Cummins (Eds) *Minority education: From shame to struggle*. Avon: Multilingual Matters, pp. 9–44.

Skutnabb-Kangas, T and R Phillipson (1989) 'Mother tongue': The theoeretical and sociopolitical construction of a concept. In U Ammon (Ed) *Status and function of language and varieties*. Berlin: de Gruyter, pp. 450–477.

Soja, E W (1996) *Thirdspace: Journeys to Los Angeles and real-and-imagined places*. Oxford: Blackwell.

Sultana, S, S Dovchin and A Pennycook (2013) Styling the periphery: Linguistic and cultural takeup in Bangladesh and Mongolia. *Journal of Sociolinguistics* 17(5): 687–710.

Sultana, S, S Dovchin and A Pennycook (2015) Transglossic language practices of young adults in Bangladesh and Mongolia. *International Journal of Multilingualism*, 12:1 93–108.

Sydney's Melting Pot of Language (2014) The Sydney Morning Herald. www.smh.com. au/data-point/sydney-languages/index.html [last accessed 16 July, 2014].

Takano, H (2012) *Imin no utage: Nihon ni utsurisunda gaikokujin no fushigina shokuseikatsu*. Tokyo: Kōdansha.

Taniguchi, N and C Murozawa (2011) Bishamonten zenkōji yuisho. *Machino omoide wo tadotte 4*. Tokyo: Ikina machizukuri kurabu, pp. 2–16.

Taniguchi, N and U Ito (2011) Arashino ema. *Machino omoide wo tadotte, 4,* Tokyo: Ikina machizukuri kurabu, pp. 26.

Tauzin, D (2009) *Tokyō no puchi pari de sutekina machi gurashi: Le petit Paris de Tokyo*. Tokyo: Seiryūdō.

Thorne, S and J Lantolf (2007) A linguistics of communicative activity. In S Makoni and A Pennycook (Eds) *Disinventing and reconstituting languages*. Clevedon: Multilingual Matters, pp. 170–195.

Thrift, N (2007) *Non-representational theory: Space, politics, affect*. London: Routledge.

Trudgill, P (1974) *The social differentiation of English in Norwich*. Cambridge: Cambridge University Press.

Van Camp, K and K Juffermans (2010) Postcolonial ideologies of language in education: Voices from below on English and local language(s) in the Gambia. In P Cuvelier, T Du Plessis, M Meeuwis, R Vandekerckhove and V Webb (Eds) *Multilingualism from below*. Hatfield, Pretoria: Van Schaik, pp. 1–20.

Velasquez, K (2013) Transcending linguistic boundaries at work. *Anthropology News* 54 (1–2): 10 & 14.

Vertovec, S (2006) *The emergence of super-diversity in Britain*. Working Paper No 25, Centre of Policy, Migration and Society, University of Oxford.

Wacquant, L (2008) *Urban outcasts: A comparative sociology of advanced marginality*. Cambridge: Polity.

Walter, H (1988) *Le français dans tous les sens*. Paris: Robert Laffont.

Watson, P (2005) *Ideas: A history from fire to Freud*. London: Phoenix.

Watson, S (2006) *City publics: The (dis)enchantments of urban encounters*. London: Routledge.

Watson, S (2009) Brief encounters of an unpredictable kind: Everyday multiculturalism in two London street markets. In A Wise and S Velayutham (Eds) *Everyday multiculturalism*. Houndmills: Palgrave Macmillan, pp. 125–139.

Webb, V (2010) Multilingualism from below? Really? In South Africa? In P Cuvelier, T Du Plessis, M Meeuwis, R Vandekerckhove and V Webb (Eds) *Multilingualism from below*. Hatfirld, Pretoria, Van Schaik, pp. 134–146.

Wesker, A (1960) *The kitchen*. London: Oberon Books.

Williams, M (1999) *Chinese settlement in NSW: A thematic history. A report for the NSW Heritage Office of NSW*. Unpublished Report.

Williams, M (nd) Wading 10,000 li to seek their fortune. 東華新報 *Tung Wah News* selections 1898–1901. Chinese Heritage of Australian Federation Project. www.chaf. lib.latrobe.edu.au [last accessed 21 October 2014].

Williams, R (1973) *The country and the city*. Oxford: Oxford University Press.

Williams, R (1980) *Culture and materialism: Selected essays*. London: Verso.

Wilton, J (2004) *Golden threads: The Chinese in regional New South Wales, 1850–1950*. Armidale: New England Regional Art Museum.

Wise, A (2009) Everyday multiculturalism: Transversal crossings and working class cosmopolitans. In A Wise and S Velayutham (Eds) *Everyday multiculturalism*. Houndmills: Palgrave Macmillan, pp. 21–45.

Wise, A and S Velayutham (2009) Introduction: Multiculturalism and everyday life. In A Wise and S Velayutham (Eds) *Everyday multiculturalism*. Houndmills: Palgrave Macmillan, pp. 1–17.

Wood, P and C Landry (2008) *The intercultural city*. London: Earthscan.

Yasmeen, G (2006) *Bangkok's foodscape: Public eating, gender relations and urban change*. Bangkok: White Lotus.

Yildiz, Y (2012) *Beyond the mother tongue: The postmonolingual condition*. New York: Fordham University Press.

Zuberi, N (2001) *Sounds English: Transnational popular music*. Urbana: University of Illinois Press.

Zuckerman, G (2009) Hybridity versus revivability: Multiple causation, forms and patterns. *Journal of Language Contact – VARIA* 2: 40–67.

Zukin, S (1991) *Landscapes of power: From Detroit to Disney World*. Berkeley: University of California Press.

Zukin, S (1995) *The cultures of cities*. Cambridge: Blackwell.

Index